The Good Parliament

THE GOOD PARLIAMENT

by Andrew
George Holmes

Clarendon Press · Oxford
1975

Oxford University Press, Ely House, London W.1.

GLASGOW NEW YORK TORONTO MELBOURNE WELLINGTON
CAPE TOWN IBADAN NAIROBI DAR ES SALAAM LUSAKA ADDIS ABABA
DELHI BOMBAY CALCUTTA MADRAS KARACHI LAHORE DACCA
KUALA LUMPUR SINGAPORE HONG KONG TOKYO

ISBN 0 19 822446 X

© *Oxford University Press 1975*

*Printed in Great Britain
by Burgess & Son (Abingdon) Ltd.
Abingdon Oxfordshire*

Contents

Abbreviations

Books cited in footnotes are published at London unless otherwise stated.

Public Record Office class numbers

C 76	Treaty Rolls.
DL 28	Duchy of Lancaster accounts, various.
E 101	Exchequer K.R., accounts, various.
E 159	Exchequer K.R., memoranda rolls.
E 163	Exchequer K.R. miscellanea.
E 364	Exchequer L.T.R., enrolled foreign accounts.
E 368	Exchequer L.T.R., memoranda rolls.
E 401	Receipt rolls.
E 403	Issue rolls.
E 404	Exchequer privy seals and warrants for issue.
SC 8	Ancient petitions.

Prologue: the problem

THE sources of information about the Good Parliament of 1376 are better than those which survive for any other English parliament in the Middle Ages and possibly superior to the sources for any comparable political episode in medieval England. The reason for this is that in addition to the usual records produced by the royal government there happen to be three independent and remarkably informative accounts of what actually happened in the parliament. The official record which the chancery clerks wrote for this as for other parliaments on the parliament roll is exceptionally long and full, containing many details not only of the grievances voiced but also of the proceedings. It was printed in the eighteenth century and runs to forty large folio pages in the printed edition. The detailed and scandalous narrative in the so-called *Chronicon Angliae*, composed by Thomas Walsingham, a monk of St. Albans, a few years later in the reign of Richard II, is an exceptionally rich and unrestrained account inspired by a lively desire to pillory the misdeeds of the Duke of Lancaster and his courtier friends. It was printed in 1874. Another narrative in the *Anonimalle Chronicle* of St. Mary's Abbey, York, was not available until it was published by V. H. Galbraith in 1927. It has the extraordinary merit of being clearly based on a day-to-day record set down by an eye-witness. It is rather surprising that these magnificent sources which offer an unusual insight into medieval political life have not received more serious attention from modern historians.

The Good Parliament does raise problems of interpretation of the evidence, as we shall see, but the reason why it has been comparatively neglected is not the inherent difficulty of understanding it but the character of the historical tradition within which it has been interpreted. The only serious modern account of the parliament was published in 1928 in T. F. Tout's *Chapters in the Administrative History of Medieval England*.[1] Tout took some pains to work out the course of events in the parliament, but

[1] Tout, III. 290–308.

his interest was chiefly concentrated on the constitutional principles which it exhibited ('It was both a political and a social development for the commons to take the leading part they played in the proceedings of this parliament') and on the place of the episode in the history of English administration ('The commons were satisfied with the institutions of the country as they were, and had no wish to make drastic changes'). His account was essentially an amplification of the mid-nineteenth-century version of Stubbs[1] for whom, considering it as a point in the evolution of institutions, the parliament was a poor successor to the crises of 1258 and 1297: 'It asserted some sound principles without being a starting-point of a new history. It afforded an important illustration of the increasing power of the commons, but, as an attempt at real reform and progress, it was a failure.' Tout's treatment was followed in more recent years by a small number of articles touching on the Good Parliament by other writers whose interest was also mainly directed to the constitutional implications and who were therefore interested in clarifying the course of events during the parliament which led to the impeachment of the courtiers and their associates and the form taken by these parliamentary proceedings.[2] The Good Parliament has thus become famous for the precociousness of the knights of the shire and their invention of the procedure of impeachment, while the political context which makes the crisis intelligible has been neglected. With the exception of M. V. Clarke, who greatly exaggerated the importance of the Irish background, Tout and the other historians have shown little interest in the political events of the period, in the cause of the political crisis, and in the issues which divided the antagonists; the parliament interested them primarily as a stage in a linear and abstract evolution of institutional forms. Such indifference to actual historical situations is of course a natural result of the study of 'constitutional history' in remote societies

[1] W. Stubbs, *The Constitutional History of England*, II (4th ed., Oxford, 1886), 448–55.

[2] M. V. Clarke, 'The Origin of Impeachment', *Oxford Essays in Medieval History Presented to H. E. Salter* (Oxford, 1934), reprinted in *Fourteenth Century Studies* (Oxford, 1937); T. F. T. Plucknett, 'The Origin of Impeachment' and 'The Impeachments of 1376', *Transactions of the Royal Historical Society*, ser. 4, xxiv (1942), and ser. 5, i (1951); J. G. Edwards, *The Commons in Medieval English Parliaments* (The Creighton Lecture in History 1957) (1958); J. S. Roskell, *The Commons and their Speakers in English Parliaments 1376–1523* (Manchester, 1965), ch. 1.

and has denatured a great deal of medieval history; the historians' treatment of the Good Parliament is a clear example of this. The purpose of the present work is to approach the events of April to July 1376 with less regard to the evolution of institutions and with the aim of understanding the nature of the political crisis. Such an exceptionally dramatic and well-documented episode as the Good Parliament promises to provide an unusual insight into the politics of medieval England. Our aim is to exploit this opportunity. The main records of the parliament contain a number of comments on the politics and administration of preceding years which cry out for an investigation into their purposes and accuracy and form an obvious starting-point for a study of the issues with which the parliament was concerned and the reasons for the peculiar explosion of anger against the court which it witnessed. Only in one sphere—the repercussions of the war in Normandy and Brittany—has a serious attempt been made along these lines to elucidate the links between the parliamentary proceedings and political situation.[1] The present study will involve more investigation of this kind.

The essential problem which faces the student of the parliament is to correlate the three main accounts of the parliament itself with the other records of English history at this period. This is not altogether easy because the records of the parliament are in some respects rather isolated. For an account of the years preceding the Good Parliament we are mainly dependent on various continuators of Higden's *Polychronicon* who give, with small variations, the same skeleton narrative.[2] The only useful accounts apart from this are in Froissart—invaluable for the French wars but not much help for English events—and the earlier pages of the *Anonimalle* itself which are rather confused. From the Good Parliament to the end of Edward III's reign

[1] C. C. Bayley, 'The Campaign of 1375 and the Good Parliament', *English Historical Review*, lv (1940); J. G. Bellamy, 'Appeal and Impeachment in the Good Parliament', *Bull. Inst. Hist. Research*, xxxix (1966), and 'Sir John de Annesley and the Chandos Inheritance', *Nottingham Medieval Studies*, x (1966).

[2] Ranulf Higden, *Polychronicon*, ed. J. R. Lumby, ix (Rolls Series, 1886); *Walteri Hemingford . . . Historia . . .*, ed. T. Hearne (Oxford, 1731), ii. 407 f.; Thomas Walsingham, *Historia Anglicana*, ed. H. T. Riley (Rolls Series, 1863–4). On this tradition see J. Taylor, *The Universal Chronicle of Ranulph Higden* (Oxford, 1966).

the situation is the same except that the *Chronicon Angliae* goes on. The rich accounts of the few weeks of the parliament itself are therefore a fertile oasis. The surrounding area is rather thinly supplied with narrative evidence. The contrast is perplexing and the difficulty of interpretation arises partly from this. For example, the financial corruption and manipulation of the court, which receive much attention in the accounts of the parliament, are unintelligible without the background of royal finance before 1376 about which the narratives are almost entirely silent. The difficulty is to get a perspective in which to see the parliament. The perspective must of course be created, as it must for other periods of medieval history, out of the institutional records.

This is a laborious process but in some respects the record sources, as opposed to narratives, are unusually good for this period. The chief bulk is provided by the usual records of the Chancery and the Exchequer. For the church there are a number of bishops' registers including those of Archbishops Whittlesey and Sudbury which include narratives of the convocations of 1373 and 1377. In addition to these standard sources there are a few which must be regarded as bonuses for the historian of this period: in particular the papal mediators who presided over the Anglo-French peace talks at Bruges from 1374 to 1377 compiled a dossier which illuminates the diplomatic history of those years, and the papal collector in England left a detailed account of his income and expenditure from 1374 to 1378 which makes his activities fairly clear. With these and other sources some progress can be made in fitting the Good Parliament into its immediate context.

The story as told in the chronicles and the parliament roll is, in the briefest outline, as follows. When the parliament met, the commons were asked as usual to make a grant of taxation for the king's wars and then sent away to deliberate apart from the lords. When they were debating on their own, the view which emerged was that the king would not have needed more money if he had not been badly and traitorously advised. The commons agreed to present this view and chose as their spokesman Sir Peter de la Mare, knight of the shire for Herefordshire and Steward of the Earl of March. When they returned to the general assembly of parliament they were faced by John of

4

Gaunt, Duke of Lancaster, in the king's place and only de la Mare and a few other members were admitted. Edward III at this time was an old and sick man—he died just a year later. The Black Prince, the king's once victorious and still greatly admired heir, had been incapacitated by illness for several years and died during the parliament. The king was represented by Lancaster, a much less respected person, who was suspected of being partial to the corrupt courtiers and, although his vice-regal position in the proceedings was not challenged, the meetings developed to some extent into duels between him and de la Mare. De la Mare insisted that all the commons should be admitted with him. He then asked for the appointment of a small committee of lords and bishops to meet with and advise the commons.

After more discussion and consultation the commons returned to attack outspokenly, again through de la Mare, a group of important courtiers and others associated with them. The main objects of their attack were, among the courtiers, William Latimer, the king's Chamberlain, John Neville of Raby, the Steward of the Household, and Alice Perrers who was notoriously the king's mistress; among the associates, Richard Lyons and several other merchants. Against these people the commons acted by impeachment; they acted as accusers and presented a case against the accused to the lords presided over by Lancaster. The accusations against Latimer and Lyons, the main culprits, were that they had sold licences to merchants which allowed them to export wool without taking it first to the Staple at Calais and that they had arranged loans to the king for which the Exchequer paid large premiums unnecessarily in order to make profits out of these transactions themselves. Latimer was also charged with another set of articles: he had done great harm to the king's cause in France by being an accomplice in the selling of the great fortress of St. Sauveur in Normandy to the French and by preventing the relief of the castle of Bécherel in Brittany which was also lost to the French, and as the king's lieutenant in Brittany he had oppressively plundered the people there. Neville was accused of misusing his position to secure payment of debts at the Exchequer for which he charged the creditors and to obtain excessive payment for his company in the war. These and other charges were argued at length in full

5

parliament with various dramatic episodes: for instance the former Treasurer was brought to testify that loans had been arranged without his knowledge, Latimer was personally challenged for his part in the loss of St. Sauveur by a knight who had a claim to inherit it, and William of Wykeham, the Bishop of Winchester, spoke up against Latimer in public. Finally the commons successfully made their case. Latimer and Neville were stripped of their offices. Richard Lyons was imprisoned and his property confiscated. Alice Perrers was banished from the court. Other criminals were condemned or fled. The commons triumphed over the court.

It is clear enough in the stories told by the *Anonimalle Chronicle* and the *Chronicon Angliae* that these contemporary writers found the conflict between the two contrasting antagonists, the traitorous courtiers and the surprisingly audacious knights of the shire who called them to account, exceptionally interesting and that they therefore gave generous treatment to the events of a few weeks. Our problem is to investigate the circumstances in which this unusual confrontation could take place; to decide what political issues made the court vulnerable and its critics antagonistic. We shall begin our investigation in what may seem to be an unexpectedly remote place, not in England but at the court of Pope Gregory XI.

I

England and the War Finances of Pope Gregory XI, 1372-1374

GREGORY XI, who was elected at the end of 1370, the last pope to reign from Avignon over a united Latin Christendom, is not, like his more famous predecessors Innocent III and Boniface VIII, commonly remembered as one of those popes whose powerful character exercised a decisive influence in English history. This is unjust. Gregory had a strong, destructive will which found in papal politics a field of action on a grand scale. Its effects are obvious in the history of the papacy—only an exceptionally forceful character could have carried the papacy back to Rome and wrecked the enormous edifice of political and administrative interests which had been built up at Avignon—but they are also important, and have not been duly recognized, in English history. English politics, for reasons which we shall see, were sensitive to shock-waves emanating from the papal *Curia* and the most convenient way to begin a disentanglement of the political moves at Westminster in the years 1375–7 is to set out the aims of the policy pursued at Avignon and their English implications.

Gregory was elected pope at Avignon in December 1370, returned with his court to Rome in the winter of 1376–7, and died there in 1378. He united in his character an idealistic determination to pursue the proper aims of the papacy as he conceived them with a proud extravagance and ruthlessness in the use of military force to promote these aims. His plans affected England in various ways. In the first place he took very seriously the duty to unite the western princes in a crusade against Islam. For this purpose it was essential in his eyes that he should spare no efforts to end the conflict between England and France, and from the beginning of his pontificate a succession of papal envoys attempted to mediate between the English and French kings.[1] English and French leaders negotiated with the help of papal mediators for long periods in 1375–7. Secondly Gregory was determined to maintain the position of the papacy in its Italian states and eventually to return to Rome. For the safeguarding of the papal states he waged large-scale wars in Italy and spent vast sums of money which could only be obtained by ambitious schemes for taxing the clergy of Europe. Thus, although in a sense he was the last of the medieval popes, Gregory filled that role with undiminished grandeur and with a characteristic combination of personal austerity and imperial assumptions about the importance of himself and his office. In his will he laid down that the subsidies which he expected to be paid for his wars by the clergy of England, Castile, and Portugal were to be used to endow his memorial chapel if the funds he set aside for it were inadequate.[2] St. Catherine of Siena observed correctly that he was too partial to his family, a great Avignon dynasty,[3] and the captivity of his brother Roger Beaufort, who fell into English hands at the sack of Limoges in 1370, gave him a keener interest in English affairs. But he was also a pious man whose actions were all the more resolute because they sprang from undeniably high-minded intentions. Throughout the period 1372–6 this very formidable statesman ensured that the claims of the papacy were a factor in English politics.

From 1371 until the early part of 1375 papal policy was in practice dominated primarily by the needs of a bitter and expensive war against the lord of Milan, Bernabò Visconti, to safeguard the papal states in Italy. The pattern of conflict was an old one. The papal states extended northwards as far as Bologna and expansive movements by the powers of Lombardy, which seemed to threaten Bologna or the Romagna and Tuscany to the south, had long been regarded as dangers which had to be resisted. The danger in this quarter was made more alarming by the rise of Milan to a preponderant position in

---

[1] A striking expression of the crusading ideal in relation to the Anglo-French conflict is the letter in which Gregory tried to enlist a Gascon noble, the Captal of Buch, as a leader in 1371 (O. Raynaldus, *Annales Ecclesiastici*, vii, Lucca, 1747–56, 201–2).

[2] L. d'Achery, *Spicilegium* (Paris, 1723), iii. 740.

[3] Cited by Delachenal, iv. 594.

Lombardy and the control of Milan by a régime which was expansive and showed a marked interest in the extension of its power into central Italy. The danger signal in 1371 was a Milanese threat to the small states of Ferrara and Modena which provided a defensive curtain to the north of Bologna. Gregory met this threat in 1371 by the revival of an anti-Milanese league including Ferrara, Padua, Genoa, and Florence in which the papacy was by far the most enthusiastic participant and in January 1372 sent one of his cardinals, Pierre de Bourges, to Bologna to manage the war. In June 1372 the forces of the league were defeated at Rubiera. Gregory countered by attracting Count Amedeo VI of Savoy, a rival of Milan in western Lombardy, into alliance with him and by building up an impressive force of mercenary troops, the most important part of which was the company commanded by the English captain John Hawkwood who was won over from the Milanese side by the promise of large financial rewards, to attack Milan from the south-east. In 1373 Hawkwood inflicted serious defeats on the Milanese at Crevalcuore and again at Montechiari, while Amedeo, with less enthusiasm, harried Milanese territory from the west. By the end of that year Bernabò's armies were so battered that he was disposed to seek peace. Gregory however was inflexible in his determination to accept only an abject submission from his enemy whom he had excommunicated and summoned on charges of heresy in January. It was not until July 1374 that he authorized his agents in Italy to treat with the enemy and not until the beginning of 1375 that he showed himself seriously inclined to make peace. Throughout this time the papal armies in Italy were kept in being at considerable expense. The conflict died down in the early part of 1375. A truce was finally made on 4 June.[1]

The papal war effort in Italy from 1372 to 1375 entailed the expenditure of very large sums of money. Part of this came from the nearby papal states where the papacy had considerable powers of taxation, but these were quite inadequate to support a major war. For this purpose the resources of the papacy in the

---

[1] The history of this war is elusive in modern historiography. Brief accounts, on which mine is based, will be found in *Storia di Milano* (published by the Fondazione Treccani degli Alfieri), v (Milan, 1955); L. Mirot, *La Politique pontificale et le retour du Saint-Siège à Rome en 1376* (Paris, 1899); J. Glénisson, 'Les Origines de la révolte de l'état pontifical en 1375', *Rivista di Storia della Chiesa in Italia*, v (1951).

church had to be called into play on the largest possible scale. The pope had to borrow money from his cardinals and from Italian bankers at Avignon, to levy subsidies from the clergy of the dioceses of Europe, to extract as fully as possible the payment of *Servitia* by newly appointed prelates and of annates by those newly provided to lesser benefices. For the duration of the war Bologna became a strategic centre of command into which the resources of both the papal states and the western church were poured in order to pay the mercenary armies operating in Lombardy. The war in Italy and the finances of the papal states in Italy do not directly concern us here. The demands of the papacy on the church as a whole are, however, a crucial factor in English politics and it is important to emphasize in the first place the intensity and scale of the papacy's financial effort during these years, of which its pressure on England was a part. The accounts of the Apostolic Chamber, which was nominally responsible for spiritual income from the church at large, are only incompletely preserved for the pontificate of Gregory XI, and the figures which can be quoted from them must be treated with the reserve which is usually necessary when quoting the records of medieval financial institutions: that is to say, it must be remembered that they do not cover all papal income and expenditure and that their purpose is to show the responsibilities of the accounting officials, not to provide material for a budget. Nevertheless they do give some idea of the scale of the general European financial policy of the papacy of which papal relations with England were a subsidiary part. The records of expenditure by the Chamber, which are fairly complete for the years 1373 and 1374, show that expenditure was then running at around 500,000 florins per annum, of which something approaching half was expenditure directly concerned with the war in Italy. So far as the fragmentary accounts reveal, it does not appear to have declined much in 1375.[1] This was an ambitious rate of activity and

---

[1] The detailed figures for 1373, for which only July is lacking, total 277,745 cameral florins, a few thousand florins of other kinds, and 252,302 francs. If the francs are converted into florins at a rate of 1·1 fl. to 1 fr., the total is 587,319 florins. The figures for 1374 consist almost exclusively of 297,532½ florins and 173,749 francs, equalling 488,655½ florins of which 234,805½ florins were said to be expended on the wars in Italy. (K. H. Schäfer, *Die Ausgaben der apostolischen Kammer unter den Päpsten Urban V und Gregor XI (1362–1378)*, Vatikanische Quellen zur

expenditure. The total expenditure recorded by the English Exchequer in the year 1374–5 was £139,617.[1] At the rate of 7 cameral florins to the pound sterling which the papal collector used for his calculations this would be about twice the expenditure of the Apostolic Chamber. Nearly all the money available to the Chamber came in one form or another from dues paid by churchmen outside the papal states. Nevertheless the pope waged war on a scale appropriate to a substantial lay power. And, in spite of the financial shocks suffered by ecclesiastical institutions since the Black Death and the increasing jealousy of lay powers, the pope was committed to action and expenditure on a scale comparable with the outlay of the most extravagant of his predecessors. So far as the evidence goes, Clement VI, Innocent VI, and Urban V seem to have spent considerably less. John XXII (1316–34), who had pursued a similar Italian policy in a period of greater financial opportunities, seems to have spent hardly any more.[2]

In order to cope with this heavy expenditure the pope resorted to borrowing from his cardinals and from the bankers' agents at the papal court,[3] but it was more important to maximize income. Papal income from the church was potentially of two kinds. First there was the possibility of requesting subsidies to be levied on the clergy. In 1372 and 1373 Gregory demanded subsidies from most of the provinces of England, France, Germany, Italy, Spain, and Cyprus.[4] Secondly there was the income derived from new appointments to benefices made through the *Curia*: the *Servitia* paid by prelates and the annates paid by lesser benefice holders. This income was difficult to collect because of the resistance of innumerable separate debtors and

Geschichte der päpstlichen Hof- und Finanzverwaltung 1316–1378, vi (Paderborn, 1937), 420–562. The more fragmentary figures for 1375 are on pp. 563–7.) A consolidated statement for 1374 is in A. Theiner, *Codex Diplomaticus Dominii S. Sedis*, ii (Rome, 1862), 556–9.

[1] E403/456, 457, eliminating book-keeping entries. See below, p. 70.

[2] The figures are compared by K. H. Schäfer, *Die Ausgaben der apostolischen Kammer unter Johann XXII, Vatikanische Quellen . . .*, ii (Paderborn, 1911), 15*–19*.

[3] H. Hoberg, *Die Inventare des päpstlichen Schatzes in Avignon 1314–1376* (Studi e Testi, iii, 1944), 523–41, contains records of a number of cases of plate and jewels taken from the papal treasury to be used as pledges for loans in the period 1372–6.

[4] The evidence is summarized by Glénisson, 'Les Origines de la révolte de l'état pontifical', 146, and L. Mirot, 'Les Rapports financiers de Gregoire XI et du Duc d'Anjou', *Mélanges d'Archéologie et d'Histoire*, xvii (1897), 113–14.

could only be increased by patient piecemeal effort in extracting debts. Some effort was made to do this. The first demand for a subsidy from England for the war against Milan was in a letter dated 10 March 1372. It was repeated on 1 July when the archbishops were offered the choice between a mandatory tenth which would bring in 120,000 florins or a charitable subsidy of 100,000 florins. On 17 December Gregory wrote ordering the archbishops on pain of excommunication to pay the subsidy in two portions at Easter and Michaelmas 1373. After a royal embassy to Avignon in the later part of 1373 the pope granted respite until Easter 1374. At the middle of 1375, more than three years after the original demand, nothing in fact had been done by the English church to meet it.[1] The other leg of papal policy was the effort to increase the proceeds of annates. This was promoted by sending to England a new papal collector, Arnaud Garnier, Canon of Chalons. He was appointed in October 1371, arrived in London in February 1372, and worked in this country continuously until 27 July 1374 when he went back to Avignon to report, returning to England nearly a year later in the summer of 1375.[2] His mission was essentially to hasten the collection of annates and he was successful to the extent that the annual yield from this source rose quite dramatically from an average of £335 per annum in 1370–2 to £1,080 per annum in 1372–4.[3] The papacy's financial plans were decidedly aggressive in comparison with its practice in the recent past. Annates had not been collected so effectively at any time in the 1350s or 1360s. The last demand for a subsidy had been in 1362 when the proceeds went straight into the king's pocket as a contribution to the ransom of King John of France. The last papal taxation from which the pope had received any money directly had been in the 1330s.[4] The general resentment and resistance which Gregory's demands evoked in England were an important part of the background to the still more surprising events of 1375 and after.

There were obvious reasons why most influential sections of opinion in England should be hostile to the papal demand for a

[1] Lunt, *Financial Relations*, 103–7.
[2] *Accounts Rendered by Papal Collectors in England, 1317–1378*, ed. W. E. Lunt and E. B. Graves (Memoirs of the American Philosophical Society, lxx, 1968), xxxix–xl.
[3] Lunt, *Financial Relations*, 379. [4] Ibid. 75–103.

subsidy. The king because he needed to tax the English clergy to pay for his own war plans: a grant of £50,000 had been conceded by them in the summer of 1371 and further demands would be made in 1373. The clergy because, if faced with the choice, they would obviously have to pay the king rather than the pope. The parliamentary commons because they would wish the clergy to bear as much as possible of the burden of taxation which would otherwise fall on them. Edward III responded to the demand for a subsidy by preventing the delivery of the papal letters which contained it to English prelates and was said in May 1373 to have arrested a Carmelite bearing such letters.[1] There were also obvious reasons why Garnier's drive for the more efficient collection of annates should provoke resistance. When Garnier was admitted to England in February 1372 he took an oath at Westminster in the presence of the chancellor, treasurer, and a number of other ministers to do nothing prejudicial to the king's interests and to export no money without licence.[2] In spite of his comparative success he clearly felt himself to be very much hampered in his work. Twice in the years 1372–4 he presented a petition to the king's council, meeting with the Black Prince presiding, asking for royal action to help him in extracting the Apostolic Chamber's rights, quoting a number of cases, mostly of benefices from which he could not get annates paid because they had lay patrons or because the incumbent had been presented by the king or the benefice itself was in royal hands.[3] Naturally he got no satisfaction. Royal resistance to collection of annates from a benefice which was in any way under royal patronage seems to have been his main frustration.[4] When he returned to Avignon in 1374 he presented a report to the Chamber which contained seven 'Excuses for the smallness of the receipt'. One of these was refusal by holders of benefices which had lay patrons, two were about benefices in royal patronage. The lords of the Chamber in their reply were cautious about royal patronage and ordered him to proceed 'in as pleasant and friendly a manner as you can'. They also ordered him not to try to upset one of the purely ecclesiastical local customs which he had found a hindrance in England—

---

[1] Lunt, *Financial Relations*, 105.   [2] *Foedera*, 933–4.
[3] *Accounts Rendered by Papal Collectors*, 477–8; Lunt, *Financial Relations*, 377–8.
[4] Lunt, *Financial Relations*, 365.

but which happened to work to the advantage of cardinals—namely that archdeacons should not pay annates on the profits of jurisdiction. The general impression conveyed by the hints in Garnier's documents is that he pushed his claims hard and, even in the eyes of the Chamber for which he was working, erred on the side of offensiveness to royal rights and local customs rather than on that of complaisance.[1]

By the summer of 1373 papal action had become sufficiently disturbing for the king to wish to make some positive response. It was probably in June of that year that a great council presided over by the Black Prince and Archbishop Whittlesey discussed the papal demand for a subsidy. According to the account—admittedly of very doubtful reliability—which has been preserved in the continuation of the *Eulogium Historiarum*, the prelates upheld papal temporal authority and therefore the right to levy a subsidy, Whittlesey summing up the matter: 'He [the pope] is lord of all, that we cannot deny.' The opposite view of a papacy without temporal lordship was put by a Franciscan, John Mardisley, and the archbishop, crumpling under the prince's withering scorn, eventually agreed that the pope was not a lord in England.[2] Whatever truth there is in this story, concern at Westminster was sufficiently strong for an embassy to be sent to Avignon in July. The delegation, which consisted of John Gilbert Bishop of Bangor, the theologian Ughtred of Boldon O.S.B., the canon lawyer John Sheppey, and a layman Sir William Burton, was delayed and arrived in Avignon late in the year and the negotiations did not reach a conclusion until December. We have several pieces of information about these negotiations. First there is a letter from the pope to Edward III, dated 21 December 1373 and important chiefly because it sets out the English demands. It also says that a written agreement is enclosed and that further replies have been given to the envoys verbally.[3] The written agreement itself is

<hr />

[1] *Accounts Rendered by Papal Collectors*, 477 (Garnier's report), 483–4 (the *Camera's* reply); cf. Lunt, *Financial Relations*, 360–1.

[2] *Eulogium Historiarum*, iii (Rolls Series, 1863), 337–9. On the chronology and authenticity of this account see J. I. Catto, 'An Alleged Great Council of 1374', *English Historical Review*, lxxxii (1967).

[3] *CPL* iv. 127, cf. E. Perroy, *L'Angleterre et le grand schisme d'occident* (Paris, 1933), 32–3; Lunt, *Financial Relations*, 352. Chronicle mentions of the mission in *Polychronicon*, viii. 379, and Walsingham, i. 316, say that it was about reservations of benefices and episcopal elections.

known from a letter from the pope to the later papal envoys designated to treat with English representatives, in which it is set out.[1] Thirdly there are verbal replies to the English demands, known from a copy later entered on the Chancery patent roll.[2]

From these sources it can be deduced in the first place that the English demands were quite far reaching. They may be roughly summarized as follows: (a) an end to interference by papal provisions with royal patronage and regalian rights; (b) unspecified complaints about papal interference with episcopal, abbatial, and other elections; (c) objections of some unspecified kind to the collations to English benefices given to aliens and the large number of benefices in England held by cardinals; (d) a demand for citations to the courts at Avignon to cease while communication was difficult during the war; (e) quashing of reservations of benefices; (f) no exercise of reservations or provisions in prejudice of rights of patronage in future; (g) no subsidy to be demanded while the war continued. These demands, if granted, would have entailed not only a complete halt to Gregory's war finance as far as England was concerned but also a substantial reduction of the rights which had been claimed by the papacy before the current financial offensive began. The papal reply to them was rather sympathetic and accommodating in tone but it gave practically nothing away. The provisional written agreement concluded with the English envoys proposed a further conference in the coming year (1374). Meanwhile the *Curia* would suspend cases in the papal courts involving the king's regalian rights until 24 June, and would suspend personal citations to the courts for a year. In return the king was expected to refrain from disturbing any clergy provided to benefices if they were already in possession of them and from using regalian rights to allot benefices which had already been allotted by papal reservation or provision. This agreement might involve the king in concessions of substance; it could involve the pope only in judicial concessions. The verbal promises as reported by the English envoys made only one concession

---

[1] *CPL* iv. 201; printed in full, Raynaldus, *Annales Ecclesiastici*, vii. 258–9, and J. Loserth, 'Studien zur Kirchenpolitik Englands im XIV. Jahrhundert', *Sitzungsberichte der Wiener Akademie*, Phil.-Hist. Klasse, cxxxvi (1897), 129.

[2] *Foedera*, 1072; identified by Perroy, *L'Angleterre et le grand schisme*, 45.

—that the payment of annates by those who received reservations (a recent innovation made in April 1371) would end on 1 March 1374. Apart from that, Gregory replied to the English demands about reservations, provisions, annates, elections, and benefices held by cardinals by saying that he would not give up any of his powers but would use them moderately, adding in the case of annates, the main issue, that he could not abandon his present practice 'because of the burdens of the wars'. The subsidy does not seem to have been mentioned. Altogether the gap between the royal and papal positions was very wide and hardly affected by the English mission to Avignon.

The parliament which met at Westminster from 14 October to 10 December 1373, while the envoys were at Avignon, demonstrated the community of feeling and interest between the king and his lay commons about these matters. The commons complained about papal reservations and provisions because of the disturbance of free elections and the outflow of money for annates which they entailed and the hold which aliens had on the English church. Embracing in their condemnation their prejudices against both Italian merchants and alien clergy, they alleged that 'alien religious, [behaving] like Lombards and other aliens living in the kingdom, by their subtleties carry off treasure from the kingdom, and reveal by their letters the secrets of the kingdom and send them abroad to the enemy.' The commons felt themselves, they said, unable to endure these extra burdens while they had to sustain the cost of the war. The characteristic mixture of self-interest and prejudice embodied in the commons petition was at this time entirely in tune with the government's feelings. The council was able to reply that 'The king has sent his honourable envoys to the court of Rome about the grievances contained in this petition.'[1]

The English church, always faced by the dilemma of choosing to displease either the king or the pope by the refusal of conflicting demands for money, was even more conscious than usual of the competing rapacity of these two plunderers of its property. On the one hand churchmen must have realized that the latest pope was one of the most demanding. On the other hand its experience of royal demands in the last few years had been painful. In the convocation of January 1370 the clergy had been

[1] *RP* 320.

browbeaten into granting the king three tenths to be paid at midsummer of successive years, 1370, 1371, and 1372.[1] Only a year later in the convocation of April 1371, after the famous anti-clerical demonstration in the parliament of the previous month which involved the substitution of a lay chancellor and a lay treasurer for the bishops of Winchester and Exeter,[2] they had been browbeaten again. They had been summoned from their proper meeting-place at St. Paul's to John of Gaunt's manor of the Savoy, where the Prince of Wales, attended by other lay lords, according to the record set down in the archbishop's register, 'first requested urgently and then demanded'[3] a grant of £50,000 to match the special grant made by the commons which was to be levied by parishes. The *Anonimalle Chronicle* also emphasizes that the clergy made the grant under threats.[4] In May the dismissed prelates, Winchester and Exeter, were summoned to council, 'their excuses notwithstanding', to take measures for hastening the collection of the tax.[5] It was to be paid in two instalments, half at Michaelmas (29 September) 1371 and half at the Purification (2 February) 1372. From the point of view of the normal clerical taxpayer it had the advantage that contributions were also to be taken from those who did not ordinarily pay, the exempt clergy, aliens holding benefices, and stipendiary priests.[6] Nevertheless it meant that in 1371 and 1372 the clergy were exceptionally heavily taxed. It is perhaps significant that the year 1372 saw a sudden expansion in the use of the hitherto rare writ *de excommunicato capiendo* for the arrest of people excommunicated for refusal to pay clerical subsidies: 90 cases are known in that year, 143 in 1373, 173 in 1374.[7]

[1] Wilkins, 82–4; D. B. Weske, *Convocation of the Clergy* (1937), 163–4.

[2] Discussed by Tout, iii. 266–77.

[3] 'Iisdem primo instanter supplicavit, et demum requisivit,' Wilkins, 91; cf. Weske, 164–5.

[4] *Anon*, 67.

[5] Issue roll entry dated 24 May of letters to them summoning them to the council at Winchester on 8 June (which was to amend the arrangements for the lay tax in the light of the discovery of the Exchequer's mistake in thinking that there were 40,000 parishes in England) 'non obstantibus excusacionibus per ipsos factis pro diligencia per ipsos appositura circa colleccionem subsidii per clerum ultimi domino Regi concessi' (E 403/442).

[6] Instructions to the bishops for the collection of the tax, 5 May 1971 (*CFR*, 1369–77, 118); the point is mentioned by the continuators of Higden (*Polychronicon*, viii. 376).

[7] F. D. Logan, *Excommunication and the Secular Arm in Medieval England* (Toronto, 1968), 55–6.

The convocation of Canterbury, which met at St. Paul's in the first week of December 1373, was much less well disposed to the king than parliament was. Soon after its assembly convocation was visited by a deputation from the council consisting of the Earls of March and Salisbury, Lord Latimer, Guy Brian, Sir John Knyvet the Chancellor, Lord Scrope the Treasurer, and Nicholas Carew the Keeper of the Privy Seal. Knyvet, speaking in English, presented the king's case for financial aid from the clergy to support his war. The deputation then withdrew. The archbishop preached in Latin. Then the Bishop of London, Simon Sudbury, expounded 'more clearly in the vernacular' the need for a subsidy and urged the clergy to vote it.[1] Next day the archbishop was sick and they met with Sudbury in the chair. The lesser clergy, after deliberation apart, returned to the prelates to say that they wished to excuse themselves from such a payment giving as reasons the money still owed by the province of York to the crown, the recent payments by themselves, and 'the sum requested by the lord pope from the prelates and clergy of the province of Canterbury which was refused because of the poverty of the clergy which was alleged to the pope' ('propter cleri impotentiam que erat domino pape in hac parte allegata')—Sudbury and other prelates who were not named urged them to think again. On 3 December proctors of the clergy granted a tenth, but it was to be paid in June 1374 and February 1375 and two days later they refused to increase it as some of the bishops apparently wished them to do.

Together with their grant the clergy presented a list of grievances and in a further meeting on 7 December the Bishop of Hereford, William Courtenay, is reported to have expressed his resentment at royal action against the clergy outspokenly, saying that 'unless the injuries done to himself and his church of Hereford in various ways unjustly by the king and his council were reformed the said lord king should not have a penny from him or his clergy on account of that grant and he expressly

---

[1] 'Dominus Londoniensis episcopus necessitatem regni et ecclesie dictis prelatis et clero nomine prefati domini Cantuariensis Archiepiscopi exposuit magis clare in vulgare eosdem prelatos et clerum ad aliquod competens subsidium in hac parte domino Regi prestandum excitando et quod super concessionem dicti subsidii plenius deliberarent' (Lambeth Palace, Register of Archbishop Whittlesey, fol. 64ᵛ). The record of this convocation is unprinted. It is summarized in D. B. Weske, *Convocation of the Clergy*, 136–8, 165–6.

rejected the grant.'[1] This is the first clear indication of the roles which Sudbury and Courtenay, the next two archbishops, were to adopt in the next few years as defenders respectively of the king and of ecclesiastical liberties in convocation. On this occasion, however, royal pressure had succeeded again and the crown had obtained matching grants of money from parliament and convocation.

These three sets of negotiations in the latter part of 1373 (parliament in October, the negotiations at Avignon, and the convocation in December) made the positions of the various parties clear enough. The crown was at one with the commons in resisting the papal financial measures. An apparently un-bridgeable gulf separated them from the papal court. The clergy, ground between the millstones of papal and royal de-mands, had to submit to the nearer and more dangerous power. This pattern was a familiar one and does not seem to have been much changed by the diplomatic manœuvres of 1374. The English embassy returned from Avignon on 20 February in that year. The crown responded to one of the pope's verbal messages, to the effect that he was not aware that he had granted any benefices to aliens except cardinals, by instituting a menacing inquiry into benefices held by aliens which did not in fact reveal any startling numbers.[2] Nevertheless the king decided to go on with the negotiations. On 11 March it was announced that the king accepted his envoys' interim agreement with the pope and that English delegates would meet those of the pope at Bruges or Calais at midsummer.[3]

Gregory named his envoys, the bishops of Pamplona and Sinigaglia and the Provost of Valencia, in May. The English envoys (the Bishop of Bangor and Sir William Burton from the previous embassy, together with the Oxford philosopher John Wycliffe,[4] Juan Guttiérrez Dean of Segovia, Castilian secretary

---

[1] 'Nisi iniurie sibi et ecclesie sue Herfordensi ut dixit multipliciter iniuste illate per regem et eius consilium essent et sint reformate quod dictus dominus rex de eo aut clero sue diocesis ratione dicte concessionis nullum haberet denarium et dicte concessioni expresse contradixit.' (Register of Whittlesey, fol. 65.)

[2] Perroy, *L'Angleterre et le grand schisme*, 34; *Calendar of Inquisitions Miscellaneous*, iii. 350–1; *The Register of the Diocese of Worcester . . . 'Registrum Sede Vacante'*, 1301–1435, ed. J. W. Willis Bund, part IV, Worcestershire Historical Society (1897) 307–8.

[3] *Foedera*, 1000; Perroy, 35.

[4] A payment for delivery of a privy seal letter to John Wycliffe at Oxford

to John of Gaunt, Simon Multon a Chancery clerk, and Robert Bealknap a lawyer) left at the end of July. They met at Bruges. These negotiations were neither long nor, on the face of it, fruitful. By 14 September Burton, Bealknap, and Wycliffe had returned to England.[1] The Provost of Valencia returned to Avignon then or soon after. There may have been further talks between the remaining envoys at the end of the year but by 10 January 1375 all the English delegates except Guttiérrez had returned home.[2]

Nothing is known about the discussions between the envoys at Bruges in 1374. Up to this point nothing suggests that the English had abandoned the hard line which they had maintained in negotiations through the previous three years. In the next few months, however, a surprising concordat was made which granted the pope his chief demand. Nothing in the previous history of Anglo-papal relations foreshadows this except the urgency of the pressure for money which Gregory XI had maintained throughout his pontificate.

summoning him 'ad consilium', presumably to discuss the mission, was entered on 3 June (E 403/451).

[1] Wycliffe had been advanced £60 by the Exchequer before leaving. His wages and expenses came to £7 17s. 9d. less than that (A. Larson, 'English Embassies during the Hundred Years War', *English Historical Review*, lv (1940), 431), which suggests that his mission was shorter than had been expected.

[2] For the chronology of the meetings see Perroy, *L'Angleterre et le grand schisme*, 34–7. He is mistaken, however, about the evidence for increased papal optimism about an agreement with England: the letter to which he refers in p. 37 n. 2 is dated 31 December 1375, not 1374 (*CPL* iv. 112; Lunt, *Financial Relations*, 110).

2

English Strategy in France,
1372-1374

WHILE the main preoccupation of the papal *Curia* was the war
in Lombardy the English court in these years was equally concerned with the war in France. Since 1369 more or less continuous warfare in France had been revived. At that time very
large areas of France had been controlled by English soldiers:
Gascony, Poitou, Brittany, parts of Normandy, Calais. But the
period with which we are concerned here was one in which
fighting was on the whole going in favour of French rather than
English forces so that the war was both expensive and politically
depressing. The great turning-point in this respect was the year
1372 when English forces suffered two major disasters. The first
was the naval battle of La Rochelle on 22 June. A fleet which
was taking the king's new lieutenant, John Hastings, Earl of
Pembroke, to Gascony was completely destroyed by a fleet
largely supplied by the king of France's ally Henry II of Trastamara, king of Castile. Pembroke himself was carried off to
languish in an apparently severe captivity in Castilian prisons
in which his health was so undermined that three years later the
journey to freedom at Calais (in return for a huge ransom)
killed him. Strategically the battle revealed that the Castilian
alliance had given Charles V of France the help of a naval
power which was inherently superior to English fleets and which
was eventually to make the Bay of Biscay, the Channel, and even
the south coast for a time dangerous for Englishmen.[1] The other
disaster—which Pembroke's expedition had been intended to

---

[1] On the Battle of La Rochelle see Delachenal, iv. 408–18; J. W. Sherborne,
'The Battle of La Rochelle and the War at Sea, 1372–5', *Bulletin of the Institute of
Historical Research*, xlii (1969), 19–23; on the implications of Castilian sea power,
P. E. Russell, *The English Intervention in Spain and Portugal in the Time of Edward III
and Richard II* (Oxford, 1955), ch. xi.

prevent—was the reconquest of Poitou, Saintonge, and Angoumois by French forces led by the Constable Bertrand du Guesclin in the summer of 1372.[1] These large areas had appeared to be firmly loyal to Edward III a few months earlier. Their reconquest for the French king brought to an end the enormously swollen Aquitaine which had been won by the military successes of Edward III and his sons and enshrined in the Treaty of Brétigny. The area of English control in south-west France was now reduced to something more like its old proportions. These two major defeats of 1372 were followed in the early summer of 1373 by the occupation of the greater part of Brittany, formerly controlled by the anglophile and English-advised Duke John IV de Montfort, again by Du Guesclin.[2] The net result of these changes was that English control and influence in France were effectively reduced to (1) Calais and the area around it; (2) the fortress of St. Sauveur in Normandy; (3) Brest and a few other strongholds in Brittany holding out against the French invasion; (4) the large area of traditional Gascony around Bordeaux. There was also the naval threat. The English in France had been placed in a severely diminished and defensive position.

How did the king and the leaders of the English court react to this situation? That question has important bearings on the political issues of 1376 but it is a difficult question to answer. A good deal is known about what they did but not very much about why they did it. Motives are not clear. And since conflicts in England about motives in war and diplomacy are important in interpreting the events of 1376 it is also important to try to elucidate as far as possible how the conflicts arose. It may be best to begin by listing the main military efforts by the English crown which followed the setbacks of 1372.

1. The first was a naval expedition by about 6,000 men, led by the king himself, the Black Prince, Lancaster, and several other nobles, in August to October 1372. The forces used in this had been intended for land operations in France and Iberia. They were diverted to the sea probably because the news of La Rochelle in June persuaded the king that he ought in some way to counter the new naval threat. The expedition was impressive in size and leadership but it was so badly hampered by

[1] Delachenal, iv. 422–39.
[2] Ibid. 474–7; M. Jones, *Ducal Brittany 1364–1399* (Oxford, 1970), 73–6.

unfavourable winds that it lasted only a few weeks, and its purpose never became clear.[1]

2. On 16 October 1372 a small force of 480 men at arms and 480 archers under John Neville of Raby, the steward of the royal household, went to Brittany. The expedition had been planned much earlier, in May and June, but was presumably held up by the king's naval expedition. Neville went to Brittany to fight in the service of Duke John de Montfort. He took over the fortress of Brest and hung on to it under French siege until some time in 1374 when he handed it over to other Englishmen.[2]

3. At the end of March 1373 quite a large force of soldiers and sailors led by William Montague, Earl of Salisbury, was sent to Brittany. It is reported to have pillaged at St. Malo and to have made an ineffective attempt to relieve Brest.[3]

4. Finally there was the famous expedition led by John of Gaunt, Duke of Lancaster. This had been planned as early as March 1373. In the end it crossed to Calais about the middle of July, nearly 6,000 men with main contingents led by Lancaster, the Duke of Brittany, the Earls of Stafford, Suffolk, and Warwick, Ralph Basset of Drayton, Hugh Calveley, Edward Despenser, and Henry Percy. The army then marched through France to Bordeaux where it arrived at the end of December.[4]

No serious military enterprise was undertaken in 1374. Indeed there was no serious military effort between John of Gaunt's march through France (July–December 1373) and an expedition to Brittany which was planned by August 1374 but did not actually go until April–July 1375.

The clearest purpose which can be seen behind these expeditions is the attempt to sustain and rescue the Duke of Brittany which evidently led to the sending of the forces commanded by Neville and Salisbury. This demands a little explanation. John IV de Montfort, born about 1340, was the claimant to the Duchy of Brittany supported by Edward III. He had been

[1] J. W. Sherborne, 'Indentured Retinues and English Expeditions to France, 1369–1380', *English Historical Review*, lxxix (1964), 725; id., 'The Battle of La Rochelle', 23–4; Delachenal, iv. 434; Walsingham, *Historia Anglicana*, i. 315.

[2] Sherborne, 'Indentured Retinues', 725–7; Jones, *Ducal Brittany*, 147; Delachenal, iv. 456–77. *Anon*, 71.

[3] Jones, 74; Delachenal, iv. 471; Froissart, viii, § 735.

[4] Sherborne, 'Indentured Retinues', 727–30; Delachenal, iv. 480–500.

brought up at the English court, married first to the king's daughter Mary and secondly to the Black Prince's step-daughter Joan Holland, and had been dependent on English support to put him in control of his duchy. On 19 July 1372 a new alliance was made between Duke John and King Edward in which the two parties promised mutual aid and Edward promised to send an armed force to help him, to give him the earldom of Richmond in England, and to wipe out his debts to the English crown.[1] The introduction to the charter by which John was granted the Honor of Richmond expressed fulsomely his close personal relationship to the English court:

Our most dear and illustrious relation John, Duke of Brittany and Count of Montfort, who as a youth was brought up in our household, then advancing to the strength of manhood, so that he should not be foreign to our royal house, bound himself to us with a double pact of kinship; and not merely accommodated himself always to all our wishes but even when he was separated from us by a great distance and surrounded by our enemies does not cease to devote his strength to our honour and advantage and moreover, applying himself as he best might to their defence against the continuous attack and power of our rivals, labours to assist us and, as we know from clear proofs, to expose himself and his property effectively and with zealous affection.[2]

The grant of Richmond to John de Montfort was in itself a large and expensive concession on the part of the crown because it had to be taken from its previous holder Lancaster and he had to be compensated by a massive grant of the honours of Tickhill and Knaresborough.[3] Though the affectionate relation-ship between Edward III and John de Montfort concealed crude political interests on both sides—the English desire to use Brittany as a foothold and field of operations, the duke's desire to secure independence by playing off the English and French crowns—still the treaty implied a good deal of keenness on Edward's part about the Breton alliance. The sending of Neville's force in October followed from the treaty. The great weakness of Duke John's position, however, was that he did not

---

[1] *Foedera*, 953–5; on this treaty and its implications see Jones, 66–70.

[2] *Registrum Honoris de Richmond*, ed. R. Gale (1722), 192–3.

[3] The exchange is described by R. Somerville, *History of the Duchy of Lancaster*, i (1953), 52–3.

command the enthusiastic support of the nobility of his duchy and when French pressure increased in 1373 he could not resist it. Neither Neville's expedition nor that of Salisbury seems to have done much to fortify him. At the end of April he fled to England leaving his wife at Auray. According to Froissart he went straight from Cornwall to Windsor 'where the king was holding court, who gave him good cheer when he saw him because he called him his son-in-law'.[1] There were still English garrisons in Brittany at Brest, Auray, Derval, and Bécherel holding out against the French, and the expedition being prepared for France under John of Gaunt was evidently intended to sail in May from Plymouth to Brittany.[2]

In the course of May 1373, however, the place of assembly of John of Gaunt's expedition was changed from Plymouth to Dover or Sandwich.[3] When it eventually left in July it landed at Calais and travelled to the east of Paris and across Auvergne to Gascony, never going anywhere near Brittany although the Duke of Brittany was, apart from Gaunt, the principal commander and took a large retinue with him. What was it intended to do? One explanation that has been offered is that it was meant to further John of Gaunt's claim to the kingdom of Castile. This hypothesis also demands some preliminary explanation. For many years the throne of Castile was disputed between two rival claimants: Peter I and Henry II of Trastamara. English interest in Iberia stemmed from an alliance between Edward III and Peter I and from the once highly successful intervention by the Black Prince. At the battle of Najera in 1367 the Prince had defeated Henry of Trastamara and reinstated Peter. Thus was established a close link between the legitimate ruler of Castile and the Black Prince's court at Bordeaux. In 1369 Peter I was ousted and killed by Henry of Trastamara. In 1370 the Black Prince returned from Bordeaux to England and his position in Gascony fell to Lancaster who had also taken part in the Najera campaign. A year later, in September 1371, still in Gascony, Lancaster married Constanza, the daughter and eldest surviving child of Peter I. In

---

[1] Froissart, viii. § 726.
[2] Sherborne, 'Indentured Retinues', 727.
[3] *John of Gaunt's Register, 1372–1376,* ed. S. Armitage-Smith (Camden Society, ser. 3, xx–xxi, 1911), i. 131.

1372 therefore, when he returned to England, Lancaster had very strong links with Gascony and Castile and the strongest reasons for being interested in that part of Europe. With his wife he had acquired a claim to the throne of Castile which he adopted and advertized persistently from 1372 onwards by using the title of 'King of Castile and Leon'. Not only did he maintain a skeleton Castilian chancery to issue documents in his name and shelter refugee adherents to his cause in his court; the interest of his family in his claim was shown also by the marriage of his brother Edmund Langley, Earl of Cambridge, to Constanza's sister Isabel in July 1372, apparently at Edward III's command. A possible expedition to Castile was envisaged in the indenture which Lancaster made with the king in July 1372 to take troops to Aquitaine and in the late summer of 1372 an English embassy went to Aragon. While Lancaster was marching through France in the autumn of 1373 another English embassy under Sir Thomas Felton, the Seneschal of Gascony, was in Aragon trying to make an alliance with King Peter III. After Lancaster arrived in Bordeaux a further embassy went from there to Aragon in the early part of 1374.[1] In the light of Lancaster's undoubted pretensions to the throne of Castile, the repeated diplomatic efforts to secure an alliance with Aragon from 1372 to 1374, and the diversion of the expedition of 1373 from Plymouth to Sandwich, it seems possible to argue that the great *chevauchée* was intended as a prelude to an invasion of Castile, or at least as a preliminary fortification of the English position in Gascony.

The purpose of Lancaster's great march of 1373 cannot be decided for certain. The only clear impression given by the chronicles is that the expedition was a grandiose failure. As the author of the *Chronique des Règnes de Jean II et de Charles V* put it, commenting on the reception of Lancaster when he returned to England after the expedition:

it is said that his father and the Prince of Wales, his brother, did not give him very good cheer because he had achieved so little in the expedition, though it was to have been the greatest ever made in France by the English. Altogether he had lost many men and horses, for he and his army had taken from England 30,000 horses

[1] For all these events see Russell, *English Intervention*, 168–217.

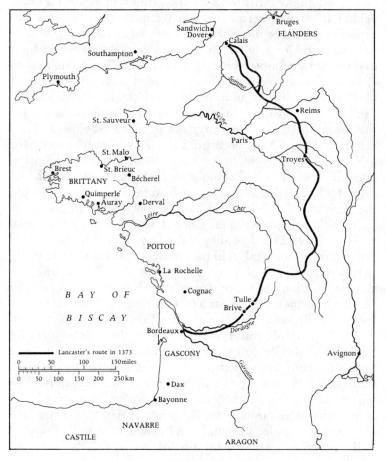

Sandwich
Dover
Bruges
Calais
FLANDERS
Southampton
Plymouth
Somme
Seine
Reims
St. Sauveur
Paris
Troyes
St. Malo
Brest
St. Brieuc
Bécherel
BRITTANY
Quimperle
Auray
Derval
Loire
Cher
POITOU
La Rochelle
BAY OF
Cognac
Tulle
Brive
BISCAY
Dordogne
Bordeaux
Lancaster's route in 1373
0   50   100   150miles
0   50   100   150   200   250 km
GASCONY
Garonne
Avignon
Dax
Bayonne
NAVARRE
CASTILE
ARAGON

FIGURE 1

and more and could only bring to Bordeaux 6,000 and he had lost the third of his men and more.[1]

Lancaster brought his army into Bordeaux with little achievement and many privations in the winter in central France behind it. It had certainly been planned on a grand scale. Froissart describes the elaborate equipment including mobile mills and bridges with which it set out[2] and the records suggest that the army numbered nearly 6,000 men.[3] Though there is no clear indication of where it was intended to go, it seems most likely that the original aim was to attack the Paris area and the French forces invading Brittany. There are various reasons for this assumption. First the command was divided between Lancaster and the Duke of Brittany, who was surely too hard pressed in his own duchy to have taken part in a campaign unconnected with it. Secondly there is the route which the army took. Starting off southwards from Calais it went round the Paris area by Reims and Troyes, south again to the upper Loire valley, then west to the Cher above Montluçon and down to Tulle, Brive, and the valley of the Dordogne. This was a very long journey, undertaken in part in the depths of winter. It can hardly have been planned as a way of strengthening the English position in Gascony or as a prelude to intervention in Iberia; it seems on the contrary likely that the route which the force actually took was the result of a diversion from its planned route. A plausible interpretation is that the commanders intended, like Knolles in 1370 and Thomas of Woodstock in 1380, both of whom attempted a similar manœuvre, to go south past Paris and then westwards to Brittany or Normandy. This would have been a manageable *chevauchée* which would also have eased the position in Brittany. It failed because the French forces under Burgundy and Anjou were well organized and successful in keeping the English out of the Paris area by gentle pressure without a showdown which might have established English superiority in a pitched battle.[4]

[1] *Chronique des Règnes de Jean II et de Charles V,* ed. R. Delachenal, ii (Société de l'Histoire de France, 1916), 174.
[2] Froissart, viii. § 732.   [3] Sherborne, 'Indentured Retinues', 728–30.
[4] The route and the character of French resistance are worked out by Delachenal, iv. 488–500. Some fifteenth-century chroniclers expressly saw the expedition as an attempt to meet the Duke of Brittany's need for relief: *La Chronique du bon duc Loys de Bourbon,* ed. A-M. Chazand (Société de l'Histoire de France,

The possibility of further English intervention in Iberia was undoubtedly in the air. A Mantuan envoy at Avignon, reporting the gossip of the papal court on 4 February 1374, said that Lancaster intended to invade Castile in the spring but his letter contained garbled accounts of both this expedition and what appears to be Edward III's expedition in 1372 and cannot in itself carry great weight.[1] The courts of Aragon and Navarre also, however, appear to have thought at the beginning of 1374 that immediate intervention in Iberia by Lancaster was a serious possibility. The negotiations with Aragon by Lancaster's envoys Sir William Elmham and Sir Walter Benedict encouraged this belief which the king apparently continued to hold until April.[2] A servant of the king of Navarre, captured by the French in 1378, reported under interrogation among other things that the king had visited Lancaster at Dax in Lent 1374 and asked in vain for military help.[3] But although Lancaster did retain his pretensions to the throne of Castile, which he invaded again in 1386, and must have wished throughout to encourage the belief that he was a serious pretender, these expectations in the southern courts of imminent action by him can only have been based on remote ignorance of the real situation at the English court and recollections of the great English deeds of the previous decade. There is no real evidence that the expedition of 1373 was intended to have anything to do with Spain.[4] It is more likely that its aim was to damage the French and help the Duke of Brittany. As it turned out it failed in both these aims.

1876), 50; *Chronique Normande de Pierre Cochon*, ed. C. de Robillard Beaurepaire (Société de l'Histoire de Normandie, 1870), 128. But their testimony cannot be taken very seriously.

[1] Lancaster 'qui se apelat regem Yspanie, discurit totum regnum Francie cum XVI millia armatorum et, ut dicitur, in vere isto venturo vult intrare regnum Castelle.' So the king of Castile is going to meet him with a big army and the king of England has collected 'gentes infinitos pedites et equites' and with all his sons except Thomas who is a minor intends to cross the sea to France. (A. Segre, 'I dispacci di Cristoforo da Piacenza procuratore mantovano alla corte pontificia (1371–1383)', *Archivio Storico Italiano*, ser. 5, xliii (1909), 54.)

[2] Russell, *English Intervention*, 209–16.

[3] E. Martène and U. Durand, *Thesaurus Novorum Anecdotorum* (Paris, 1717), i, col. 1572.

[4] Russell, *English Intervention*, 205–6, refers to a partially legible copy of a letter issued in June 1373 when Gaunt was appointed Lieutenant and Captain General in France asking for prayers for his expedition (*Historical Manuscripts Commission, Various Collections*, i. 221). The text is probably that printed in full in *Foedera*, 983

In 'Le Libvre du bon Jehan, duc de Bretagne', a verse history composed by Guillaume de Saint-André, one of the duke's servants, there is a passage describing a quarrel between Lancaster and John de Montfort towards the end of their long expedition. According to this story Lancaster suddenly demanded that Brittany should pay half the wages of the troops they had with them if he wished to continue to share the command. Brittany replied that he had spent all he had borrowed on advance payments before setting out on the expedition and had no money left. If Lancaster would lend him money for present needs he would enter into written obligations and pay later. Lancaster refused: Brittany must either pay or give up command. Brittany therefore with a force of only sixty men left the main army apparently somewhere in the upper Dordogne valley above Sarlat. By skill and good luck he evaded the French and got to Bordeaux by himself.[1] This story may reflect quite faithfully a quarrel about the command of the army with the penniless Duke of Brittany in a weak position. There may have been behind it some difference of opinion about the route, though there is no hint of this in the narrative. It is particularly interesting, however, for the student of English policy and strategy because it suggests strongly that Lancaster and Brittany were not entirely in harmony in 1373 and, after such an episode, are not likely to have been on good terms in later years. This may be helpful in attempts later on to explain divisions in English policy.

It is not clear just when in 1374 John de Montfort returned to England after leaving the expedition in France and visiting his wife at Auray on the way. Evidently, however, he went back to use his influence at the court to get an expedition to Brittany.[2] By 10 May an expedition to Brittany for him was being discussed. An entry on that day records the sending of a privy

(cf. *CCR*, 1369–74, 563), which contains no reference to an intended invasion of Castile. I am indebted to the late K. B. McFarlane for drawing my attention to this.

[1] 'Le Libvre du Bon Jehan, duc de Bretagne' in *Chronique de Bertrand du Guesclin*, ed. E. Charrière (Collection de Documents Inédits sur l'Histoire de France, 1839), ii. 489–502. Cf. Delachenal, iv. 497; Jones, *Ducal Brittany*, 77.

[2] According to the *Chronicon Briocense* (P. H. Morice, *Mémoires pour servir de preuves à l'histoire ecclésiastique et civile de Bretagne* (Paris, 1742–6), ii. 47) he went by sea from Bordeaux to Brittany, joined his wife at Auray, fortified that castle and Derval and Brest, but found the Breton nobility corrupted by the king of France. He therefore returned with his wife to the honor of Richmond in England.

seal letter 'with a note enclosed concerning certain articles touching the passage of the Duke of Brittany to the parts of Brittany' to Lancaster, the Archbishop of Canterbury, the Bishop of London, the Earl of Arundel, and the Bishop of Winchester, asking for their advice.[1] By August of that year, as we shall see, preparations for such an expedition were in full swing. John of Gaunt left Bordeaux for England early in April 1374 and was in London early in May.[2] He appears from his register to have remained in or near London except for a journey to his northern estates between late August and early October. He was therefore in contact with Westminster throughout the planning of the next phase of English policy. He lost 66s. 8d. playing dice in Lord Latimer's house in London in July.[3]

During the summer of 1374, while the first steps towards an expedition to Brittany were being taken, another factor in the diplomatic situation was also becoming more important: papal efforts to secure peace between England and France by mediation. Intermittent efforts by Gregory XI to persuade the two kings to lay down their arms had taken place throughout his pontificate. A new phase of effort started in early September 1373 with the appointment of two legates, the Bishop of Carpentras and the Archbishop of Ravenna. They are said to have made their first move immediately by approaching Lancaster in the middle of his *chevauchée* in the field near Troyes at the end of September. This approach was rebuffed.[4] Lancaster did, however, use the pope's intervention early in 1374 to secure a brief local truce to end on 21 May between his forces and Du Guesclin's in Gascony, presumably to enable him to get away from Bordeaux without further catastrophe.[5] The papal peace offensive continued in the summer.

From the obscure story of English strategic policy—to use an inappropriate modern phrase—only tentative conclusions can be drawn. The main impression which it leaves is that the most prominent objective of English military planning in 1373 and after was probably the defence of Brittany. This may have been because John de Montfort had much personal influence at

---

[1] E 403/454 (18 May), 'cum quadam cedula inclusa de certis articulis tangentibus passagium Ducis Britanniae versus partes Britanniae'.

[2] Delachenal, iv. 500, and entries in *John of Gaunt's Register 1372–1376*.

[3] *Register 1372–1376*, ii. 302.   [4] *Anglo-French Negotiations*, xiii.

[5] Ibid. xiv–xv.

court; he was a favourite of the old king and it is interesting that Froissart in his, admittedly rather confused, account of the expedition planned in August 1374 says that de Montfort arranged it through the influence of Alan Buxhill, a courtier knight who was constable of the Tower.[1] It may have been because courtiers had an interest in safeguarding the two great threatened fortresses of Bécherel (which Latimer held of the king) and St. Sauveur (which Buxhill held of the king);[2] or because strategic considerations suggested that Brittany, with its puppet duke and its harbours useful for warfare in the Channel, was both defensible and worth defending. Whatever the reason, the court seemed to be committed to the support of John de Montfort as its chief sphere of activity in the Anglo-French war.

[1] Not chamberlain, as Froissart says (§ 760), though he had been under-chamberlain in 1369–70 (Tout, vi. 47).

[2] For the significance of Bécherel and St. Sauveur see below, p. 37.

3

The first reversal of court policy
in 1375

I. THE NEW PEACE TALKS

By midsummer 1375 the main objectives of English policy
which have been described in the two previous chapters had
been abandoned. The court had apparently capitulated to the
pope's financial pressure and the attempt to support the Duke
of Brittany by military force had been replaced by a humiliating
truce with the French king. It was this dual reversal of policy
that created the essential conditions for the Good Parliament of
1376. The agreements between the king and the pope and
between the king and his French adversary were made in the
course of negotiations at Bruges in which there were three sets
of negotiators, representing England, France, and the pope, and
in which the English and papal envoys were both concerned
with two separate sets of questions: the differences between
England and France, in which the papal legates were mediators,
and the differences between England and Gregory XI, in
which they represented the pope. The progress of these negotiations against the background of continued fighting is complex
and obscure but it contains the essential key to the Good
Parliament and we must do our best to understand it.

The initiative in the preparation of the conference at Bruges
was taken by the pope but the English must already in the
summer of 1374 have shown enough favour to the idea of peace
talks to encourage the pope to persist. The Archbishop of
Ravenna visited England as papal mediator to prepare the
ground for the new round of Anglo-French peace talks in June
and July 1374. He seems to have been well received. Lancaster
ordered a present of plate to be given to him,[1] and he attended

[1] *John of Gaunt's Register 1372–1376*, ii. 224 (1 June).

he consecration of Alexander Neville, the brother of John Neville, steward of the royal household, as Archbishop of York at Westminster Abbey.[1]

On his return he reported that the king was willing to consent to a truce for the purpose of negotiations and for envoys to meet at Bruges. He may have been in England again in October.[2] On 1 December the legates wrote from Paris to Edward III saying that the king of France had agreed to the suggestion of a meeting at Bruges during a local truce in the Calais area. They asked Edward to send his envoys to Bruges on 13 January 1375.[3] Edward replied promising that his envoys would be at Bruges by 9 February[4] and he empowered the Captain of Calais to make a temporary, local truce which was done on 11 February.[5] On 20 February powers were issued to the English envoys: Lancaster, Simon Sudbury, Bishop of London, the Earl of Salisbury, John Lord Cobham, Sir Francis de Hales, Sir Arnold Savage, and two clerks, John Sheppey and Simon de Multon.[6] The delegation actually crossed to Calais in March and arrived in Bruges on 24 March, the day after the French delegation led by the Duke of Burgundy.[7]

The negotiations then proceeded in three short bursts of activity separated by two gaps during which the envoys at Bruges consulted with the courts which they represented. A good deal can be deduced about the progress of the talks from the reports which the papal mediators sent back to Avignon. Roughly, it seems that during the first round of talks from 27 March to 8 April the delegations stated their positions about the English claims in France without making much progress. In the second round, extending from the beginning of May to 26 May, they agreed on a temporary truce instead of a long-term peace. In the third round between 17 June and 27 June they made detailed changes in the truce agreement. Sometime in this period the Anglo-papal concordat was also made. The timing of this is much more obscure but two crucial dates are the papal permission for the translation of Sudbury from

---

[1] *Registrum Palatinum Dunelmense*, ed. T. D. Hardy (Rolls Series, 1873–8), iii. 528 (4 June).
[2] *CPL* iv. 133–4; *Anglo-French Negotiations*, 1, 76.
[3] *Anglo-French Negotiations*, 1–3.　　　　　　　　　　　[4] Ibid. 3–4.
[5] *Foedera*, 1021, 1022–3.
[6] Ibid. 1024–5.　　　　　　　　　　　　　　　[7] *Anglo-French Negotiations*, 9–10.

London to Canterbury, given on 4 May and suggesting, as we shall see, that some agreement had been reached before then, and the papal order to levy the subsidy, issued on 15 July and suggesting that the English agreed to permit it as soon as they were sure of the truce.

The legates first proposed two alternative peace plans to both sides on 31 March: (1) That the Duke of Lancaster should become Duke of Aquitaine, renouncing his English lands, and that he should become a feudatory of the French crown, the English king retiring from the scene in exchange for Lancaster's English property. (2) That Gascony should be partitioned between the kings of France and England, England retaining the core of lands in the dioceses of Bordeaux, Bayonne, Dax, and Aire in full sovereignty, the rest going to France. The English rejected (1) and preferred (2). The French took the opposite line. It was also reported that Lancaster rejected the first alternative 'most strongly (*potissime*) on account of the homage to be done to the king of France which did not please him'. This may possibly mean that Lancaster was personally tempted by the idea of ruling an independent Gascony, although his delegation rejected the proposal. Apart from that the division between the two delegations appears to have been clear-cut.[1]

On 8 April the envoys of the two kings sent messengers home to report on two further plans: (1) a French proposal to divide Gascony into three parts, one to be held freely by the king of England, one by the king of France, and one by a son or nephew of the king of England from the king of France; (2) an English proposal for division into two parts, one to be held, in full sovereignty, by the king of England, one by his son or nephew, of the king of France.[2] This was the end of the first phase of the talks. The negotiations were then broken off for nearly a month while the messengers reported and returned.

The rest of April was a gap between two sets of talks, during which the courts prepared their plans. On the English side John Sheppey went home 'to make relation to us and our council on behalf of our son the . . . Duke of Lancaster and our other envoys . . . in Flanders on account of the treaty of peace between us and our adversary of France concerning the state of the said treaty, waiting in our city of London for the reply of us and our

<hr/>

[1] *Anglo-French Negotiations,* Ibid. 11.   [2] Ibid. 14.

council to repeat it to our son and our other envoys'.[1] He returned to Bruges at the end of April, accompanied by William Latimer, the king's chamberlain and a central figure at court, who had not been one of the envoys accredited to the negotiations but now appears to have joined them to represent the court's or his own views in what was to be the crucial phase of the Anglo-French negotiations.[2] On the resumption of talks the English expressed themselves unwilling to surrender any of Aquitaine completely to the French. The French had nothing more to say. In the interval Charles V's refusal to yield an inch to English demands about sovereignty in Gascony had been fortified by a specially summoned *Grand Conseil*.[3] The legates then suggested, as an alternative to peace, a long truce of forty or fifty years during which further negotiations would take place. The English would not have this either: they said they had no power to discuss anything but peace proposals.[4] This was where matters stood on 16 May. But by that time other things had happened which were related to the peace negotiations. The English had launched an expedition into Brittany and another papal representative, Arnaud Garnier, had arrived with messages from the pope.

[1] From the letter of 10 October 1375 ordering the Exchequer to pay Sheppey for his journeys: 'des temps que a ses dieux retours en Engleterre des parties de Flandres pur faire relacion a nous et a notre conseil depart notre filz le Roi de Castile et de Leon duc de Lancastre et noz autres messages esteantz nadgaires en Flandres a cause du tretee de pees dentre nous et notre aduersaire de France de lestate du dit tretee demoroit a notre citee de Londres attendant la response de nous et de notre dit conseil pur la repeter a notre dit filz et noz autres messagez susditz'. (E 159/152, Brevia directa baronibus, Michaelmas, rot. 2.)

[2] Sheppey's account with the Exchequer (E 101/316/38) mentions three separate voyages to Bruges in 1375. 1. He left London on 23 January and returned on 22 February. No indication is given of the purpose of this mission. 2. He left London on 28 February 'in negotiis domini Regis cum duce Lancastrie ad tractandum de pace cum adversario Francie' and returned on 14 April. 3. He left London on 25 April 'cum domino le Latymer versus Brugges in negotiis domini regis', returning only on 17 July. On 18 April, before he left, the Exchequer paid wages to him as an envoy 'pro expediciione quorundam negotiorum inter dominum papam et ipsum dominum Regem perveniencium' and on 5 June 'existenti apud Brugges in comitiua Ducis Lancastrie super expeditione pacis'. These documents confirm the legates' report that Latimer went over for this phase of the talks (*Anglo-French Negotiations*, 19) and also show that the Anglo-papal and Anglo-French discussions were in the same hands.

[3] Delachenal, iv. 572–3; *Chronique de Jean II et Charles V*, 176–7.

[4] *Anglo-French Negotiations*, 15, 17–18.

II. THE EXPEDITION TO BRITTANY AND THE TRUCE OF 27 JUNE 1375

While the English court was taking part in the diplomatic manœuvres leading to the meeting at Bruges, it was also promoting a large military expedition. After returning from Lancaster's *chevauchée* early in the year, the Duke of Brittany had fairly quickly got royal support for the expedition he wanted. Indentures were made on 1 August 1374 with the duke himself, Edmund Langley, Earl of Cambridge, Edmund Mortimer, Earl of March, and Edward Lord Despenser to take a force of 4,000 men for a year. Documents granting legal protection during their absence from the country were issued for the duke's retinue in expectation of their going to France on 23 August.[1] The indentures specified that the commanders were to be paid wages for six months. For the rest of the year they were to be recompensed from ransoms ('de redempcionibus provenientibus tam in Britannia quam in Francia per annum supradictum'). It was foreseen that the expedition might be cut short, for the indentures also contained the explicit provision that if this happened on the order of the king or the council the commanders should not be charged with money which they had received in advance and had already paid out in wages to their troops.[2] It seems therefore to have been envisaged from the beginning that the expedition might be abandoned as a result of the diplomatic moves which were to be made at the same time.

English forces were still holding out at Brest, commanded by Robert Knolles and John Devereux,[3] at the important castle of Bécherel in north-east Brittany, and across the water in Normandy in the great fortress of St. Sauveur-le-Vicomte south of Cherbourg. But they were increasingly hard pressed by Du

---

[1] *Foedera*, 1009, 1011.

[2] 'Et in casu quod dictum viagium versus Britanniam quouismodo sit impeditum per ordinacionem Regis vel consilii sui seu aliter non in defectu predicti comitis Marchie tunc de illis summis quas idem comes receperit de Rege causa dicti viagii vnde ipse comes solucionem fecerit cum hominibus de dicta retinencia sua talem qualem sibi facta fuerat per predictum Regem vel infra idem comes Marchie et heredes sui essent quieti et exonerati erga regem imperpetuum.' The indentures do not survive but passages from them are quoted in the enrolled accounts with March, Despenser, and Cambridge, E 364/10, m.4, 4d., 7d. The particulars of March's account are E 101/34/6. Cf. Sherborne, 'Indentured Retinues', 730.

[3] Jones, *Ducal Brittany*, 147.

Guesclin's French and Breton army and the envisaged expedition was a long time in coming to their aid. The commanders of Bécherel made an agreement with the French that obliged them to surrender if not relieved by 1 November. The day came without help and the castle was lost.[1] This allowed the French to concentrate on the more formidable problem of St. Sauveur. St. Sauveur was a mighty fortress which had been built by the great captain Sir John Chandos and had been for a long time a centre for English plundering in Normandy. Charles V was now in a position to concentrate substantial forces against this stronghold which he must have regarded as a monstrous offence to the kingdom of France. The castle was commanded by Thomas Catterton, deputy for Sir Alan Buxhill, a courtier who held it from Edward III.

The first evidence of a serious French effort to deal with the problem of St. Sauveur also comes from August 1374 when Charles V put the admiral Jean de Vienne in charge of an army to besiege it.[2] Between that date and the following summer a series of taxes was voted by the estates of Basse Normandie to pay for the removal of this standing menace to their security.[3] In January 1375 Charles decided to press the siege very seriously, using advanced and expensive cannon, and the siege started in February.[4] After enduring severe siege and occasionally heavy bombardment for several months Catterton decided to come to terms. An agreement dated 21 May 1375 said that the besiegers would pay Catterton 40,000 francs for the surrender of the fortress on 3 July.[5] Sometime, possibly then, possibly later, it was also agreed that in addition Catterton would receive a personal gift of 12,000 francs and two of his companions in the fortress, Sir Thomas Trivet and Hannequin Vallebreton, 2,000 and 1,000 francs respectively.[6]

The English expedition, which might have been expected to relieve the pressure on Brest, Bécherel and St. Sauveur, was held up through the winter. Edward III appointed Brittany and Cambridge his lieutenants and captains general in France on

---

[1] C. C. Bayley, 'The Campaign of 1375 and the Good Parliament', *English Historical Review*, lv (1940), 371; Froissart, viii, §752, 750.

[2] L. Delisle, *Histoire du château et des sires de Saint-Sauveur-le-Vicomte* (Valognes, 1867), 212–15; Delachenal, iv. 524.

[3] Delisle, 216–17, 220–1, 226–33, 239–40, etc.

[4] Delachenal, iv. 525–7.   [5] Delisle, 242–5.   [6] Delisle, 261.

24 November 1374.[1] Substantial sums had already been paid out to the commanders as wages in advance: the Issue Roll records under 20 September £7,111 2s. and £5,743 12s. 4d. for Brittany, £3,555 11s. and £2,937 15s. 8d. for Cambridge, the same for March, and a similar sum for Despenser.[2] Under 28 October payment is recorded to a messenger sent to Plymouth to make payments to sailors in the ships to carry the army. Further payments to the commanders were made at the end of the year: on 18 November £1,000 to Brittany, on 15 December £2,000 to Despenser, on 23 December another £1,000 to Brittany, £300 to Cambridge, and £8,700 taken by a messenger to pay out to troops at Plymouth. On 20 January 1375 an entry records further letters sent to Plymouth to the Earl of March, one of the commanders, to Guy Bryan and Ralph Ferrers in charge of the muster, and to the Exchequer officials in charge of payments. More money was sent on 17 February.[3]

On 2 March there is a record of a letter sent to the commanders at Plymouth 'to make haste with their retinues'.[4] By this time people at court were becoming extremely impatient and vexed because of the failure of the commanders to set off. A privy seal letter which must have been sent by the king early in 1375 to Guy Bryan at Plymouth indicates the degree of impatience.

Very dear and faithful. Although, because of the complete trust which we had in your good sense and loyalty, we appointed you by the advice of our council to see the muster of men at arms and archers to go in our service in this next voyage of war overseas in the company of our sons the Earl of Cambridge and the Duke of Brittany and have since written by other letters both to our same sons and to you to hasten their passage in contingents according to the capacity of the boats prepared for their passage, still the muster has not been done nor the passage at all advanced by you, so that time is running by without any action in this matter to our great damage and cost, for which we are very displeased and marvel at your slackness since we have written to you so forcefully about it earlier. We therefore order you again and charge you firmly on the faith and allegiance you owe

[1] *Foedera*, 1018–19.   [2] E 403/451; E 364/10, m.4, 4d., 7d.
[3] E 403/456. On 22 January a letter was sent to the authorities of London ordering proclamation to be made that all men in retinues must be at the coast within a week on pain of imprisonment (*Letter Book H*, 4).
[4] 'De se festinando cum Retinencia sua versus partes predictas' (E 403/456).

us to use your good pains and diligence towards our sons and the other lords who are to pass over so that the muster is done and the passage of them and their men hastened as much as can be by any way in the world according to the purport of our said letters, with no default, doing so much for your part that we may truly know that it is so. And take this matter fully to heart so that it shall be put in effect with all speed as we trust in you and on all the pain and indignation that you may incur from us.[1]

The Commons of Devonshire were probably justified in complaining next year in the Good Parliament that 'the Duke of Brittany and others of his retinue on his last passage to Brittany stayed a long time in the county, where many of his retinue and other retainers took by night as well as by day from various people beef cattle, cows, sheep, corn, hay, oats, and other victuals for most of which they paid nothing.'[2] Not until 25 April did the expedition, after crossing from Plymouth, land at Finisterre. In the early part of May they were probably besieging St. Brieuc.[3] The delay of the expedition through the winter is explained nowhere. All the evidence suggests that the court,

---

[1] 'Treschers et foialx. Combien que pur lentiere affiance quele nous auiens en voz sens et loialtee nous vous feismes assigner par lauys de notre conseil de veoir la montreson dez gentz darmes et archers a aler en notre service en cest prochein viage de guerre par de la en la compaignie de noz filz lez Conte de Cantebrugge et Duc de Bretaigne et depuis eons escrit par noz autres lettres tant a mesmes noz filz come a vous de haster leur passage par parties solonc ce que les niefs prestes pur leur passages purrient suffire si nest vncore la montreson faite ne la passage aucunement par vous auances einz coert toutdys le temps sanz aucun exploit en celle partie a grantz damages et coustages de nous de quoi nous nous tenons tres mal content et meruaillons de votre lachesse en ce cas meement depuis que nous vous auons sur ce tant effectuelment paravant escrit. Si vous mandons de rechief et chargeons fermement sur la foy et ligeance que vous nous devez que vous mettez votre bone peins et diligence enuers noz ditz fitz et les autres seigneurs qi passeront que la dite montreson soit faite et que le passage de eux et de leur gentz soit hastez a tout le plus que lem purra par aucun voie du mond solonc le purport de noz ditz lettres sanz nulle defaute, ffesant tant de votre part que nous puissons vraiement sauoir que ensi soit. Et ceste chose preignez entierment a cuer a fyn que ele soit a toute haste mise en oeure come desus siccome nous nous fions de vous et sur toute la peine et indignacion quele vous purrez encurrer enuers nous. Done souz notre etc.' (Entered without name of recipient or date in a privy seal formulary book, Cambridge University Library MS. Dd. 3, 53, fol. 42–42ᵛ.)

[2] *RP* 354, § 180. SC 8/655, which appears to be the original version of this petition, has some variations including a particular complaint against the retinue of Sir Robert Ashton: 'la retenue monsieur Robert de Aysshtone et plusours autres dautri retenue'. Ashton was granted royal protection because of his intention to go abroad in the duke's company (*Foedera*, 1010).

[3] Delachenal, iv. 516–17; Jones, 78.

40

having paid out considerable sums of money to the commanders in the autumn, wanted the army to go and finally became very impatient. If the expedition was to achieve anything, it must do so—from the court's point of view—while the negotiators at Bruges could still use it as a bargaining piece. What hesitations or disagreements among the commanders held it up it is now impossible to say—perhaps they distrusted the courtiers or Lancaster, perhaps they simply did not want to campaign in the winter. The result of the delays, however, was that when the talks at Bruges were well under way the expedition was only just beginning its operations in Brittany.

On 20 March 1375, before the start of the negotiations, the pope wrote to his mediators at Bruges encouraging them in their efforts for peace and also telling them that he was sending the Collector, Garnier, to them with further instructions ('cui aliqua vobis referenda comisimus'). They were to give him help and especially in the matter of the subsidy to be collected in England, 'above all in the levying of the subsidy imposed by us, as you know, sometime ago upon the clergy of England for the necessities of ourself and the Roman church, about which we have also written to our brother Simon, Bishop of London, and to certain others'.[1] In their letter to the pope dated 16 May, after Garnier had arrived at Bruges, the two legates mentioned two matters of papal interest apart from the peace negotiations with which they were concerned. The first was the release of Roger Beaufort, the pope's brother, who was a prisoner in English hands. The pope had sent letters in March and April to Princess Joan, to the king's daughter Isabella, Countess of Bedford, and to Latimer and Henry Wakefield, the Keeper of the Wardrobe, asking them to use their influence for the release of Beaufort and another relation Jean de la Roche.[2] He must have been anxious that any agreement between France and England should include provision for the release of these prisoners. The second matter was the subsidy which the legates said they had been dealing with as well as they could. These

---

[1] *Lettres secrètes et curiales du pape Grégoire XI (1370–1378) relatives à la France*, ed. L. Mirot and H. Jassemin (Paris, 1935–57), no. 1843. The pope wrote on the same day to Wykeham, asking him to use his influence on the side of peace in the Bruges negotiations and on the side of payment of the subsidy and similarly promising further information from Garnier (*Wykeham's Register*, ed. T. F. Kirby, Hampshire Record Society, 1899, ii. 245).   [2] *CPL* iv. 146.

two issues appear from the terms in which they wrote to the pope to be the only ones about which Garnier had brought messages to them. Garnier himself was on his way back to England but he spent ten days at Paris delivering papal letters to the king and ten days at Bruges delivering letters to the negotiators. These visits cannot be precisely dated but must have fallen in April and early May.[1] During the crucial months of May and June 1375 the peace negotiations and the Anglo-papal negotiations were in the same hands.

The next firm date in the negotiations is 26 May when the envoys at Bruges, surprisingly in view of the earlier concentration on major peace proposals, agreed on a truce for one year.[2] The Anglo-French negotiations now bifurcated into two separate areas. The plans and proposals for a peace settlement or a long truce continued to be debated while the short truce was being arranged. At some time, probably before 26 May, the legates put forward new peace proposals in an attempt to break the deadlock over their earlier ones. These were (1) a division of Aquitaine by a commission of four or five nominees of each side; (2) that the king of England should retain the lands in Aquitaine at present in his power and receive an annual pension from France; (3) that there should be a long truce of twenty-five or thirty years at the present *de facto* boundaries. In order to facilitate discussion of these plans there was to be a one-year truce. The negotiators should consult immediately with their kings about these proposals and reassemble at Bruges by 22 July.[3] The date for reopening of peace talks eventually agreed on was 15 September.[4] The peace conference was thus kept alive without anything effectively being done on that front until later in the year.

But the most serious business was now the establishment of the short-term truce and on this immediate action was taken. It was agreed on 26 May that the truce was to start at different

[1] 'Item exposuit dictus collector redeundo de Avinionia ad Angliam de mense Martii et Aprilis et Maii anno ab incarnatione et cetera LXXV in quinquaginta diebus quibus in via et multum plus stetit, cum familia et quinque equitaturis, quorum dierum decem diebus stetit Parisius de mandato domini nostri pape cum certis literis etiam credentie ad Regem, et aliis decem diebus et plus Brugiis cum aliis consimilibus literis ad tractatores pacis, etiam sperando ubique eorum responciones.' (*Accounts Rendered by Papal Collectors*, 537.)

[2] *Foedera*, 1033.

[3] *Anglo-French Negotiations*, 19–20.   [4] *Foedera*, 1034.

dates in different parts of France, in Normandy on 2 July, in Brittany on 7 July, further south on later dates up to 2 August. In addition to this: (1) Henry of Trastamara and John de Montfort were to be included in the truce; (2) the Duke of Brittany was to withdraw his army from Brittany retaining only 200 men to hold the fortified places in his hands; (3) the French would raise the siege of St. Sauveur for the duration of the truce; (4) Cognac in the Charente valley was to be put into the hands of the pope. The Captal of Buch, Roger Beaufort, and Jean de la Roche were to be released during the truce to raise their ransoms.[1] The main detailed provisions in this agreement about Brittany and St. Sauveur involved a disbandment of the two armies. After consultation with their kings the envoys in fact reassembled on or soon after 17 June to make modifications in these truce arrangements which were then published on 27 June.[2] The modifications were these: (1) During the truce the Duke of Brittany was to have ransoms and *pattis* as they stood at 27 June, not when the envoys left Bruges. The significance of this is not clear. (2) Brittany was to take part in the peace negotiations. (3) The clause about St. Sauveur was very explicitly replaced by another according to which it was to be handed over to the keeping of papal mediators on payment to the English of 40,000 francs (in addition to 20,000 which the king of France had already paid to the English), and at the end of the truce the king of France was to get the castle, and the king of England a further 40,000 francs. This superseded both the earlier Bruges clause about St. Sauveur and the local arrangements made by the English and French troops at St. Sauveur. (4) Beaufort and de la Roche, not the Captal, were to be released for four months.

Such evidence as there is suggests that the truce was not made without consultation between the English envoys and the English court and nobility. Early in May, when the outcome of the first phase of the Bruges negotiations must have been known in England, the nobility and prelates were summoned to a council on the sixteenth of that month.[3] When the decision on

---

[1] *Foedera*, 1033.   [2] Ibid. 1031–2, 1034.

[3] E 403/457, 3 May, payments for messengers carrying letters of summons to the Bishop of Winchester and the Earl of Arundel to council; 7 May, letters of summons to bishops, earls, and others to council on 16 May.

26 May to conclude a truce was reported back to England, Lancaster was granted powers to proceed with it on 8 June with the advice and consent of the great council, *par l'avis et consentement de nostre grant consail*.[1] There was also concern about the fate of Brittany and St. Sauveur and last-minute efforts to save them. It may be surmised that the modification of the truce arrangements to make the Duke of Brittany a party to eventual peace negotiations was the result of representations on his behalf made in England. As late as 8 May hopes of success were entertained for the Brittany expedition; on that day the bishops were asked by the king to arrange prayers for its success.[2] At the end of May an attempt was being made to send help of some kind to St. Sauveur—it is not known what troops were to go but ships were certainly being collected. This was abandoned on 5 June.[3] But communication between the English negotiators at Bruges and the soldiers at St. Sauveur and in Brittany was slight or non-existent and military events there seem to have taken an independent course. According to Froissart the French besieging St. Sauveur refused to accept the terms of the truce obliging them in the first draft to lift the siege and in the final version to allow the fortress to remain in the hands of the papal envoys. They forced the English garrison, by the threat of killing hostages, to observe the local agreement of 21 May by handing over the castle and receiving 53,000 francs in return. This is confirmed by a certificate recording the payment of the money on the French side on 3 July.[4] Catterton, the captain, did well out of the deal and may not have been an unwilling participant in

[1] *Foedera*, 1029.

[2] Ibid. 1028.

[3] An Exchequer official, Thomas Durant, was commandeering ships and sailors in Dorset, Devon, and Cornwall at the beginning of June, sent 'per preceptum consilii ipsius domini Regis pro vadiis marinariorum in comitatibus Dorset Devonie et Cornubia soluendis pro rescussu Sancti Salvatoris in Normannia'. He was paid wages for the period 31 May–20 June (E 101/34/10). The termination of his mission is recorded in a payment on 5 June (E 403/457), 'Johanni Cook valeto misso versus Plymuth et Dertmuth et per costeras maris ibidem cum vna littera de priuato sigillo et vna littera domini Thesaurarii directis Thome Durant et aliis in comitiva sua existentibus nuper missis versus easdem partes pro marinariis arestandis et pro vadiis eorundem soluendis pro quodam viagio ordinato versus partes transmarinas pro rescussu castri de Seint Sauueours in Normannia de se festinando versus London et pro dictis arestationibus et solucione cessandis causa treuge capte inter dominum Regem et aduersarium suum Francie.'

[4] Froissart, § 768; Delisle, *Saint-Sauveur-le-Vicomte*, 272–3; cf. Bayley, 'The Campaign of 1375', 378–80.

it, but presumably the main reason why it was carried out was that Charles V did not enforce the terms of the truce to which his envoys had agreed at Bruges.

The position in Brittany at the end of June, according to Froissart, was that Montfort and Cambridge were concentrating their attention on besieging Quimperlé. They made an agreement with the French garrison of that stronghold similar to the one which Jean de Vienne had made earlier with the English at St. Sauveur—it was to surrender if not relieved by a certain date. But the truce in both the original and the revised forms provided for the cessation of hostilities by Montfort in Brittany on 7 July. According to Froissart this news was conveyed by messengers to Montfort's army before Quimperlé just in time to rob them of the fruits of their siege. For the substance of the events at Quimperlé which ended the Brittany expedition we are dependent on Froissart but there is no reason to doubt the general correctness of his account.[1] The reluctance or expected reluctance of the commanders in Brittany to give up their campaign is reflected in the tone of royal letters sent to them from England ordering them to return at once. The Earl of March's account with the Exchequer for his wages of war still has attached to it a privy seal letter dated 20 July which presumably reached him in Brittany and ordered him firmly to return home: 'desisting from all acts of war return with all your retinue into our kingdom of England so that you and the retinue shall be there with no default with the greatest possible haste.'[2]

---

[1] Froissart, § 766–8; Bayley, 375–8; Jones, 78–9. The account of the end of the Brittany expedition by Bayley contains two assumptions for which I can see no justification in the sources cited: (1) that the date on which the Quimperlé garrison was to surrender was 3 July—this seems to be based ultimately on a hypothetical reconstruction by A. le M. de la Borderie, *Histoire de Bretagne* (Rennes, 1896–1914), iv. 37–40; (2) that the final version of the truce included a new stipulation that fighting should cease immediately in Brittany, i.e. before 3 July. When these two points are removed, however, it remains true that Quimperlé was saved by the truce.

[2] 'De par le Roy Treschier Cousin et foial. Savoir vous fesons que a la mediacion des honurables pieres en dieu Larceuesque de Ravenne et Leuesque de Carpentras Messages notre seint piere le Pape trieves generales sont prises parentre nous et notre Adversaire de France et touz les adherentz de nous et de lui a durer par vn certein temps, par queles trieves est acordez et ordenez que cessez soit de tout fait de guerre dune part et dautre et que tretee se face de pees finale deinz mesme le temps. Par quoy nous voloms et vous mandons et chargeons fermement que en cessant de tout fait de guerre come desus, retournez ouesque toute votre retenue en notre roialme Dengleterre sique vous et mesme votre retenue y soiez sanz nulle defaute a toute la haste que vous plus purrez par la cause susdite. Et ce en nulle

The English leaders had to come back leaving the duke in Brittany.

III. THE ANGLO-PAPAL CONCORDAT

The making of the truce was known at Avignon and the pope was giving it as a reason for postponing his return to Rome on 8 July.[1] On 15 July the pope sent letters to England ordering the collection of a subsidy at a reduced rate of 60,000 florins. Since the levying of the tax was not now hindered by the English crown we may suppose that the order of 15 July was issued in the knowledge that it had been accepted.[2] This is the earliest piece of evidence showing that an Anglo-papal concordat had been arrived at, presumably at Bruges, about the same time as the Anglo-French truce.

On 1 September papal bulls were issued making concessions to the English crown on a number of points connected with appointments to English benefices.[3] Presumably these concessions also followed from an agreement between the English and papal representatives at Bruges in June. Taken together these concessions amounted to a general settlement of differences between Westminster and Avignon which must have been concluded about the same time and in the same place as the truce between England and France. The terms of the agreement may be analysed as follows:

1. The English agreed to set Roger Beaufort at liberty to facilitate the raising of his ransom.[4]

2. The English agreed to allow the raising of a papal subsidy from the clergy of 60,000 florins, about £9,000, to be paid in two instalments in December 1375 and June 1376.

3. The pope conceded that clerks appointed in the past by royal presentation or collation were not to be impeded by any papal collations which might have been made.

manere ne lessez sur la foy et ligeaunce que vous nous deuez. Entendant que pur le repassage de vous et des autres seignurs noz liges esteantz es parties ou vous estes asqueux nous escriuons aussi sur ceste matire et de les retenues de vous et de eux nous avons fait charger notre Amiraille deuers le Suthe et le West denuoier hastiuement de nauye vers mesmes les parties. Done souz notre priue seal a Guldeford le xx. jouer de Juyl.' (E 101/34/6.)

[1] *Lettres secrètes et curiales du pape Grégoire XI*, 624–5; *CPL* iv. 139.
[2] *CPL* iv. 218; Lunt, *Financial Relations*, 108.
[3] Perroy, *L'Angleterre et le grand schisme*, 45.   [4] *Foedera*, 1034.

4. Ten suits between royal and papal nominees to benefices were settled in favour of the royal nominees. In at least eight of these cases the beneficiaries were clerks in the royal administration: Richard Ravenser, Keeper of the Hanaper (two cases); Henry Wakefield, Keeper of the Wardrobe, made Bishop of Worcester about the same time; John Sleaford, Clerk of the Works at Westminster and the Tower; John Fordham, Keeper of the Privy Seal to the Black Prince; Thomas Orgrave, a clerk of the Exchequer of Receipt; Richard Beverley, Cofferer of the Wardrobe; William Borstall, Keeper of the Rolls of Chancery.[1]

5. A general reservation of benefices resigned by pluralists made in 1366 by Pope Urban V was revoked.

6. Arrangements were to be made for cases in papal courts to be heard at Bruges if Englishmen were impeded by war from attending at Avignon.

7. The English archbishops were given powers to enforce repairs to ruinous benefices held by cardinals.[2]

These were the formal agreements of the concordat. Taken by themselves they would be very puzzling because the pope conceded practically nothing of significance in return for the generous permission to levy the subsidy. But the picture looks rather different if we take into account a group of appointments made to English bishoprics in 1375 which of course required papal approval. Permission was given for the translation of Simon Sudbury from London to Canterbury on 4 May.[3] A rather cryptic remark in a letter by the legates at Bruges to the pope on 30 March ('By Boerius, your Holiness's messenger, who remains here at our wish and will soon return, we shall write again to your Holiness giving the fullest information we can on the matter of provision to the churches of England and whether Hereford would be content with that which was mentioned in your Holiness's letter')[4] seems to imply that William Courtenay, Bishop of Hereford, who had been difficult in the convocation of 1373 about the royal subsidy[5] and was to be a notable defender of the church later, was considered a rival candidate for Canterbury. Canterbury had been vacant since

---

[1] Tout, iii. 215–16; 273–4; iv. 384; 189–90; iii. 369; iv. 156.
[2] *Foedera*, 1037–9.
[3] Wilkins, 97–8. [4] *Anglo-French Negotiations*, 13. [5] See above, p. 18.

the death of Whittlesey in June 1374. According to the Chronicles, the monks had incurred the king's fury by trying to re-elect Simon Langham who had held the see from 1366 to 1368 and resigned on becoming a cardinal.[1] The appointment of Sudbury who would appear from the record of the 1373 convocation to have managed the grant of subsidy and was now entrusted with the embassy to Bruges must have been highly satisfactory to the royal court. He was to live up to expectations as an archbishop exceptionally sensitive to royal wishes.

The provision for Courtenay's translation to London as a consolation prize was issued on 12 September. By letters with the same date he was replaced at Hereford by John Gilbert, Bishop of Bangor, who had been the main English envoy in the Anglo-papal negotiations of 1373 and 1374.[2] The electors at Worcester were treated like those at Canterbury. There the bishopric had been vacant since November 1373 and the monks had elected their prior whose election had been confirmed by the king. This election, however, then remained in suspense for nearly two years while, presumably, the king, knowing that the Prior of Worcester, unlike Cardinal Langham, would have no influence at Avignon, manœuvred for the substitution of a royal nominee by papal provision. The nominee was a royal clerk, Henry Wakefield, who had been Keeper of the Wardrobe since 1369 and had earlier, in June 1373, been elected at Ely but superseded there by the papal provision of Thomas Arundel, the twenty-year-old son of the Earl of Arundel, whom as a leading magnate and also one of the chief lenders to the crown the king did not wish to offend. Wakefield's letter of provision to Worcester was issued on 12 September 1375, the same day as the provisions for Courtenay and Gilbert. Apart from a brief visit to Worcester for installation in the following spring, he appears to have remained at the court for the rest of Edward III's reign.[3] On 12 October Ralph Erghum, John of Gaunt's

[1] 'Propter quod factum contra predictos monachos rex tantam arsit in iram, quod procurantibus aemulis omnes monachos dictae ecclesiae disposuit exulasse.' (*Polychronicon*, viii. 380; cf. Walsingham, *Historia Anglicana*, i. 317.) 'Et monachi Cantuariae postulabant cardinalem cui Rex noluit assentire, sed offensus priorem et monachos graviter vexavit laboribus et expensis. Cardinalis non volens archiepiscopatum cum bona gratia regis habere resignavit juri suo. Et papa dedit eum Simoni Sudbury advocato Curiae.' (*Continuatio Eulogii*, 339.)

[2] Lunt, *Financial Relations*, 744, 738.

chancellor, was provided to the see of Salisbury—as the *Poly-chronicon* continuator succinctly put it 'contemplatione ipsius ducis, auctoritate papali'—with an additional order that his consecration was to precede that of Wakefield.[1] With the exception of Courtenay's appointment, the new bishops—Sudbury, Gilbert, Wakefield, and Erghum—all look as if they were chosen to please the court and strengthen its following in the church. These appointments illustrate the truth of the comment by the contemporary continuator of the *Polychronicon*, who showed much interest in episcopal elections, that papal power in such matters was untouched by the concordat because some people found it easier to secure election through provision obtained by influence at the papal court than by free election by the cathedral chapter. If the two courts were in agreement papal provision was much the easiest way for the king to promote his nominee.[2]

IV. THE REASONS FOR THE ENGLISH VOLTE-FACE

The agreements made at Bruges in June 1375 were a notable double landmark in English policy. The truce with France was a change to peace after a lengthy period of war. Military activity had indeed already declined since 1372 and the court had shown itself more disposed to peace, at least since the summer of 1374. But it had also mounted a large expedition to Brittany which was now cut short. The clause in the indentures with the commanders providing for payment if the expedition were cut short suggests that the court had entered into the negotiations at Bruges with the genuine intention of making a break in the war. It was hoped that the expedition would strengthen the position in Brittany, save the English garrisons there before peace or truce was concluded, and strengthen the negotiators' hands at Bruges. Hence the impatience of the court to get the expedition moving at the end of 1374. The apparent lack of co-ordination of policy in the summer of 1375, however, is still

---

[3] W. P. Marett, *A Calendar of the Register of Henry Wakefield Bishop of Worcester 1375–95* (Worcestershire Historical Society, n.s. vii, 1972), xxxiii–xxxviii; *Poly-chronicon*, viii. 383.

[1] *CPL* iv. 144; *Polychronicon*, viii. 383.

[2] Walter Hemingford, *Historia*, ed. T. Hearne, ii. 441, 'Sed de electionibus, superius tactis, nihil actum est; et hoc ascribitur aliquibus, qui sciebant, se posse citius per Curiam Romanam, quam per electiones, ad dignitates episcopales, quas ambiunt promoveri.'

mysterious. It seems possible that there may have been deep suspicion on the part of Brittany and his fellow commanders of the intentions of Lancaster. Moreover once the expedition was in Brittany the commanders and negotiators had physical difficulties of communication and events at Bruges moved too fast. It is also fairly clear that in the final stages of the drafting and implementing of the truce the English were outplayed by Charles V who secured both the surrender of St. Sauveur and the withdrawal of Montfort's army, both of which might conceivably have been avoided. Charles drew confidence from the knowledge that French power at St. Sauveur and Cognac made it impossible for the English to enforce their claims to these places. He had recently made highly satisfactory arrangements for the succession of his eldest son, the future Charles VI and for a marriage by which his younger son, Louis, would acquire a prospect of gaining the kingdom of Naples.[1] His kingdom was gaining in strength and unity while England in both respects was on the decline. French policy was directed with firmness from the centre. English policy was not. When all allowances are made, however, the lack of co-ordination between the English negotiators and the army, the delay in getting the expedition under way, and willingness to sacrifice it indicate that Brittany and his fellow commanders had half-expected to be betrayed and that in the end they were betrayed.

The granting of permission to the pope to levy his subsidy is also surprising because it was so unprecedented. Did the English get reasonable concessions in return? Gregory XI conceded none of his rights in the future in the matters of reservations and provisions. His concessions in the field of provisions related entirely to the past and mostly to cases in which the king as a collator had an interest. The concessions about hearing cases at Bruges and repairing churches in the hands of cardinals were entirely trivial. We have seen that in the cases settled out of hand in favour of clerks presented by the crown the majority of beneficiaries were royal clerks and that the new bishops were mostly close associates of the court and its policy. The king's court and its friends did get some solid return for the concessions over taxation. But others, as we shall see, thought the bargain was a bad one.

[1] Delachenal, iv. 543–5, 575.

Why did the English court make this double treaty with the pope and France? There are first of all two possible lines of explanation which ought to be rejected. Bruges might be easier to understand if one could assume that Lancaster's eyes were still firmly fixed on Castile and that he was securing a breathing space in order to plot further intervention there. That approach seems, however, unfruitful. The security and strength of his opponent, Henry of Trastamara, which, as we have seen, had been mounting since 1372, though temporarily set back by the ignominious failure of an attack on the English fortress of Bayonne in the summer of 1374, reached new heights with marriage alliances with Aragon and Navarre concluded in April and May 1375.[1] By the time Lancaster agreed to the truce it must have been clear to him that he had no effective friends in the Iberian peninsula. This was the result of Lancaster's own inability to help his friends and his virtual abandonment of attempts to do so. As we have seen, both Aragon and Navarre were anxious for English help in the spring of 1374. There are also hints of attempts by King Charles of Navarre to make closer contact with England later in that year. According to a rather puzzling passage in the confession of a servant of Charles captured by the French in 1378, the king of Navarre sent an envoy to England *entre l'an lxxiv et l'an lxxv* proposing an alliance, which was also favoured by the Black Prince.[2] The English Chancery on 8 June 1374 issued a safe conduct for the king to visit England from Cherbourg[3]—as far as we know it was not used. We are brought back to the fact that at least from the spring of 1374 Lancaster had accepted his inability to find the resources to act in Iberia: his Iberian policy was temporarily in abeyance and it seems very unlikely that events in that peninsula had a decisive effect on his actions at Bruges.

Secondly there is the possibility which was aired at the time that Lancaster was hoping to mobilize support for a plan to secure his succession to Edward III in place of the Black Prince's son, Richard. Flemish envoys visiting the court of the king of Navarre, probably in 1375 or early 1376, were told of a secret treaty between the king of France and the Duke of

[1] Russell, *English Intervention*, 217–21.
[2] Martène and Durand, *Thesaurus Novorum Anecdotorum,* i, col. 1546.
[3] *Foedera,* 1004.

Lancaster in which Charles V had agreed to help secure the succession to the throne of England after the death of Edward III by persuading the pope to declare Richard illegitimate. It was also said that Charles had promised to stand aside while Lancaster attacked Henry of Trastamara in Castile.[1] In fact Charles V did not at any point behave as if he was doing other than pressing the interests of France against England. The rumour may indicate that the agreements at Bruges were puzzling to contemporaries, and other people certainly believed that Lancaster was aiming at the English crown,[2] but there is nothing in the negotiations to suggest a secret agreement. There is in fact no good evidence that Lancaster ever did aim at the throne.

The Bruges agreements probably ought to be explained from the English side on the basis of ordinary calculations of political advantage to the English crown. The urgent need for a truce, once the Brittany expedition was too late, and also the timing of it, were probably dictated mainly by the crown's financial prospects. The parliament of 1373 had granted lay subsidies to be paid unconditionally in 1374 but in the second year, 1375, they were to be paid in two instalments on 2 February and 10 June only if the king was still at war and the grant was expressly stated to be annulled if the war ceased.[3] The conclusion of the truce on 27 June allowed the king to claim the whole of the lay subsidy. It put at risk half of the second year of tunnage and poundage (1375) and the whole of the second year of wool subsidies (Michaelmas 1375 to Michaelmas 1376) which had been granted under the same condition. These were collected at the ports and the policy makers probably calculated that they could raise them without parliamentary authorization if

[1] 'Item, a-il un traittiet bien secré entre le roy de France et le duc de Lancastre, et est par toutes voyes accordé entre eulx que pais se fera entre les II roys à leur pooir, adfin que le dit Laencastre entent estre roy d'Engleterre après le moort son père, considéré que le prinche ne se puet aidier et que par l'ayde dou roy de France on pourcachera en la court de Romme les enfans le dit prince estre non légitime, dont dès maintenant on a prié à no Saint-Père le pape, et dou droit que ledit duc de Laencastre puet avoir au royalme d'Espainge il en fera par le conseilz le roy de France, et, se le roy Henri ne le volra faire, le roi de France ne se mellera point de le guerre entre eux.' (*Œuvres de Froissart*, ed. Kervyn de Lettenhove, Brussels, 1867–77, viii. 461, from an undated report to the Count of Flanders.)

[2] *Chronique des quatre premiers Valois*, ed. S. Luce (Société de l'Histoire de France, Paris, 1862), 259; *Anglo-French Negotiations*, 60.

[3] *RP* 317, § 12.

necessary, as indeed they did; but they could not have collected a lay subsidy arbitrarily without the help of the shire gentry nor, more importantly, could they support further serious military activity without a new grant from parliament. The calculation in the autumn of 1374 therefore must have been that they had to have either striking military success or peace by the early summer. As the Brittany expedition failed to materialize, it became clear that they must have peace as soon as possible after 10 June. Though humiliating, it offered a breathing space and was better than the rapid loss of all that remained of English-held France under the apparently relentless pressure of Charles V's armies. In spite of this rational explanation, however, it remains true that there are strong indications of a serious lack of co-ordination between the commanders of the Brittany expedition and the managers of the peace negotiations. It looks as though Lancaster's willingness to abandon the expedition may have been the fulfilment of fears of treachery, perhaps based on hostility between Lancaster and John de Montfort, which had held the commanders back throughout the winter. Perhaps Lancaster, with his Gascon background and Castilian dreams, never had been enthusiastic about Brittany. Alternatively, the commanders had their own reasons, which we cannot discover, for waiting. Whichever it was, they were not in step. The division of opinion about the Brittany expedition which caused recriminations in the Good Parliament must have gone back to the time before the expedition set out.

In the world of ecclesiastical politics the English were faced by a pope as determined as the king of France. The vacancy at Canterbury after the death of Whittlesey in June 1374 must have been the deciding factor here. Lancaster and his associates probably calculated that they would find the English church unmanageable, and in particular the levying of taxes from it impossible, unless they had a reasonably co-operative archbishop. But Gregory, greatly in need of money for his Italian projects, could be expected to pursue his subsidy as relentlessly as Charles V waged war for the reconquest of France. A subsidy reduced by agreement to £9,000 may have seemed a reasonable price to pay for the improved control of the church through Sudbury, especially when Courtenay, who had shown his teeth as an opponent of the crown in the convocation of 1373, was the alternative and several compliant bishops were added to the bench at the same time. In effect the king would be sacrificing the church to the pope temporarily in order to improve the prospects of taxation in future years.

How far were the two agreements with France and the pope interdependent? At the court where Gregory XI pursued his ambitious and interlocking plans to humble Milan, to return to Rome, and to unite the princes of the west in a crusading endeavour the diplomatic threads of Christendom met and the interconnection of the various local European patterns could be surveyed more easily than anywhere else. Some people there thought that the two agreements at Bruges were parts of one settlement. On 7 April an envoy from the court of Mantua wrote from Avignon:

There is news here of peace to be made between the lord kings of France and England and it is hoped that there will be peace firmly established between them. For the Duke of Burgundy and the Duke of Lancaster, the son of the king of England, are in a place called Malines in a parliament with four ambassadors of the lord pope who longs for that peace and it is thought that before they move from there peace will be made.

Apart from the confusion of Bruges with Malines, this was correct.[1] On 30 April he wrote an even more optimistic letter forecasting a general settlement of European problems which would shortly make the Milanese war the only obstacle to a crusade against the sultan. The disputes of the Iberian peninsula he said, had been set at rest by the recent peace between Castile and Aragon and the marriage alliances made by Castile with Navarre and Portugal which had established Henry of Trastamara firmly. Then he went on,

It is said that peace will shortly be made between the kings of the French and the English in this way. The pope gives a certain census which he has in the kingdom of England to the said king and that king gives the pope all the cities and places which he holds on this side of the sea. The king of France gives the Dauphiné to the church and the church gives the king of France all the things which he has from the king of England.[2]

[1] Segre, 'I dispacci di Cristoforo da Piacenza', 73.

[2] 'Dicitur quod pax fiet in brevi inter reges Francorum et Anglicorum per istum modum. Nam papa dat certum censum quot habet in regno Anglie dicto regi et

54

This report is far removed from any actual peace plan and certainly from the plans promoted by the mediators at Bruges and the truce eventually agreed upon, but it does contain recognizable echoes of what was happening at Bruges. It offers some support for the impression conveyed by the succession of events at Bruges that agreements between England and the pope and between England and France were connected by showing that this deduction could be made at the time.

There is in fact no good evidence for a general three-cornered settlement of the kind suggested by the Mantuan envoy. Though the English and papal envoys were concerned simultaneously with both sets of negotiations, these were not linked together in the legates' dossier except for the rather subsidiary issue of the release of Roger Beaufort from captivity in England about which Garnier carried some message from the pope to Bruges. In one other respect, however, the two agreements must have been interdependent. The English crown could not have allowed the collection of the subsidy unless it was sure of the cessation of war. Gregory therefore had a good reason for using his influence with the French court to secure the truce. There is no evidence that his influence in this direction was any more effective than it had been over the previous four years: he had always been anxious to stop the war. Nor is there any evidence that Charles V granted the truce to please the pope. But on the English side the concession of the papal subsidy must have been dependent on the truce. The humiliating submission to the French and the expensive submission to the pope must therefore have been connected in the minds of knowledgeable Englishmen.

The holding of a Great Council in May 1375 suggests that Lancaster and the court were careful to secure the general consent of bishops and magnates for their policy. In spite of this, later events were to prove that both the bargains were interpreted by contemporaries as political mistakes and in combination produced a strong reaction. Until the summer of 1375 the policy of the court, though it was unsuccessful, had at least been conventional. Its resistance to papal pressure and promotion

ditus res dat pape omnes civitates et loca que tenet citra mare. Rex vero Francie dat Delfinatum Viane ecclesie et ecclesia dat regi Francie omnes res quas habuit a rege Anglie.' (Ibid. 75.)

of war in France were traditional policies which commanded general acceptance. After June 1375 it was associated with policies which were unusual, humiliating, and offensive to some important interests which might otherwise have been willing to tolerate a corrupt court pursuing normal political aims. The diplomatic volte-face of 1375 is an essential part of the background to the Good Parliament because its effect on English opinion made the court exceptionally isolated and friendless.

V. ANGLO-FRENCH RELATIONS AUGUST 1375–APRIL 1376

In the succeeding months of truce with France no lucky turn of fortune came to relieve the gloom. A new and unfavourable strategic factor was appearing which had to be added to the failure of English arms in France. This was the naval threat from Castile which was becoming a positive danger to English shipping and the English coasts. England and France each had an ally whose objections to the truce of 27 June could be used as an argument in bargaining and might easily cause friction. But while England's Duke of Brittany was relatively powerless and dependent, France's king of Castile had means in his navy to make his own will effective. Secure in his new alliances with Aragon and Navarre and in the knowledge of Lancaster's inability to press his claims, Henry of Trastamara was an unwilling keeper of the truce. At the beginning of August 1375 a fleet of English merchantmen impressed into royal service was returning from a voyage on which they had taken Sir Thomas Felton, the seneschal of Gascony, and Sir William Elmham, the governor of Bayonne, to their posts. They made for the Bay of Bourgneuf to load for the home run. At La Rochelle they were attacked by a Castilian fleet under the Admiral Fernán Sánchez de Tovar. According to a French source this was retaliation for the pillaging of Spanish ships by the English. Although it took place on 10 August, a week after the truce should have been effective, the Castilians rejected English appeals to the truce and captured or sank a number of English ships. An official list contained thirty-five ships with a total estimated value of over £15,000. They came from various ports around the coast from Bristol to Yarmouth and two were the property of Richard Lyons, the court financier. The only English chronicle to mention the episode called it 'the greatest loss that England ever suffered on sea'.[1] This spectacular exhibition of Castilian sea power was the prelude to a period of several years in which the English felt themselves in serious danger of attack on sea or even of invasion, first from Castile whose adherence to the truce was precarious, then, after the final end of the truce period at Easter 1377, from Charles V who had built up his navy in preparation. Of course the danger of Castilian sea power had been dramatically shown at La Rochelle in 1372 and had been a factor ever since. Nevertheless the conclusion of the truce of June 1375 marks the beginning of a period in which the strategic situation must have been peculiarly depressing for both the nobility and everyone concerned with ships and trade. Not only had English armies been driven out of large parts of France, but there was a serious threat of invasion from the sea and naval defence was a more prominent factor in English politics than aggressive attempts to recover control in France.[2] Henry of Trastamara, with extensive naval power, was restive under the limitations of the truce and breaking it. Charles V was known to be building a fleet to attack England when the truce came to an end.

The diplomatic shadow of Castile hung over the renewed negotiations at Bruges. Henry of Trastamara sent his Chamberlain Pedro Fernández de Velasco to take part in the treaty. *En route* by sea from Bermeo to La Rochelle he fell in with some ships carrying Edward III's Gascon ally Florimund of Lesparre whom he took prisoner—another violation of the truce. After delivering the lord of Lesparre back to his master he set out again and eventually presented the Castilian case to Charles V.[3] The king of Castile also had an enthusiastic supporter of his

---

[1] *Chronique des quatre premiers Valois* (80 Spanish ships attacked 84 English); *Anon*, 79 (72 ships lost). Other English chroniclers ignore the episode. N. H. Nicolas, *History of the Royal Navy* (1847), ii. 510–13 (official list). *RP* 346.

[2] Sherborne, 'The Battle of La Rochelle and the War at Sea, 1372–5', 25–8, points out that the English position at sea was not weak down to 1375.

[3] Pedro Lopez de Ayala, *Cronica de los reyes de Castilla*, ii (Madrid, 1780), 77. The chronology of the embassy is obscure. The capture of Florimund must have happened after 2 August 1375 (*Anglo-French Negotiations*, 36). It is connected in an English source with the fiasco of 10 August 1375: at the end of the list of ships taken by the Castilians on that date is the entry 'Item une nief pris ovesque le seignour de lespre' (Nicolas, *History of the Royal Navy*, ii. 513). Charles V made presents to the embassy on 18 May 1376 (L. Delisle, *Mandements et actes divers de Charles V*, Collection de documents inédits sur l'histoire de France, 1874, no. 1234), but there seems to be no evidence that it went to Bruges (cf. Russell, *English Intervention*, 224–5).

cause at the French court, and at Bruges, where he was one of the French envoys, in Louis Duke of Anjou. Anjou, who was like Lancaster a royal duke in search of a kingdom, was relying on Castilian support for his claim to the kingdom of Majorca which he bought in 1375 from the sister of the last independent King, James III (d. February 1375). He said at the end of October that he was going to Bruges 'to guard there, after the rights of the king of France, the rights of the king of Castile and to hold for him at the said treaty the place of brother and special friend'.[1]

During the first three months of 1376, while the negotiators were talking at Bruges, measures were being taken to deal with the threat of invasion. In the first week of January orders were issued to array men in the south of England, to set up beacons on the hills for defence and to assemble commandeered ships at Southampton and Sandwich by 1 march.[2] At the end of March lords of estates on the sea coast from Lincolnshire to Cornwall were ordered to be on their lands with their retinues by Whitsun and more ships were to be pressed into the king's service.[3] Evidently the English council thought there was a serious possibility that Castile would attack, whether or not England was at peace with France, and their fears are justified by the fact that the dukes of Anjou and Burgundy promised to use their influence to stop the king of Castile breaking the truce when it had been extended.[4] It seems probable that the months before the Good Parliament and the negotiations during that period were overshadowed by the naval threat in a way that could not be guessed from the English chronicles or from the records of the Parliament itself.

The agreement about the truce included a provision for the negotiators to meet again at Bruges on 15 September. In fact it was much later when they finally came together again. The English envoys—Sudbury, Lancaster, the earls of Cambridge and Salisbury, Latimer, and John Lord Cobham—were appointed on 20 September, with the addition of specific power to make or prolong truces which may reflect the view of the

[1] A. Lecoy de la Marche, *Les Relations politiques de la France avec le royaume de Majorque* (Paris, 1892), ii. 392; cf. 207–21.

[2] *Foedera*, 1045–6; *CCR* 1374–7, 290.

[3] *Foedera*, 1049; *CCR*, 1374–7, 302.

[4] *Anglo-French Negotiations*, 41–2; Russell, *Intervention*, 225.

council that a renewal of truce was the best aim.[1] Cobham left on 29 September, Sudbury crossed the Channel on 20 October.[2] Then there was a dispute about the rendezvous, the English insisting on Bruges, where Lancaster had established himself at the latest by 7 December, but which the French at first rejected.[3]

Pope Gregory had received the news of the truce in July with elation. Under the influence of the Duke of Anjou he thought that the prospects of peace between England and France which it offered were sufficiently convincing for him to put off his return to Rome, which had appeared imminent, until the spring of 1376 so that he could attend better to the pressing business of northern Europe. This change of plans was announced on 28 July. On 12 August a Sienese correspondent at Avignon wrote that Anjou and the cardinals and relations of the pope crowded round him asking 'Holy Father, why do you want to go to Rome? When those kings who have warred for so long that the world was almost destroyed want to make peace and be in concord you ought not to go away, rather if you were at Rome you ought to come here to make peace between them.' He was told that the king of England's son, the king of France or his brother, and the emperor would meet to complete the business. Under the influence of these entreaties and hoping to achieve one of his life's ambitions, Gregory dismissed the Venetian and Neapolitan galleys which had been waiting to take him to Italy.[4] Doubtless Anjou exaggerated the likelihood of agreement. The negotiations, however, continued under the auspices of the same papal mediators, Guillaume Lestrange, Bishop of Carpentras, raised to the archbishopric of Rouen on the eve of the resumed negotiations in December 1375, and Pileo de Prata, Archbishop of Ravenna, reinforced by Gil Sánchez Munionis, provost of Valencia, who was sent back to Bruges to

---

[1] *Anglo-French Negotiations*, 24–5, 77. Powers were issued to the envoys on 20 and 23 September and 10 October (*Foedera*, 1039–41). Latimer, John Knyvet, Robert Ashton, Nicholas Carew, and other officials were at work at Westminster for 27 days in September 'pro secretis negotiis Regis ibidem expediendis' (E 403/459, 8 October) which suggests unusual conciliar activity.

[2] Deprez et Mirot, 'Les Ambassades', 194; Lambeth Palace, Register of Sudbury, fol. 10ᵛ.

[3] *Anglo-French Negotiations*, 25.

[4] G. Mollat, 'Rélations politiques de Grégoire XI avec les Siennois et les Florentins', *Mélanges d'Archéologie et d'Histoire*, lxviii (1956), 168. Cf. Mirot, *La Politique pontificale et le retour du Saint-Siège à Rome en 1376*, 78.

continue the negotiations about Anglo-papal relations which had been in progress since 1373.[1] The chief envoys of France were the dukes of Burgundy and Anjou.[2] Their clerical colleague, Jean de Lagrange, Bishop of Amiens, received news of his promotion to the college of cardinals on the day that he entered Bruges with the French delegation for the renewed negotiations.[3] The papal blessing lay over their proceedings and their outcome was eagerly awaited at Avignon.

A Florentine merchant trading at Bruges wrote a letter home describing the reopening of negotiations at the end of December which both portrays the ceremonious world of aristocratic diplomacy and also reveals the easy superiority of French prestige and wealth. Lancaster had appeared a few days earlier 'with several lords and with twenty-two knights and others, about 300 horse altogether; and they came in with many weapons like men at arms and the duke with a hawk on his wrist, so that they were not much praised.' The aggressive and down-to-earth English approach was in striking contrast to the carefully staged procession of the French which delighted the Florentine on 29 December. The French ambassadors were preceded by 200 big horses carrying their harness each ridden by a valet in the livery of the Duke of Anjou, 250 other valets on horseback, 30 carts full of luggage pulled by four horses each, 40 falconers on horseback, one of them carrying a leopard on the crupper, 150 squires in satin and silk, 80 knights in the same livery, 8 mace-bearers of the king of France, 30 minstrels, and finally a specially grand group of knights bearing the swords of the dukes of Anjou and Burgundy. The newly promoted Cardinal of Amiens came in with the dukes. The English envoys, utterly outclassed by this display, 'had stationed themselves in a house at the windows behind curtains so as to watch without being seen, but when the dukes came opposite this house they were told of it and halted and then the English lords had the curtains lifted and for some time they exchanged greetings and conversed with cheerful faces.' The following day they met formally in the collegiate church of St. Donatien as in previous

---

[1] *CPL* iv. 218.

[2] On their approach to the Bruges negotiations, Delachenal, iv. 584–7.

[3] He was promoted on 20 December 1375 (C. Eubel, *Hierarchia Catholica Medii, Aevi,* i, Monasterii (1898), 21).

negotiations, the dukes greeting each other with elaborate courtesy, 'embracing, kissing each other on the mouth, and kneeling and each begging the other to rise'. After discourses by the Cardinal of Amiens and the Archbishop of Ravenna they adjourned, Anjou taking Salisbury to dinner and Lancaster taking Bureau de la Rivière. After this, according to the Italian, the negotiations proceeded at a leisurely pace, regular morning meetings being interrupted by periods in which the envoys were waiting for instructions from home and therefore gave themselves up to hawking and hunting and dancing.[1]

The negotiations lasted from the end of December to the later part of March and appear to have centred around a detailed proposal for a forty-year truce submitted by the papal mediators.[2] The mediators' idea was that the territorial position should be accepted as it was at present and stabilized, the English being compensated by a substantial grant of money from the French king and the Duke of Brittany by a pension. Both sides sent members of their mission home during a gap at the end of January and the beginning of February, presumably to receive reactions to this idea; Anjou, Rivière, the Cardinal of Amiens, and the papal nuncios all went to Charles V, Latimer and Sudbury probably to the English court.[3] Before departing, the French promised to give Latimer an answer about the immediate prolongation of the truce for another year by 8 February: presumably the English were anxious to obtain this and were in the position of suppliants to Charles V for it.[4] It was agreed and formally enacted at Bruges on 12 March.[5] The ambitious plan for a forty-year truce, however, presented much greater difficulties. The English wanted far more money than the French were prepared to offer; they wanted to keep French outposts isolated rather than rationalize the boundary line; above all the French attachment to full royal sovereignty and the English attachment to the title of king of France remained fundamental obstacles. At the end of March they could only agree to disperse after a tournament at Ghent provided by

---

[1] *Lettere di mercatanti toscani scritte nel sec. 14 non mai fin qui stampate,* ed. P. Ferrato (Venice, 1869), 28–38.
[2] The proposals are printed in *Anglo-French Negotiations,* 26–35, the reactions to them, ibid. 37–41.
[3] Ibid. 36; Sudbury's expense account, Mirot and Deprez, 194–5, Larson, p. 428.
[4] *Anglo-French Negotiations,* 35.   [5] Ibid. 37.

Burgundy from 31 March to 3 April and to meet again on 1 July.[1]

Apart from the renewal of the truce, the only positive advantage which the English gained from the negotiations was an agreement by Charles V to pay the 40,000 francs which had been laid down the previous year as the price of St. Saveur. A special delegation of Sir Thomas Harleston, the captain of Guisnes, and William Ermyn, the treasurer of Calais, was sent to Bruges in January to press for payment[2] and the money seems to have been paid in the summer.[3] The renewed truce did give the English court a long breathing space until 1 April 1377 and the assurance of French help to restrain the Castilians until then. In the meantime something must be done to meet the ultimate inevitable menace of French and Castilian attack. The first summons to a parliament was issued on 28 December 1375 for 12 February; on 20 January it was postponed to 28 April, presumably so that the diplomatic results of Bruges should be clear and the envoys home before it assembled.[4] Paradoxically the prolongation of the truce probably made the prospects of a successful parliament still worse. With hostilities due to be resumed in almost a year's time, the courtiers could claim neither success in war nor immediate necessity. In addition to this Lancaster had spent a good part of the time since the conclusion of the original truce in ostentatious junketing with the country's enemies which could not have improved his standing either with merchants or with soldiers.

---

[1] *Anglo-French Negotiations*, 40, 42.

[2] 'Domino Johanni de Harleston militi et Willelmo de Eiremyn Thesaurario ville Calesie missis de Calesia vsque Bruges per ordinacionem consilii domini Regis ad prosequendum pro quadam summa xl Ml francorum recipiendorum pro redempcione ville Sancti Salvatoris in Normannia', for 8 days in January (E 101/180/4, fol. 10).

[3] *Foedera*, 1051, 1059.

[4] *Reports of the Lords' Committees . . . touching the Dignity of a Peer of the Realm* (1820–9), iii. 662–6.

4

The court and the royal finances
1372-1375

I. THE OFFICERS AND THE COURT

BEHIND the strategies and policies executed in the name of the crown, with which the previous chapters have been concerned, loomed the king's court in which they were framed and authorized. The proceedings of the Good Parliament were essentially an indictment of the court and the courtiers for squandering the king's money and surrendering his conquests. When we try to probe these accusations, however, we are faced with many difficulties, some of which are insuperable. There is no doubt that the court was the hub of the political world but there is no way of entering it. There is no 'secret history' of the English court: that is why the glimpses offered by the Good Parliament proceedings are so fascinating and tantalizing. At this period there are no records of the council or the Chamber. The accounts of the Wardrobe which survive contain little information of political significance. The process of the formulation of policy therefore can only be reconstructed to a very limited extent on the basis of tenuous inferences. It is for practical purposes simply impossible to say who was responsible for the decisions about the Brittany expedition or the concordat; the most that can be said is that presumably those whom we know to have been prominent at court were generally held responsible and must have acquiesced. In two respects, however, we can advance our understanding of the court by consulting the extraneous records: first we can identify some of the people who stood out at court, secondly we can outline the court's financial policy, against which the charges made in the Good Parliament were particularly directed, and to some extent identify its beneficiaries.

The individuals who most obviously managed the king's government were the chief ministers. During the years immediately preceding the Good Parliament they were the following: Sir John Knyvet, Chancellor from 5 July 1372; Richard Scrope of Bolton, Treasurer from 27 March 1371, succeeded on 26 September 1375 by Sir Robert Ashton; William Latimer, Chamberlain from 27 October 1371; John Neville of Raby, Steward of the Household from 20 November 1371. Lists of the witnesses of important governmental acts commonly include these men together with a selection of great magnates on the one hand and lesser courtiers on the other, and give us some idea of the people who had a hand in the high politics of the court. Thus in June 1372, when Robert Thorp, the old Chancellor, was dying in the house of the Bishop of Salisbury in Fleet Street, he had the Great Seal sealed in a purse by Knyvet and two Chancery clerks. They took it to Westminster and handed it to Latimer, Scrope, and Nicholas Carew, the Keeper of the Privy Seal, in the Star Chamber. A few days later the king gave it to Knyvet in the presence of his son Edmund Langley, Henry Percy, Latimer, Scrope, Neville, and Carew.[1] In December 1373 the king's case for a grant of money was presented to Convocation by a deputation consisting of the earls of March and Salisbury, Latimer, Knyvet, and Scrope, Guy Brian, a household knight, and Carew.[2] The repayment of the big loan of August 1374 (which was raised to pay for the Brittany expedition and came under attack in the Good Parliament) was guaranteed by a long list of people, four bishops, the Black Prince, Lancaster, and six earls, Latimer, Neville, Brian, Knyvet, Scrope, Carew, John Cavendish a judge, Richard Sturry a Chamber knight, William Tank a baron of the Exchequer, and William Dytton clerk of the Privy Seal.[3]

Some of the central group of ministers and courtiers were administrators rather than independent noblemen. Knyvet the Chancellor was a lawyer who had been Chief Justice of King's Bench since 1365. Nicholas Carew the Keeper of the Privy Seal was a squire of no great importance.[4] This leaves us with Scrope, Latimer, and Neville. Richard Scrope of Bolton in Wensleydale was a nobleman who had been very active in the wars since

[1] *Foedera*, 951.   [2] Lambeth Palace Library, Register of Whittlesey, fol. 64[v].
[3] *CPR*, 1374–7, 6.   [4] Tout, v. 44–5.

Neville's Cross in 1346. Since 1367 he had been a feed retainer of Lancaster and went on an expedition with him in 1369. This connection very likely explains his appointment as Treasurer in the anti-clerical crisis of 1371. He stayed in the office until September 1375 when he left it to become Warden of the West March.[1] There was no suggestion in the Good Parliament that he was implicated in the scandals; on the contrary he and the previous treasurer, the Bishop of Exeter, were called upon to give evidence about the loan of August 1374 on which much of the accusation of corruption by the courtiers turned and, according to the *Anonimalle Chronicle* which quotes his words, he promised that if the king released him from his oath of secrecy as a councillor 'I will not spare any living man but will say the truth entirely to my knowledge as I have conceived and heard and learnt it.' A few days later, after receiving the royal command to speak, he said that the loan of August 1374 had been made by William Latimer and Richard Lyons without his knowledge: 'Come ieo suppose par le seignur de Latymer qe issy est et Richard Liouns, saunz sew de moy.'[2] Since the loan, as we shall see, is clearly traceable in the records of the Exchequer, it hardly seems plausible that the Treasurer should have been ignorant of it. On the other hand it is conceivable that such a man as Scrope, probably with very little interest in or aptitude for such dull clerkly business, genuinely did not know much about what was going on in the Exchequer and was happy to leave the responsibility for financial policy to others. In September 1375 he gave up the office to become joint warden of the West March. He was succeeded as treasurer by a more obscure West Country knight, Robert Ashton, who had been Chancellor of Ireland under Clarence (1364–7), Admiral to the West (1369–72), and then Lieutenant of Ireland (1372–3) and had just come back from the Brittany expedition. The office of Treasurer therefore was not held at this period, as it usually was, by an experienced and weighty clerical administrator, nor by a very powerful lay politician; this may have left the field rather open for courtier financiers.

There is no reason to doubt the implication of the Good

---

[1] His biography in *Scrope and Grosvenor Controversy*, ed. N. H. Nicolas (1832), ii. 17–39 (where it is mistakenly said that he accompanied Lancaster to France in 1373), and *Complete Peerage*, xi. 539–41.　　　　　　　　　　　　[2] *Anon*, 87–9.

Parliament proceedings that Latimer and Neville, who held the household offices throughout the period from the autumn of 1371, had some special power at court. Although Neville's second marriage (*circa* 1378–81) was to Latimer's daughter, the two men were of about the same age and had led similar active lives. The marriage itself must have been the result of a close association between the two men. Latimer had no son and on his death in 1381 most of his property went to Neville.[1] Latimer was born in 1330. Starting with the battle of Crécy at the age of 16, he spent many years in France and was the most prominent English soldier and official in Brittany in the decade after 1359.[2] At the end of the sixties he came back to England and made a place for himself at court, being Steward of the Household from 1368 to October 1370 before he became Chamberlain. He was also from 1368 Warden of the Forests, and from 1372 Constable of Dover. He agreed to buy the wardship of the lands of Edward Courtenay in August 1372 for a lump sum of 1,000 marks and those of Henry Beaumont in December 1373 for £1,500 paid over two years, transactions which suggest that he had accumulated a considerable amount of money.[3] This wealth may just as well have been the result of his highly profitable career in France as of the use of his position at court. His relationship to the financial manipulations of the court is, as we shall see, almost entirely obscure, as far as the records go, but the sources for the Good Parliament agree in reporting that his accusers said he supplied some of the money and took some of the profit. According to the parliament roll the accusation was that 'the money of the king himself in his Chamber of which the said lord was keeper or treasurer and also the money of Latimer and Richard [Lyons] themselves was advanced to make the said loan.' John Pyel said that the loan of August 1374 in which he and Lyons were the official lenders was actually made 'from the goods of our lord the king or of Lord Latimer'.[4] Latimer was in fact, as Chamberlain, the official receiver of the 10,000 marks p.a. which were regularly paid from the Exchequer to the Chamber[5] and was normally noted in the issue roll of the Exchequer as the recipient of the money. He was also

---

[1] *Calendar of Inquisitions Post Mortem*, xv. 155–60.
[2] *Complete Peerage*, vii. 470–5.   [3] *CFR* viii. 171, 224.
[4] *RP* 325, § 24; *Anon*, 90; *CA* 78.   [5] Tout, iv. 313–18.

occasionally recorded officially in the Exchequer rolls as lending the Exchequer cash from the Chamber.[1] It is therefore quite possible that he lent Chamber money unofficially for his own profit. In the absence of any Chamber accounts it is impossible to guess what quantities of money were available to Latimer in this capacity but it is certain that, in addition to the regular Exchequer income, miscellaneous receipts of various kinds were paid into that office without the knowledge of the Exchequer. When the city of Bristol paid for a new charter, for example, it paid the Chamber.[2] It also seems that the payments for licences for evasion of the Staple, which at eleven shillings a sack must have amounted in some years to over £7,000, were paid into the Chamber. When Richard Lyons, Latimer's merchant associate, was pressed in the Good Parliament about this extra imposition and about the tax of 4*d*. in the pound on letters of exchange, he said that he had the king's authority to collect them,

but he produced no warrant or authority in parliament except only that he said he had the command of the king himself and of his council to do it. And on this evidence was given openly in parliament that our lord the king had said expressly the previous day to some lords present here in parliament that he did not know how or in what manner he [Lyons] had come to hold such an office from him and moreover he never knew him to be his officer.[3]

As Chamberlain, Latimer was well placed to manage a sector of the royal finances as he pleased without the knowledge of the king or of the Treasurer. He was a greedy man who probably made the most of the opportunity.

The other courtier who figured prominently in the Good Parliament impeachments, John Neville of Raby, was not implicated in the general financial charges about the Staple and loans. Accusations against him were confined to two points: that he acted as broker of royal debts and that he had committed various misdeeds as captain of a company going to Brittany. Neville's background was rather similar to Latimer's.[4] He was

---

[1] e.g. 14 June 1373 the Exchequer receives a loan of £1,333 6*s*. 8*d*. from the Chamber by the hands of Latimer (E 401/513); 3 November 1373 Exchequer repays to Latimer 5,000 marks which had been lent from the Chamber (E 403/451); 6 November 1375 Exchequer repays to Chamber by hands of Latimer and Adam Hertyngdon £300, part of 500 marks loaned 18 April (E 403/459).
[2] Below p. 134.   [3] *RP* 324, § 18.   [4] *Complete Peerage*, ix. 502-3.

a northern baron who had been an active fighting man starting in the same year as Latimer at Neville's Cross under his father. He had been on various expeditions to France and was made a Knight of the Garter in 1369. Since November 1370 he had been like Richard Scrope an indentured retainer of John of Gaunt. Although he became Steward of the Household in 1371, Neville spent a long stretch of time in 1372-3 in Brittany and this suggests in itself that he was less deeply involved in court politics than Latimer. Like Latimer he seems to have had money to spare. The Duke of Lancaster borrowed 1,000 marks from him in 1372 and £500 in 1373,[1] and the Duke of Brittany raised more than 2,000 marks by mortgaging lands to him.[2] The correct picture seems to be that Neville was a beneficiary from influence at the court but not one of its main managers.

Finally there is the colourful and legendary figure of Alice Perrers. Alice's origins are obscure and need not concern us here. There is plenty of evidence, however, that by the 1370s she had achieved a position of extraordinary pre-eminence and influence at court as the king's concubine. In payments by the wardrobe for gifts of clothes she was coupled with the king's own daughter Isabella, Countess of Bedford.[3] While the Good Parliament itself was taking place the court was hopefully planning a tournament at Smithfield which would have taken place in the first week of June—a sad week as it turned out when the Black Prince was on his death-bed and the court faction was being thoroughly routed—and for which special clothes were again ordered for the same two ladies.[4] In 1374 the king had a barge called 'La Alice'.[5] She bore the king a son who was acknowledged at court as 'John Sotherey'[6] and, with respect equal to that accorded to his mother, was given clothes with the young noblemen in the king's wardship as a squire of

---

[1] *John of Gaunt's Register 1372-6*, i. 75, 78.

[2] *CPR 1377-81*, 74.

[3] e.g. 'In Cameram domini nostri Regis apud Shene ad dandum dominis Comitisse Bedeford filie eius et Alicie Perrers de dono Regis pro diuersis garnamentis . . .' (E 101/397/20 under 19 October 1375, and again 10 November).

[4] Payment to the king's tailor 'Eidem in Cameram domini Regis apud Westmonasterium ad dandum domine Comitisse Bedeford et Alicie Perrers pro apparatis earundem de dono Regis pro hastiludiis que ordinata fuerunt ad essendum in Smethefeld post Pentecostam sed non completis per manus proprias xx die maii' (E 101/397/20). [5] *Foedera*, 996.

[6] M. Galway, 'Alice Perrers's son John', *English Historical Review*, lxvi (1951).

the Chamber.[1] Outsiders assumed that this position at court gave her great influence. When the abbot of St. Albans was in dispute with her over the ownership of a manor in 1374 he was advised that it would be useless for him to persist with the case: 'This Alice de Perers had such power and eminence in those days that no one dared prosecute a claim against her. And so all those of the abbot's council advised that it would be better for the abbot to desist from an action to establish his right and to wait until kinder fortune smiled upon him.'[2] Even the pope did not disdain to ask for her influence to help in the release of his brother from captivity.[3] No estimate can be made of the extent of her winnings but by the end of her career she had amassed enough property to rank as a substantial landowner.[4] In November 1375 she could afford to lend Walter Fitzwalter £1,000 on a mortgage of the castle of Egremont.[5] Naturally she had received many gifts from the king: for instance in August 1373 she was given some or all of the late queen's jewels.[6] In the following month she was granted an annuity of £100 to sustain her son.[7] She occasionally received sums of Exchequer money which must in reality have been royal presents. For instance in April 1372 the Exchequer paid her £397 ostensibly for jewels bought from her for the king's use at Christmas 1370 and 1371;[8] in February 1376 £120 out of the regular Exchequer income for the Chamber was paid into her hands.[9] Obviously her position in the court must have given her all kinds of opportunities for influence and corruption but they cannot be specified and beyond this point her role is impenetrable.

II. ROYAL BORROWING 1372-5

The general pattern of royal income and expenditure at this period can be seen from the following analysis of payments into and out of the Exchequer recorded in the receipt and issue rolls

[1] e.g. 1 October 1375, gowns 'pro domino de Beaumond Johanne Sothereye et filio domini de Gomenyz de dono Regis de secta aliorum scutiferum camere sue' (E 101/397/20).
[2] *Gesta Abbatum Monasterii Sancti Albani,* iii (Rolls Series, 1869), 228-9.
[3] *CPL* iv. 96.
[4] *Calendar of Inquisitions Miscellaneous,* iv. 1-5, 6-17, 23-4, 44-5, 48, 59-60, 73.
[5] *CPR* 1385-9, 204.   [6] *Foedera,* 989.   [7] Galway, op. cit.
[8] E 403/446, 15 April.
[9] E 403/459, 29 February.

for the year Michaelmas 1374 to Michaelmas 1375.[1] Payments
in totalled £112,187. The main headings were

customs and subsidies	£34,734
lay subsidies	32,522
clerical subsidies	9,140
loans	8,548
issues of lands, castles, and farms	7,837
payments by sheriffs	4,140
alien priories	3,548

Payments out totalled £139,617. The main headings were

wages of soldiers and sailors	£64,183
payments to Wardrobe	18,618
advances to Treasurer of Calais	13,377
repayment of loans	12,906
annuities	6,992
payments to Chamber	6,667
costs of embassies	5,814

The financial policy of the king, like that of the pope, was,
as these figures show, dominated by the demands of war. Peace-
time finance was comparatively easy, wartime finance was
punctuated by crises. The nature of English military activity,
in which the major part was played by expeditions sent abroad
at irregular intervals, determined the pattern of expenditure.
The dispatch of each expedition, when money had to be found
to pay the first instalments of the soldiers' wages and the cost of
transporting them, was a short crisis of high expenditure followed by a longer lull in which the Exchequer had only to meet
the costs of Calais and other permanent garrisons and the
arrears of wages for earlier expeditions until the next big effort
was made. The supply of money for war depended on two
things: the granting of taxes, chiefly lay subsidies and wool
customs voted by the commons in Parliament and clerical subsidies voted by Convocation, and the willingness of lenders to
advance the large sums of ready money needed to fit out an

[1] E 401/518, 519; E 403/456, 457. Both cash payments and assignments on as
yet uncollected sources of income are included but fictitious loans and other book-
keeping entries of assigned *prestita soluta* and of prests which had not been repaid
are omitted. The figures are rounded to the nearest pound.

expedition in return for promises of repayment from taxes to be paid in the future. Without these two conditions—the granting of taxes and the availability of loans—serious military activity would sooner or later become impossible. Grants of taxation were made by Parliament and Convocation. They depended on the ability of the crown to persuade, cajole, or coerce those assemblies and these grants of course determined in general the availability of money. Loans, however, were an essential part of the mechanism of royal finance because revenue was slow to come in. The arrangement of loans was a field in which the court had opportunities for manipulation.

In the early 1370s the pattern of royal finance had certain distinctive features which came under attack in the Good Parliament. In order to understand these features it is necessary to follow through some of the stages in the financial history of the period so far as it is known from the records of the Exchequer. The first big military effort of 1372, Pembroke's expedition which ended with the destruction of his fleet at La Rochelle in June, was managed without substantial borrowing. Although he took with him, in addition to a small force, £12,000 to be used for raising troops in Gascony, the money seems to have been found by drawing in cash payments of the customs voted for the three years 1370–2 by the Parliament of 1369 and the lay and clerical subsidies voted by the Parliament and Convocation in 1371 without raising any large loans.[1] The next effort was Edward III's abortive naval expedition in August to October 1372 for which more than £20,000 was paid out in the autumn.[2] This involved the raising of two large loans both entered under 16 August on the Receipt Roll. One was entered as a straightforward short-term loan of 5,000 marks by the Earl of Arundel repaid to him at his castle at Lewes a month later.[3] The other one was more complicated. John Pyel, a merchant of London, advanced 10,000 marks in cash and repaid a royal debt of 5,000 marks to the Bardi company of Florentine merchants which had been incurred nearly thirty years earlier. In

---

[1] Sherborne, 'Indentured Retinues', 733–4; considerable payments of taxes into the Exchequer in March and April are recorded on the Receipt Rolls, E 401/506 and 508.

[2] E 403/446 (August and September).

[3] E 401/508 (16 August); E 403/446 (16 September), 'per manus proprias apud Lewes'.

return for this he was to be repaid the total sum of 15,000 marks (£10,000) from the customs at London.[1]

The next big expedition, John of Gaunt's foray through France, was marked by payments from April to July 1373[2] which necessitated a loan of the same kind at the beginning of July, apparently balancing a very large payment to the other chief commander of the expedition, the Duke of Brittany, on 13 July. Richard Lyons, a London merchant, together with other unnamed Londoners, was credited with a loan of £9,000 of which it appears that £6,000 was cash paid to the Duke and the other £3,000 repayment of an old debt to the Bardi. £9,000 was to be repaid to Lyons from the customs at London.[3] A month earlier on 4 June, Arundel had made another short-term loan repaid on 29 October.[4]

At the end of 1373 the crown's prospects of income were improved by the grants made by Convocation and Parliament in December which promised unconditionally a clerical subsidy to be paid in June 1374 and February 1375, a lay subsidy to be paid in the first half of 1374, and continuation of tunnage and poundage and wool customs to Michaelmas (29 September) 1375; if the war was still being fought the king was to get a further lay subsidy in the first half of 1375 and continuation of the other taxes until Michaelmas 1376. Fortified by these grants the crown raised another big loan of the same kind from Lyons and another Londoner, Richard Francis, on 6 February 1374. It consisted of 8,354 marks paid to the Exchequer in cash and 4,177 marks (50 per cent of the cash loan) credited to the lenders

[1] 'De Johanne Pyel cive et mercatore Londonii. x ML li. de mutuo. Inde habet letteras Regis patentes de magno sigillo super custumas Londonii. Inde soluit ad Receptam x ML marcarum et pro mercatoribus de societate Bardorum v ML marcarum', E 401/508 (16 August); *CPR*, 1370–4, 196–7; A. Beardwood, *Alien Merchants in England, 1350–77* (Cambridge, Mass., 1931), 129; the original debt to the Bardi, *CPR*, 1343–5, 467–9.

[2] E 403/449 (especially 13 July).

[3] 'Mutuum de Ricardo Lyons et aliis mercatoribus civitatis Londonii ix ML librarum de mutuo, satisfactum est eis inde per letteras patentes super custumas Londonie. pro Roberto de Morton pro Duce Britannie.' E 401/513 (13 July). The letters patent dated 7 July (*CPR*, 1370–4, 319) mention the division into cash and repayment of debts as does the final account with the Bardi (Beardwood, *Alien Merchants*, 467–9).

[4] E 403/459 (29 October) repayment to Arundel by the hands of his son John and John Philpot of £10,000 loaned on 4 June. I have not found a record of the original loan.

for repayment of an ancient debt to *Pancius de Controne* who had been the king's physician in the 1330s.[1] This was followed six months later in the autumn of 1374 by a burst of borrowing for the expedition to Brittany. On 23 August Lyons and Pyell were credited with a loan of 30,000 marks, of which exactly 20,000 marks was cash and 10,000 marks repayment of debts, this time a collection of debts, of which the major one was £5,854 15s. 8d. to the Bardi made up by a number of small ones to the exact round figure.[2] Repayment was to be made from the customs at London, Hull, Boston, and Yarmouth. Under 18 September four more loans are recorded on the Receipt Roll. The Earl of Arundel lent £10,000 which was repaid to him by the hands of John Philpot a London merchant on 31 January and 5 June 1375.[3] Lyons made another loan of the same variety, two-thirds cash and one-third repayment of debts. The sums this time were £2,215 17s. and £1,107 18s. 6d. in debts, mostly to the Bardi.[4] Repayment was to be from the tonnage and poundage and petty custom, all of which were farmed out to Lyons. John Hedyngham of London lent £2,000 cash and received payment of £1,000 of debts, some of them to himself, none to the Bardi. Finally, Michael de la Pole lent

[1] 'De Ricardo Lyons, Ricardo Fraunceys et sociis suis. viii ML cccliiii. li. de mutuo. Satisfactum est eis inde per litteras Regis patentes super custumas Regis de Lenne, Jernemuthe, Boston et Hulle per manus dicti Ricardi Lyons Inde soluerunt v ML d. lxix li. xi s. viii. d. et pro magistro Pancio de Controne ML ML d. ccc iiiixx. iiii. li. xiii. s. iiii. d.', E 401/514 (6 February). Cf. *CPR*, 1370–4, 411; E 403/451 (6 February) and for debts to Pancius who died before 20 September 1340 (*CPR* 1340–3, 33), entries in *CPR* and *CCR* in the 1330s.
[2] 'Petro de Barde et Waltero de Barde mercatoribus de societate Bardorum at attornatis eiusdem societatis per manus predictorum Ricardi Lyons et Johannis Piel in allocacione eis facta infra summa xx ML li. predictarum super debita in quibus dominus Rex eisdem mercatoribus tenetur ut patet per litteras acquietanciales ipsorum Petri et Walteri nomine predicte societatis factas remanentes in hanaperio de hoc termino et ut patet per litteras patentes quas dicti Petrus et Walterus inde penes se habent indorsatas de summa subscripta. Respondebunt— v ML d ccliii. li. xvs. viiid unde.' (E 403/454, 23 August.) The other debts paid were to John Daywatre of Bredon (£20 5s. 3d.), John Burghard of Lynne (£34 3s. 1d.), the Prior of Bredon (£12), John Cokyn of Ashburnham (£10), Richard Heruy (£11 10s.), the Prior of the Hospital of St. John (£694 1s. 2d.), John de Ravensholme (£30 8s. 2d.). The loan itself is recorded in E 401/515 (23 August); cf. *CPR*, 1374–7, 6; *CCR*, 1374–7, 41; Beardwood, *Alien Merchants*, 129, 131.
[3] E 401/515 (18 September); E 403/456, 457 (31 January and 5 June).
[4] 'Alexandro Bartholomei de Bardes et Bartholomeo domini Radulphi de Bardes' £924 11s. 10d.: E 403/454 (18 September) E 401/515. *CPR*, 1374–7, 5.

£1,200 cash and was credited with a payment of £600 due to himself in return for which he got tallies to the value of £1,800.[1] On 6 November two Londoners, John Hedyngham and Richard Wandesford, advanced £1,000 and repaid £500 of debts owing from the years 1370 and 1372.[2] The last big loans were on 23 December when Lyons advanced £4,000.[3] The courtier soldier Guy Brian paid £632 3s. 8d. in cash and was credited with £316 1s. 10d. paid for an old debt to Hugh de Courteney.[4] Finally there are some slightly mysterious entries about a loan by a group of London merchants. A patent dated 10 December 1374 promised repayment of £3,000 to William Walworth, John Bernes, Nicholas Brembre, John Bures, and John Hadlee of which £733 6s. 8d., just a quarter, was to be repaid from the lay subsidy levied in London and the rest from the customs there after Lyons and Pyel had been satisfied for their loans. An entry on the receipt roll dated 23 December recorded a loan of £2,266 13s. 4d., just three-quarters of £3,000, 'De Willelmo Walleworth Johanne Bernes Adam Staple et aliis probis hominibus Civitatis Londonie'. A possible explanation is that they were the same loan and that the king was paying a premium of one-third for it, but this is hypothetical.[5]

It has been necessary to recapitulate the loans of the period 1372–5 in some detail both because they were a crucial issue in the Good Parliament and because they provide some important leads into the obscure politics of the court which must now be followed up.

The biggest individual lender to the crown in these years was not a merchant but a great landed magnate, Richard, Earl of Arundel, who appears to have built up an unusual accumulation of wealth by the successful exploitation of very large estates and avoidance for the last fifteen years of his life of any involvement in the costly business of fighting. Arundel had much increased the large ancient property of his family by adding the Warenne inheritance. He was a landowner on an enormous scale in both the Welsh Marches and Surrey and Sussex.[6] There

[1] E 401/515 (18 September), E 403/454 (22 September).
[2] E 401/518; E 403/456. [3] E 401/518 (23 December).
[4] E 401/518; E 403/456. [5] CPR, 1374–7, 36; E 401/518 (23 December).
[6] He rented the Warenne lands in the Welsh Marches from the last earl of Warenne's widow for £900 a year in December 1347 (CPR, 1345–8, 434–7). When she died in 1361 he inherited in fee simple both these and the extensive properties

are hints too of a policy of positive estate management. The commons petition in the Good Parliament complained that he had farmed the sheriff's tourn in the rapes of Chichester and Arundel from the king, created 'a new court called Shire-court at Arundel', and made a profit of £30 a year from it.[1] In 1362 he had acquired from Christ Church, Canterbury, the right of mining ironstone on the manor of Merstham.[2] His regular financial agent seems to have been John Philpot, the prominent London merchant, who is said to have been responsible for selling wool from his estates to the value of more than £2,000 in one year.[3] Whatever the means, he had acquired an enormous stock of money: it was reckoned that at his death he had 45,000 marks' worth of coin in bags in a chest in the High Tower at Arundel, apart from considerable sums stored elsewhere or due to him as debts which added up to as much again.[4] The breadth of Arundel's estates was not unique but his accumulated wealth was probably very unusual for a lay magnate. He had been a lender to the crown at least since 1351.[5] John of Gaunt borrowed 1,000 marks from him to pay his household wages in June 1372, £1,000 apparently for his war expenses in April 1373, 4,000 marks in July 1374, and an unspecified sum in February 1375.[6] Arundel was an outstandingly powerful magnate. His son Thomas was provided to the see of Ely in August at the age of 20 at his father's request and over the heads of two candidates with royal favour because the pope wished to use the earl's influence in England.[7] But there is no evidence that he was a directing force in politics: he had long

in Surrey and Sussex which she had held jointly with her husband (*Calendar of Inquisitions Post Mortem*, xi. no. 215; *CPR*, 1361–4, 123; 1364–7, 198).

[1] *RP* 348.

[2] *Literae Cantuarienses*, ed. J. B. Sheppard (Rolls Series, 1889), ii. 420.

[3] 'Item fait assavoir qe les leines en la Marche en Surrey et Sussex esteantz en pyle le Jour de sa mort et venduz depuis par J. Philpot amontent en tout la quart part donez par mon dit Seigneur que dieux assoille al dit J. Philpot nient rebatuz £ML ML x li li. xiii s. iiii d. . . . .'. This is in an 'Inventaire des toutes les biens et chateaux moebles appurtenantz au noble Seigneur Monseigneur Richard Counte Darundell et de Surrey le xxiiii jour de Janvier lan du Regne le Roy Edward tiercz xlixme' (24 January 1376, the day of his death) in a seventeenth-century transcript in British Museum Harleian MS. 4840 fol. 393.   [4] Ibid.

[5] *CPR*, 1350–4, 106, loan of 4,000 marks; 1354–8, 511, £2,000 in 1357; 1358–61, 24, £3,000 in 1359; etc.

[6] *John of Gaunt's Register 1372–6*, i. 74–5, 77, 79; ii. 36, 62, 93, 154, 189, 303.

[7] *CPL* iv. 119, 129; M. Aston, *Thomas Arundel* (Oxford, 1967), 9.

ceased to be active in war, he was an old man of about 60, and he does not figure much in the court circle.

Arundel's were short-term loans fairly quickly, sometimes very quickly, repaid and do not seem to have involved him to the same extent as the merchant lenders in recovering his money from taxes. There are, however, some pieces of evidence which suggest that some of his loans were not as straightforward as appears at first sight and may have been closer to the 'two-thirds plus one-third' pattern observed in the merchants' loans. An earlier loan of June 1370 is recorded as 20,000 marks on the receipt and issue rolls but a close roll entry records an obligation for £20,000 acknowledged in two bonds, one for 20,000 marks, the other for 10,000 marks, and orders repayment of the whole from the customs.[1] Possibly the 10,000 marks was payment for the loan. Secondly there is an undated letter preserved in a privy seal formulary book which acknowledges the receipt of a loan of 10,000 marks from Arundel for which certain royal jewels have been pledged ('certeins noz corone et vesselle dor') and promises repayment 'en les trois semaignes de Pentecoste prochein venant'. The guarantors of repayment are Latimer as Chamberlain, Knyvet as Chancellor, Scrope as Treasurer, and Carew as Keeper of the Privy Seal, so the document must fall in the period 1372-5 and the only known loan to which it could refer is that of £10,000 recorded on 18 September 1374 and repaid in two instalments entered on the receipt rolls, 5,000 marks on 31 January 1375 and 10,000 on 5 June, five days before Pentecost.[2] In view of the Duke of Lancaster's assertion in the Good Parliament that a charge of 50 per cent for a loan might be unavoidable,[3] it is possible that Arundel was being paid 5,000 marks for his help. But there is still a further complication. On 31 January Arundel was repaid not £3,333 6s. 8d. (5,000 marks) but £4,333 6s. 8d., £1,000 extra,[4] and on the

[1] E 401/501 (28 June); E 403/444 (14 November); F. Palgrave, *Ancient Kalendars and Inventories of the Exchequer* (1836), ii. 226-7; *CCR*, 1369-74, 149-50.
[2] Cambridge University Library MS. Dd. 3.53, fol. 40ᵛ. E 401/515 (18 September) 'De Ricardo Comite Arundellie x Ml Li. de mutuo. Inde sol. xxi die Januarie anno xlix v Ml li. Item quinto Junii proximo sequente x Ml. marc. in persolucionem.' E 403/456 (31 January) see below; E 403/457 (5 June) to Arundel by hands of his son John and John Philpot 10,000 marks 'in persolucionem x ML. marcarum quas domino Regi ad receptam Scacarii xviiiᵒ die Septembris Anno xlviiiᵒ mutuo liberavit'.
[3] *Anon*, 86.
[4] E 403/456 (31 January) 'Ricardo Comiti Arundellie In denariis sibi liberatis

same day he was said to have repaid £1,000 to the Bardi. The meaning of these entries may be that Arundel advanced 15,000 marks on 18 September, of which only 10,000 was covered by the privy seal letter, and that his only reward was the discount on £1,000 of royal debts. It is possible, however, that he advanced 10,000 marks for which he received as premium 5,000 marks, in addition to discount on the £1,000 of Bardi debt.

The position of the other lenders is different. In the cases where repayment of debt was involved it is highly probable that they made a profit by receiving full payment at the Exchequer for the face value of debts which they could probably have bought at a discount, especially if these debts were thirty years old. The practice of brokerage of royal debts was alleged and admitted in the Good Parliament and some of the specific cases mentioned may be relevant to the loans of this period.[1] Lyons was alleged to have acted as broker for a debt to the Prior of St. John for a payment of 80 marks (£53 6s. 8d.).[2] It might be the debt of £694 1s. 2d. repaid as part of the bargain for the loan of 23 August 1374. Neville was alleged to have had similar dealings with Lady Margaret Ravensholm who died on 10 September 1375.[3] His explanation was that she had a debt to him for which, since she had no money, he accepted tallies for £200 'for which he was later paid by the help of his friends around the king. But it was with great difficulty . . .' In gratitude she gave him £95. True or not, this explanation illuminates the system. One of the debts involved on 23 August 1374 was £30 8s. 2d. due to John de Ravensholm, Lady Margaret's husband who had died in 1353.[4] This may be part of the debt referred to in parliament.

The loans made to the crown by merchants in this period were as follows:

per manus Johannis Philippot in parte solucionis X ML librarum quas domino ad Receptam scaccarii xviii° die Septembris anno xlviii° mutuo liberauit vt patet in Rotulo Recepte de eodem die iiii ML iiic xxxiii li. vi s. viiid.'

[1] Some examples of dealing in royal debts earlier in the reign are given by A. Steel, 'The Negotiation of Wardrobe Debentures in the Fourteenth Century', *English Historical Review*, xliv (1929), and G. Sayles, 'A Dealer in Wardrobe Bills', *Economic History Review*, iii (1931–2).

[2] *RP* 324.

[3] *RP* 328–9; *Calendar of Inquisitions Post Mortem*, xiv, no. 193.

[4] *Calendar of Inquisitions Post Mortem*, x, no. 73.

Date	Lenders	Loan	Debt Repayment	
July 1372	John Pyel	10,000 m.	5,000 m.	All Bardi debt
July 1373	Richard Lyons and others	£6,000	£3,000	Bardi debt
February 1374	Lyons and Richard Francis and others	8,354 m.	4,177 m.	Debt to Pancius de Controne
August 1374	Lyons and Pyel	20,000 m.	10,000 m.	£5,854 15s. 8d. Bardi debt
September 1374	Lyons	£2,215 17s.	£1,107 18s. 6d.	£924 11s. 10d. Bardi debt
,,	John Hedyngham	£2,000	£1,000	
November 1374	Hedyngham and Richard Wandesford	£1,000	£500	
December 1374	Lyons	£4,000		
,,	William Walworth and others	?£2,266 13s. 4d.		(?£733 6s. 8d. premium)

Features to be noted in this list are the prominence of two merchants, Lyons and Pyel, in the loans combined with debt repayment and the prominence of Italian creditors, especially the Bardi, in the debt repayment itself. It appears that the practice of brokerage of royal debts, which was commonly used for relatively small sums like Lady Ravensholm's debts, was applied over several years in some system of lending which involved the liquidation of one particular group of ancient debts—those to the old Bardi company.

Among these mercantile lenders, all London merchants, two men stand out, John Pyel and Richard Lyons. Pyel, as far as one can tell, was an ordinary member of the London patriciate. He was a mercer and had been an alderman since 1369.[1] In the Good Parliament he gave evidence against his former associate Lyons, though that did not save him, as we shall see, from suffering serious damage from the affair. The case of Lyons was a different matter: he was accused, together with Latimer, of being one of the main architects of the crown's financial policy in relation to both the evasion of the wool staple and the loans. Lyons does not seem to have been an ancestral Londoner or a long-established member of the patriciate. His origins are un-known but he was evidently an upstart.[2] One of the earliest references to both him and Alice Perrers is an entry in the London Plea and Memoranda Roll on 9 December 1364 when five men mainprized for him to keep the peace with Alice Perrers and not to interfere with her on the king's business and her own.[3] This tantalizing entry stands alone and is unexplained. Lyons was a vintner but his rise to importance in the city seems to follow from his association with royal finance rather than to precede it. He had evidently been well-to-do for some years— in 1368 he had a licence to go overseas with four yeomen[4] and in 1371 he owned a ship[5]—but he did not become an alderman until April 1374. In addition to his loans, he farmed the tunnage and poundage and petty custom together with John Hedyng-ham from Christmas 1372 to Christmas 1373 and by himself for the following two years, 1373–5.[6] From 1372 on he had a central position in the mercantile side of royal finance.

III. FINANCIAL POLICY AND COMMERCE

Apart from the borrowing system, one of the most conspicuous features of the government's financial plans during this period, and one which was also attacked in the Good Parliament, was

[1] R. Bird, *The Turbulent London of Richard II* (1949), 18–19.
[2] Biographical sketch in A. R. Myers, 'The Wealth of Richard Lyons', *Essays in Medieval History presented to Bertie Wilkinson*, ed. T. A. Sandquist and M. R. Powicke (Toronto, 1969).
[3] *Calendar of Plea and Memoranda Rolls of the City of London, 1364–81*, ed. A. H. Thomas (1929), 11; cf. *Chaucer Life Records*, ed. M. M. Crow and C. C. Olson (Oxford, 1966), 5.
[4] *CPR*, 1367–70, 129.   [5] *CCR*, 1369–74, 225.
[6] *CFR* viii. 197–8, 227, 231, 273; *CPR*, 1370–4, 382–4.

the granting of licences for the evasion of the Staple. The Staple had last been officially restored to Calais, as a mart through which all exporters were compulsorily obliged to send their wool, in 1370[1] but a new commercial breach with the Flemish towns which arose in 1371 led to renewed difficulties about the transport of wool from the town which were not settled until March 1372.[2] It was probably this commercial breach which led the government in the first place to issue licences for the export of wools *ad partes exteras*, without restriction to Calais, to avoid the hindrance to traffic through Flanders; but the freedom these licences gave was so advantageous to some merchants that the policy was continued long after the dispute with the Flemings had been settled, and a very large number of such licences is enrolled on the Fine Rolls.[3] Apart from the licences themselves we have two sources of information about the extent of this policy. The accounts of the Treasurer of Calais for the year May 1371 to May 1372 record the amount of wool disembarked at Calais: 2,805 sacks (counting fells at the rate of 240 to the sack) which is only about 11 per cent of the total export from England in the year 1371–2.[4] From 1371 the enrolled customs accounts of the collectors at the English ports distinguished between shipments to Calais and shipments elsewhere. The earliest Exchequer year for which this is done runs from 29 September 1371 to 29 September 1372 and therefore half-overlaps the Calais account and half-covers the period following the agreement with the Flemings when trade presumably picked up. During that period 8,170 out of 25,378 sacks, about 32 per cent, were recorded as exported to Calais. The figures for the whole period are on p. 81.

These figures show that, after the impact of the crisis in relations with Flanders had passed, there were three years 1372–5 in which most of the wool export trade was diverted from Calais and much was in the hands of aliens. In 1375 the volume of trade began to decline and the proportion taken by Englishmen to Calais increased. Over the whole period 1371–6,

[1] *CFR* viii. 92. Order of 11 August 1370 for the renewal of Calais Staple.
[2] E. Perroy, 'L'Administration de Calais en 1371–1372', *Revue du Nord*, xxxiii. (1951).
[3] *CFR* viii. 149–end, *passim*.
[4] E. Perroy, *Compte de William Gunthorp* (Memoires de la Commission Départementale des Monuments Historiques du Pas-de-Calais, x[1], Arras, 1959), 12.

SACKS OF WOOL EXPORTED FROM ENGLISH PORTS[1]

	Total	To Calais	Elsewhere
1371–2	25,378	8,170	17,208
1372–3	26,214	11,483	15,731
1373–4	23,647	5,975	17,662
1374–5	27,637	11,221	16,416
1375–6	20,995	14,054	6,941
1376–7	14,209	10,653	3,556
		(up to June 1377)	(or less)

SACKS OF WOOL EXPORTED FROM LONDON[2]

	Calais		Elsewhere	
	By Denizens	By Aliens	By Denizens	By Aliens
1371–2	3,154	150	3,762	5,773
1372–3	4,766	—	1,121	5,111
1373–4	4,064	87	1,301	5,153
1374–5	6,481	402	919	4,321
1375–6	5,705	1,550	307	2,204
1376–7 (to June 1377)	4,663	1,215	82	—

if the customs figures can be trusted, less than half the wool exported from England went through Calais. One of the interesting features of these wool export figures is the link between the aliens and the evasion of the Staple. This phenomenon, together with the recurrent mention of the Bardi debt in the royal loan transactions, suggests that we should take into account the relations of the court with the Italian merchant community in London.

Although a great deal of trade with England was done by Genoese, Venetians, and others, the Italian community in London was mainly Florentine. Unlike other Italians, who

[1] Totals from E. M. Carus-Wilson and O. Coleman, *England's Export Trade 1275–1547* (Oxford, 1953); Calais figures from A. Beardwood, *Alien Merchants in England 1350–1377* (Cambridge, Mass., 1931), 142–59.

[2] Figures from Beardwood, 150–1.

were generally occasional visitors, the Florentines included a number of settled residents, partly because a large sector of their business was international exchange, the transfer of money by letters of exchange from one part of Europe to another, which involved having correspondents permanently residing in different trading centres. The most prominent Florentine residents in London at this time were the representatives of two major trading families, the Alberti and the Strozzi. Some of their factors can be fairly easily identified and appear frequently in the English records, though the particular partnerships or companies which they represented are not easy to identify. In the case of the Alberti the most commonly named representatives were called Piero di Messer Jacopo Marchi and Niccolò di Luca.[1] The most commonly named Strozzi representatives were called Giovanni Credi and Niccolò di Rossello Strozzi.[2] There were also a number of other Florentines who were active in this country at one time and another. Among the more prominent in the existing records are Giacopo Giacomini, Lodovico di Andrea, Bernardo di Antonio Ursi,[3] Gualtiero de' Bardi, the Master of the Mint, Arnaldo and Niccolò di Giovanni Peruzzi, and two Biancardi whose activities, as we shall see, caused a special stir in the Good Parliament.[4]

[1] The papal chancery named as factors of the Alberti in London in January 1372 Raniero di Domenico, Bartolommeo di Giovanni, Piero Marchi, and Niccolò di Giovanni (*CPL* iv. 100–1). A letter from the comune of Florence to Edward III dated 24 October 1375 making clear that certain Florentines were not connected with the Biancardi company (see below, p. 122) referred to the Alberti thus: 'cum Andrea benedicti de Albertis et sociis ciuibus florentinis pro quibus Nerozius de Albertis Pierus domini Jacobi Marchi et Nicholaus Luce compatrioti nostri in regni vestri finibus conversantur' (Florence, Archivio di Stato, Missive 16, fol. 35ᵛ). In this letter Niccolò di Giovanni Peruzzi is said to have no connection with the Alberti. Raniero di Domenico, in addition to Marchi and Niccolò di Luca, appears in English records; Bartolommeo di Giovanni and Nerozzo degli Alberti do not.
[2] The letter of 24 October 1375 says 'cum Azolino Caroli de Strozis et sociis qui super eorum negociis Vbertum Caroli de Strozis, Johannem Credis, Franciscum Johannis et Sandrum Boni de Florentia in partibus Anglie profecerunt . . . Aut cum Nicholao Rosselli de Strozio et societate sua cum quo Pierus Geri Peraglie in Anglia negociandi causa commoratus.' Uberto, Sandro, and Piero do not appear in English records; Giovanni Credi, Francesco di Giovanni, and Niccolò di Rosselli do. English records also refer to Bernardo di Giorgio de' Bardi and Michele Strozzi as Strozzi representatives.
[3] Identified in Missive, 16, fol. 56 (22 December 1375).
[4] Below, p. 121. For other Florentines named in the records and the Anglicizations of their names see G. A. Holmes, 'Florentine Merchants in England, 1346–1436', *Economic History Review*, ser. 2, xiii (1960), esp. 201–3. An entry on the Issue

The extent of Italian, and in particular Florentine, participation in the wool export trade can be deduced to some extent from the licences for the export of wool directly to the continent, without the necessity of going through the Calais Staple, many of which are entered on the Fine Rolls for the years 1371–6.[1] Licences are recorded for the export of the following numbers of sacks according to Exchequer years from Michaelmas to Michaelmas.

1371–2	21,362 sacks
1372–3	24,270
1373–4	25,645
1374–5	4,392
1375–6	8,330

The total number was 83,999 as against a total number of 76,514 sacks reported as exported in this way in the enrolled customs accounts for 1371–7, so that it looks as though the record of licences granted may be fairly complete. Some of the Florentines who are well known in other English records are prominent among the holders of these licences. In 1371–2 licences for 6,714 sacks, nearly a third of the total, were granted to identifiable Florentines who are mentioned also elsewhere in English records. Then the proportion drops: in 1372–3 to 3,268, about an eighth; in 1373–4, 2,150; in 1374–5 only 500; in 1375–6 none.[2]

The broad outlines of the evolution of the wool export trade in these years may then be summarized as follows: in 1371–3

Roll for 22 December 1372 distinguished between two companies, the 'old' and 'new' Strozzi represented respectively by Niccolò di Rossello and Giovanni Credi: 'Nicholao Russell mercatori de noua societate de Stroze de Florencia et Johanni Credi mercatori de antiqua societate de Stroze de Florencia in denariis eis liberatis per manus proprios super quibusdam secretis negotiis domini Regis de quibus idem dominus Rex dictos Nicholaum et Johannem specialiter oneravit per breue de priuato sigillo inter mandatos de hoc termino—vj Ml. li.' They repaid £2,000 on 4 Oct., £3,371 13s. 4d. on 7 Nov., £608 6s. 8d. on 21 Nov. 1373 (E 403/447).

[1] CFR viii. 149–51, 161, 163–6, 171, 182–4, 193–7, 233–7, 276–9, 329–31, 378–9. There are none for 1376–7.

[2] This calculation assumes that the major Florentine exporters have been identified. There are, however, two mysterious figures prominent in the period 1372–6 who have not been identified. 'Francis Mariole' had licences to export 4,800 sacks in 1372–3 and 3,700 in 1373–4, 'Thomas Bees' or 'Besse', described in one place as a Lombard (CFR viii. 276), had licences for 5,100 sacks in 1373–4, 1,800 in 1374–5, 4,500 in 1375–6. 'Mariole' may well have been a member of the Marignolli family of Florence so perhaps the Florentine or Italian share is larger.

a heavy annual export (25,000–26,000 sacks), well over half avoiding Calais, considerable participation by Florentines in this evasion. In 1373–5 level and pattern of trade maintained, issue of licences falls sharply from 1374. In 1375–7 volume of trade sharply reduced (21,000–14,000 sacks), Calais Staple controls more than two-thirds, issue of licences for evasion declines to zero.

The reasons for this course of development are not very clear. There were, however, some events in the period which may have contributed to it. For one thing there was piracy directed against Italian shipping. One striking case of this took place apparently in the early summer—probably May or early June since the first reference is in a letter of 18 June—of 1374, when three *tarits*, one Catalan, one Genoese, and one Neapolitan, were captured by pirates from the Kent ports. They were sailing from Bruges and two of them at least were going to Pisa, with goods of Catalan, Genoese, Florentine, Milanese, and Neapolitan merchants. The Alberti company, which had goods in the ships, quickly secured a letter of protest from the pope to Edward III.[1] The two main Italian cities which normally sent galley fleets to northern waters, Genoa and Venice, both decided soon after they received news of the episode, and at least partly as a result of it, to send embassies to north-west Europe.[2] Florence was not a maritime power but Florentine merchants were deeply concerned. Some fragments of correspondence about the affair conducted by the Calimala (cloth traders') guild of Florence and the community of Florentine merchants at Bruges have survived.[3] A second major shock came in the following year, 1375, when the partners of one of the Florentine companies operating in England, the Biancardi, fled

---

[1] *CPR*, 1370–4, 445, 492; *Foedera*, 1005.

[2] *Calendar of State Papers Venetian*, i. 13–17, decision to send an ambassador to England, 14 July, later withdrawn 17 August. *Foedera*, 1008, 1025, appointment of Genoese envoys 9 August and safe conduct for them 23 Feb. 1375. The purpose of the embassy was 'ad exponendum . . . querelas de injuriis et dampnis, illatis per gentes dicti domini Regis, contra Januenses navigantes ad partes Flandriae, praesertim super captione et aresto plurium navium oneratarum mercibus mercatorum Januensium . . .' A special tax was levied in Genoa to pay for the embassy (J. Day, *Les Douanes de Gênes, 1376–7*, Paris, 1963, i. 7).

[3] Archivio di Stato, Florence, Carte Strozziane, Serie I, filza 136, fol. 113 (Calimala—Florentines in Bruges, 16 December 1374), filza 137, fols. 193–194ᵛ (agents at Genoa, probably to the Calimala, 13 December 1374).

the country owing considerable sums to English merchants and reprisals were taken against other Florentines.[1] The third was the imposition of the papal interdict on Florence on 31 March 1376 which released debtors to Florentines from their obligations and seriously disrupted Florentine trade.[2] It is impossible to judge how seriously these events affected Italian activities in northern Europe and the English wool export trade. It does look, however, as though the participation of the main Italian colony, the Florentines, in the wool export trade slumped for some reason from 1374. The only identifiable Florentine purchasers of licences in the year 1374–5 were Credi and Marchi.

These two men were leading representatives of the Strozzi and Alberti companies which also operated in this country on a large scale as financial agents, experts in the transfer and exchange of money, and were therefore less susceptible to fluctuation in trading in commodities, though of course they were profoundly affected by the papal interdict of 1376. Though we only occasionally find detailed evidence of it in the records, the Italians, especially Florentines, performed the essential service of transferring money by letter of exchange from one part of Europe to another. Thus, for example, an English merchant, Gilbert Boulge of Ipswich on 28 September 1371 paid £200 to Giacopo Giacomini at London so that a payment could be made for him at Middelburg for woad which he hoped to buy there.[3] The Alberti were in an especially favoured position as the bankers who transferred to the continent most of the money collected in England for the papal Chamber. In December 1371 Garnier the collector was ordered to pay all the money he collected in England in the next twelve months to the Alberti for transfer.[4] In fact, as can be seen from his accounts,[5] Garnier generally did send money to Avignon through the Alberti as long as it remained possible to use Florentines at all. When Garnier left England temporarily in 1374–5 he left his affairs in the hands of Master 'Laurencius de Nigris', Bachelor

---

[1] See below, p. 122.　　　　　　　　　　　　　　[2] See below, p. 125.

[3] E 368/144, Michaelmas Recorda, m. 15.

[4] *CPL* iv. 150. On the Alberti as papal financial agents in general see Y. Renouard, *Les Relations des papes d'Avignon et les compagnies commerciales et bancaires de 1316 à 1376* (Paris, 1941), 284–6; idem, *Recherches sur les compagnies commerciales et bancaires utilisées par les papes d'Avignon avant le grand schisme* (Paris, 1942), 33–9.

[5] e.g. *Accounts rendered by Papal Collectors*, 475–6.

of Law, a Roman who was also proctor of Cardinal Orsini in England and who was to act with his brother Angelo and also Piero Marchi, the Alberti factor.[1] This ecclesiastical business, in which the Strozzi also had a share,[2] included a vast amount of work for ecclesiastical persons and institutions with affairs at Avignon which probably far exceeded in scale the work done for the papal Chamber itself. Thus, for example, in October 1375 Wykeham appointed two Alberti representatives to act at Avignon as proctors to report to the pope on the oath of allegiance of the Abbot of St. Augustine's, Canterbury.[3] That election, as we happen to know from an abbey chronicle, cost the abbey £398 4s. 6d. in payments which had to be made to the pope and cardinals and £6 15s., a surprisingly low rate, for converting this money from sterling into florins.[4]   We are not told who made the exchange; it was probably the Alberti or the Strozzi. We find the Strozzi representatives Michele Strozzi and Giovanni Credi receiving 20,000 florins due in England to Cardinal Langham for transfer to him at Avignon on 14 December 1372.[5] A defendant in a case in King's Bench confessed how in 1372 he gave £30 to a member of the Strozzi company in London so that they should arrange to acquire a benefice for his son who was a scholar at Oxford.[6] Not very many examples of these ecclesiastical financial activities come to light but they are obviously typical of a very large number of others. They were presumably profitable. Since they mostly involved payments out of England by letters of exchange, one obvious implication of them is that the Florentines, especially the Alberti and Strozzi, must, from time to time, have accumulated large sums of cash in London. It is important to remember this aspect of the London world both because of its strictly financial implications and because the Florentines were correctly identified in the public mind as conspicuous beneficiaries of the papal financial system.

[1] *Accounts rendered by Papal Collectors*, 479; Vatican Archives, Instrumenta Miscellanea 2850 (the notarial document recording the arrangements, issued at Garnier's house in London, 24 July 1374).

[2] e.g. Garnier paid £45 through the Strozzi on 11 March 1373 (*Accounts rendered by Papal Collectors*, 476).   [3] *Wykeham's Register*, i. 68.

[4] R. Twysden, *Historiae Anglicanae Scriptores X* (1652), 2152.

[5] Westminster Abbey Muniments, 9224.

[6] *Select Cases in the Court of King's Bench under Edward III*, vi, ed. G. O. Sayles (Selden Society, lxxxii, 1965), 170–2.

The only Italian who figured in the court's borrowing at this period was Gualtiero de' Bardi. The Bardi were famous in English, and indeed in Florentine history, for their participation in the royal borrowing schemes in the early years of the Hundred Years' War and the consequent collapse of their over-extended companies in the 1340s with grave consequences for the whole Florentine financial world. They were never so conspicuous again. Their interests in England, however, were re-formed in 1357 by the creation of a new company which took over the paper debts and credits of the old ones so far as they related to this country. The management of it was put into the hands of Piero di Rodolfo de' Bardi who appears to have remained in England intermittently until the 1390s. So did another member of the family, Gualtiero or Gualterone di Filippo, the man who figures in loans to the crown. Not very much is known about the nature of Piero's business interests though he appears to have been actually resident in London in the early 1370s. Gualtiero, however, is a prominent person because from 1363 he held the office of Master of the Mint which must have put him in a central position in the London mercantile community as well as in an official relationship with the court.[1] Over the years these two men recovered quite a lot of the debts owing from the crown which had been put into Piero's hands in 1357. Thirty-four years later in 1391 they jointly made a final settlement with Richard II.[2]

From the final agreement of 1391 it appears that, in the whole period from 1357, 1372–5 were the years when they were, on paper at least, most successful in recovering their debts and that all the payments to them were connected with the big loan transactions. The nominal payments to them of 5,000 marks in August 1372, £3,000 in July 1373, £5,853 15s. 8d. in August 1374, and £1,000 in January 1375 amounted to £13,197 2s. 4d. within three years. What is the significance of these payments? Clearly they could serve the purpose of providing a concealed premium for the lenders, or others involved, in the shape of the

[1] T. F. Reddaway, 'The King's Mint and Exchange in London 1343–1543', *English Historical Review*, lxxxiii (1967), 6.
[2] A. Sapori, *La crisi delle compagnie mercantili dei Bardi e dei Peruzzi* (Florence, 1926), 86–9; A. Beardwood, *Alien Merchants*, 5–9, 122–33. Piero had letters of protection for 12 months from 10 December 1372 (*CPR*, 1370–4, 183), renewed 18 November 1373 (p. 368) and 29 October 1375 (*CPR*, 1374–7, 188).

brokerage which they charged to the Bardi in return for securing payment. But, even if the brokerage was substantial, the
Bardi must have counted themselves lucky to get some payment
of such bad debts. Were the Bardi an essential part of the process in some other way; had they helped to raise the money
which was loaned?

There is unfortunately no reliable evidence about the ultimate source of the money lent to the crown, whether it came
from Italians or Englishmen. It is, however, worth mentioning
another hint of the close involvement of Gualtiero Bardi in the
affairs of the court. This is contained in the evidence which was
revealed by inquisition when the Exchequer in 1384 instituted
inquiries into the concealed debts which had been due to Alice
Perrers at the time of her condemnation to forfeiture in 1377.
According to the jurors, Latimer owed her £40 which she had
given him 'to her use' and another £40 which she had paid on
his behalf for precious stones.[1] Robert Ashton owed her several
sums of money: £400 which he had received from Sir Peter
Veel[2] to Alice's use and with which he had been supposed to
buy the manor of Frome from her; 200 marks for the lands of
Sir John de Kyngeston which he had promised to sell to Alice;
200 marks with which he had been supposed to procure a
release of the manor of Frome from Stephen de Wynslade;[3] and

[1] 'Willelmus dominus le Latymer defunctus debuit et adhuc debet prefate
Alicie Perrers xl libras eidem Willelmo domino le Latymer ad opus suum proprium
per prefatam Aliciam per manus Nicholi Rounhey tunc capellani ipsius Alicie
accomodatas. Et eciam xl libras quas prefata Alicia ad rogatam dicti Willelmi
domini soluit pro eodem Willelmo domine Marie Sencler pro uno Nouche garnifi-
cato cam lapidibus preciosis videlicet Rubies Saphires perles Diamandes et Balois
quod quidem Nouche idem Willelmus dominus le Latymer emit de predicta Maria
Sencler et vnde dicta Alicia nondum fuit resoluta per prefatum Willelmum
Dominum nec per aliquem alium nomine suo.' (Inquisition, London, 16 September
1384, E 368/159, Hilary Records, m. 21.) Nicholas Rounhey, here described as
Alice's chaplain, was given the archdeaconry of Meath by the King on 5 March
1375 (CPR, 1374–7, 88).
[2] One of the Black Prince's knights, constable of Gloucester castle (he sold the
life tenure of the constableship to the Chamber knight John Beauchamp in
November 1376), M.P. for Gloucestershire in the Hilary 1377 parliament (CPR,
1377–81, 192; 1374–7, 76; CCR, 1369–74, 536). He alienated the castle of St.
Fagans in Glamorgan (CPR, 1374–7, 440).
[3] He had been lord of the manor of Frome Braunche and had apparently been
selling land there (CCR, 1369–74, 95, 119; CPR, 1370–4, 330). He granted a life
interest in the manor to one John Payn, after whose death the king granted the
wardship of the manor to Alice and she granted her interest in it, according to
another inquisition, to Robert Ashton (Calendar of Inquisitions Post Mortem, iv. 44–5).

130 marks which she lent him 'to her use'. She had lent Lady Joan Mohun £100.[1] A quantity of jewels estimated to be worth £20,000 had been taken over by William of Windsor after her conviction. A 'frensshebakere' of London, William Gilmyn, owed her £28 which she had advanced to him. Finally Richard Lyons had, some time before her conviction, owed her £300 by the assignment of Gualtiero Bardi. The words are these: 'Richard Lyons formerly citizen of London, deceased, in his life for his concession by assignment of Gualtiero Bardi of the Tower of London was debtor to the said Alice Perrers long before Alice was convicted . . . of £300 of which Richard Lyons on the day Alice was judged owed her 100 marks clear.'[2] They are obscure but they seem to mean that Bardi owed £300 to Alice which he met by assigning to her a debt of that amount from Lyons to himself.

Apart from the further light which it sheds on Alice's affluence and her land purchases, this document shows that Gualtiero Bardi had some sort of dealings with her. That is not very surprising. He was a very favoured alien drawing an annuity at the Exchequer[3] and may have dealt in the jewels she loved— his partner Piero took jewels to the court in 1358.[4] The £300 debt could conceivably be a payment due for Alice's services in arranging the loan repayment, discharged by diverting to Alice some of the money which Lyons would have owed Bardi as intermediary between him and the Exchequer. But this is speculation. All we can say for certain is that Gualtiero was on the fringe of the charmed circle which could influence royal finance. The repayment of Bardi debt and the issue of licences for Staple evasion were clearly advantageous to Italians. The court was a friend to Italians and this was probably of political

[1] 'Johanna Domina la Mann debet prefate Alicie Perrers causa veri mutui ad opus dicte Johanne Domine ut supra c libras in moneta quas eidem Alicie nondum resoluit.' The lady was presumably the widow of John de Mohun of Dunster who died in September 1374 (*Calendar of Inquisitions Post Mortem*, xiv. 304).

[2] 'Ricardus Lyons nuper Civis Londonie defunctus in vita sua pro concessione sua propria ex assignacione Gauteronis Bardes del Tour Londonie fuit debitor prefate Alicie Perrers diu ante ipsa Alicia convicta fuit ut supra de iij c libris de quibus idem Ricardus Liouns ad diem quo prefata Alicia adiudicata extitit debuit eidem Alicie in claro c marcas sterlingorum que adhuc debentur et que ad diem supradictum quo ipsa Alicia erat convicta fuerunt a domino Rege concelata et nunquam postea soluta erant dicte Alicie nec alicui alio ad opus ipsius Alicie.'

[3] *CPR*, 1364–7, 222.   [4] Sapori, *La crisi delle compagnie*, 89.

importance to a wide circle of people who objected to Italians as commercial rivals or as agents of papal financial administration. The Italians were convenient allies for the courtiers because they commanded large resources and in their vulnerable position as aliens they were happy to pay for favours. Unfortunately for the courtiers the period 1374–6 was one of declining trade and declining alien participation. We shall return to this theme later.

The time has come to summarize the evidence about the court's loan policy. First it is clear that the loans were arranged in such a form that there were obvious opportunities for profit by the lenders. Secondly the Bardi company must have been to some extent a beneficiary and presumably had arranged this through contacts at the court. Thirdly there is no evidence to show where the capital really came from and no real reason to question that in the case of the loan of August 1374 it came, as the accusers later claimed, from Latimer and Lyons. This may also be true of the other main loans nominally made by Lyons and Pyel. In the case of Arundel's loans he presumably supplied it himself. One of the odd results of this investigation is to suggest that the crown did not necessarily rely for the bulk of its credit facilities on commercial capital though it could derive considerable financial advantages from dealings of various kinds with individual merchants and commercial groups.

IV. THE COURT AND IRELAND

While Latimer and Alice Perrers may well have had a dominant influence on the financial policy of the court, there is no reason to suppose that they controlled the general political strategy of the government in relation to France and the papacy which has been discussed in previous chapters. In the period when both Edward III and his son the Black Prince were increasingly withdrawing from war and politics, one because of age, the other because of illness, the political strategy must have been increasingly dominated by Lancaster, the oldest active prince of the royal blood. After Edward III's last military effort in the autumn of 1372 there is not much evidence of his controlling hand. The king seems in his later years to have spent a large proportion of his time at his country castles and manors, Windsor, Havering, Sheen, Eltham, coming only occasionally to Westminster. But the business of government was still concentrated at Westminster and even the household officers spent long periods at work there unsupervised by the king.[1] As a result of these circumstances government and policy must have been very loosely directed. It must have been relatively easy for Lancaster and Latimer to follow their own inclinations in certain spheres, for the lack of a single controlling hand to lead to divided policies, and for some aspects of government to be neglected and uncoordinated.

There is one aspect of English policy which in a smaller way illustrates this general inefficiency rather well. While the negotiations were grinding on at Bruges and affairs were largely at a standstill in France in the winter of 1375–6, one of the preoccupations of the English court was the condition of Ireland where a crisis was reached in the early months of 1376, centring on the conduct of the governor, a knight called William of Windsor who was also an intimate of the court circle. Ireland was not of course a major preoccupation of the court. The number of important people interested in its fate and the sums of money which might have to be spent on it were very much smaller than in the case of France or even Scotland. The Irish crisis of 1376 was, however, in some ways linked with the general crisis of English policy, and also it happens to have led to the production of rather a large number of records—the Exchequer paid for a special coffer to hold the written evidence against Windsor in July 1376[2]—which make it a particularly well-documented sector of the activities of the court group. For both these reasons it is worth examining for the light it may shed on the situation at Westminster.

English-held Ireland had its own administration, a system of courts, chancery, and exchequer at Dublin, to which the English population was subject, presided over by a justiciar or governor sent out from Westminster. The administration in Ireland had at one time been self-supporting. But the native Irish revival of the fourteenth century changed that, both by making constant warfare necessary to protect the English part of the half-conquered country and by reducing the local resources from which the English had to pay for warfare.[3] In the later

<hr />

[1] Tout, iv. 182–4.   [2] F Devon, *Issues of the Exchequer* (1837), 200.
[3] H. G. Richardson and G. O. Sayles, 'Irish Revenue 1278–1384', *Proceedings of the Royal Irish Academy*, lxii (1962).

fourteenth century even a modest retinue for the governor could only be maintained either by subsidies from England or by exactions in Ireland which were very much resented by the English population there. This was the dilemma which faced the court. Ireland in the years 1369 to 1376 was dominated by the controversial figure of William of Windsor who was lieutenant from 1369 to 1372 and governor, the same role with a different title, from 1374 to 1376,[1] and became still better known as the later husband of Alice Perrers.

Windsor was a knight from a Westmoreland family with a normal military background.[2] His connection with Ireland began when he served there under the king's son Lionel, Duke of Clarence, who was lieutenant from 1361 to 1364 and from 1365 to 1366. In 1369 Windsor himself was appointed lieutenant, a rather honorific title for one of his rank, though it had been common for such men to perform the same duties as justiciars. In sending Windsor, Edward III accepted the principle that he was to have a retinue heavily subsidized from the English Exchequer. £20,000 was promised to him.[3] Windsor actually took more than the number of men specified in his indentures with the king and the money that he received from England was quite inadequate. He therefore resorted to taxing the Anglo-Irish. A parliament at Kilkenny in January 1371 granted him £3,000. Another at Ballyduagh in June (which he was later said to have held in a remote place with no houses so that the representatives could not put up a long resistance)[4] granted him £2,000. These impositions caused much indignation among the Anglo-Irish. The reaction was so strong that in September and October 1371 king and council in England ordered that the collection of the taxes should cease because of the complaints they had received.[5] In April of the following year, 1372,

---

[1] There are several modern studies to some extent overlapping: M. V. Clarke, 'William of Windsor in Ireland, 1369–76' in *Fourteenth Century Studies* (1937); H. G. Richardson and G. O. Sayles, *The Irish Parliament in the Middle Ages* (2nd ed., Philadelphia, Pa., 1964); J. F. Lydon, 'William of Windsor and the Irish Parliament', *English Historical Review*, lxxx (1965); A. J. Otway-Ruthven, *A History of Medieval Ireland* (1968).

[2] A mass of information about him and his connection with Alice Perrers is collected unsystematically in G. F. Duckett, *Duchetiana: or Historial and Genealogical Memoirs of the Family of Duket* (1874), 283–306.

[3] Richardson and Sayles, *Irish Parliament*, 80–1.

[4] Clarke, *Fourteenth-Century Studies*, 190.   [5] Ibid. 149.

Windsor was summoned back to consult with the council and did not return to Ireland. The office of keeper or justiciar was filled successively, as stopgaps, by the Earl of Kildare, Robert Ashton, and the Prior of Kilmainham in the two years from April 1372 to April 1374.[1] Meanwhile the opposition of the Anglo-Irish forced the English government to make quite searching investigations into Windsor's behaviour as lieutenant: proceedings at the Exchequer about the money for which Windsor was responsible there dragged on from July 1372 to October 1373,[2] while Ashton as keeper held inquests in Ireland into the alleged offences against the Irish population in May and June 1373.[3] The complaints which emerged in a considerable mass of testimonies were that Windsor had acquired consent to taxation by coercion, had raised money and food for his retinue by illegal impositions and seizures, and had misused the king's money.

It is not surprising that these investigations were inconclusive and obviously it is quite impossible now to estimate whether Windsor or his enemies were the more reasonable in their attitudes, given the need for some sort of defence against the natives. Behind the issue of Windsor's personal conduct lay the fundamental disagreement about whether the English exchequer or the Anglo-Irish people should pay for the lieutenant's retinue. Whether or not Windsor was in the right, however, it is remarkable that in the autumn of 1373 he was reappointed to the command from which he had been driven by public opinion. Why was this done?

There is some evidence that the man whom the Anglo-Irish would have preferred to rule over them was Edmund Mortimer, Earl of March, who was also Earl of Ulster and a great landowner in Meath, Ulster, and Connaught. In the course of later investigations it was stated that at a parliament at Kilkenny held by Ashton in January 1373 the representatives agreed to send envoys to England to plead for the appointment of March and for the rejection of Windsor.[4] A statement by Robert Holywood, Baron of the Irish Exchequer, in 1376 puts the

[1] H. G. Richardson and G. O. Sayles, *The Administration of Ireland 1172–1377* (Dublin, 1963), 90.
[2] *Parliaments and Councils of Medieval Ireland*, ed. H. G. Richardson and G. O. Sayles (Dublin, 1947), 39–48.
[3] Clarke, 220–32.   [4] Ibid. 203.

request in its English context and is worth quoting. The bishops of Meath and Cloyne, the Prior of St. John's in Ireland, and Holywood himself, he said,

> sued before our lord the King and before his council that the coming of the earl of March be agreed and indentures made between our lord the King and him and his purveyors sent to Ireland with commissions announcing his coming. And they asked for the keeping of the lands of our lord the King by a son of the King, or if this could not be, Lord Latimer or another suitable and sufficient lord to give justice in the land and keep it. At that time when this petition was being submitted the Duke of Lancaster with nearly all the great lords of the land were on their passage towards France with a great number of men, the Earl of Salisbury was ready for his passage with various lords and others to recover the castle and town of Brest, Sir Nicholas Tamworth with a great number of men was ordered to pass over to Spain,[1] so that few captains were then left in the land. And, though the council of our lord the King treated and spoke with some lords and knights to have had governance of the land, they could not find a sufficient person who would undertake the governance, except the said Sir William who undertook it after being persuaded with great difficulty and urgency on the part of the said council (*a graunt peyn et exitacoun du dit conseil*) as those who were lords of the council then will testify.[2]

Holywood seems to be recalling the situation in the spring, though Lancaster's force did not go until July, of 1373. Military activity on the continent was planned on a fairly large scale and the opportunities there were much more attractive to suitable candidates for military commands. The post had been offered at the very beginning of 1372 or earlier, when Windsor's unsuitability became apparent, to Richard Pembridge—a distinguished old courtier soldier, Knight of the Garter, and sub-Chamberlain—who refused it even though he incurred such severe displeasure by doing so that the king and council deprived him of the constableship of Dover, the wardenship of Bamburgh Castle, and the keepership of the New Forest.[3] Edward issued a document saying that he had ordered March

---

[1] Tamworth's force, originally intended for Portugal, actually joined Lancaster's expedition to France (Russell, *English Intervention*, 197–8).

[2] Clarke, 214.

[3] *CCR*, 1369–74, 420; Richardson and Sayles, *Irish Parliament*, 83; Tout, vi. 47; G. F. Beltz, *Memorials of the Order of the Garter* (1841), 163.

to go to Ireland as soon as possible to defend his own extensive lands, but in the same document—dated 20 September 1373—Windsor was reappointed.[1] He was appointed on his own terms after some argument about the conditions.[2] The taxes which had led to his recall were to be collected in spite of Irish opposition.[3] His indenture stipulated a retinue of 200 men-at-arms and 400 archers (more than twice as big as the 80 men-at-arms and 150 archers of the previous tour of duty).[4] Except that his nominal rank was reduced from lieutenant to 'Governer and Keeper', Windsor seems to have had everything his own way.

A hostile witness later alleged that Windsor, the Bishop of Meath, and Holywood 'plotted that the said governor should have the whole land of Ireland from the lord king for life without paying anything for it, imagining that the said governor with his whole retinue should live on the subjects of the king of Ireland for his life without paying anything for their keep'.[5] The contemporary records suggest a somewhat different picture of a reluctant commander, probably greedy and tactless, determined to make the best profit out of an unpromising assignment but also greatly hindered by inadequate backing from home. Money from England was not forthcoming to pay the wages stipulated in his indenture so he fell back again on various forms of exaction from the Anglo-Irish. He landed in Ireland on 18 April 1374. Later accusers stated that he waited for seventeen weeks at Dublin after his arrival, although the plundering by the native O'Briens called for action by him, refusing to lift a finger until the taxes due from his last tour had been paid: 'and said openly that even if the whole country of the lord king was burnt he would never arm himself or resist the attack of the Irish until he was paid the tallages conceded to him at the parliament held before him at Kilkenny and Balliduagh.'[6]

---

[1] *Foedera*, 990. [2] Richardson and Sayles, *Irish Parliament*, 83.
[3] *Foedera*, 995, 999. [4] E 101/33/3, m. 3.
[5] On 19 March 1375 at Dublin, 'Conspiraverunt inter se quod predictus Gubernator haberet totam terram Hibernie de predicto domino Rege Auo ad terminum vite sue absque aliquo inde reddendo imaginantes inter se quod preductus Gubernator cum tota retinencia sua vixeret super ligeos domini Regis Hibernie durante vita sua absque aliquo pro sustentacione sua eisdem soluendo' (E 368/157, Recorda, Hilary, m. 23, stated in an inquisition held at Dublin in 1378).
[6] '. . . pacifice in castro domini Regis Dublin' cum tota comitiva sua iaceret et palam dixit se an si tota patria domini Regis combusta extitisset quod ipse nunquam armare voluit nec malicie Hibernicorum resistere quousque solutus extitisset de

Whether or not this accusation is true, it is certainly true that Windsor and his council decided in September 1374 to wage war in Munster by raising money and food arbitrarily.[1] These actions may have been offensive, but it was also true that the king was unable to fulfil his obligations to Windsor. Some time before 20 January 1375, when the letter was publicized at a parliament at Dublin, the king wrote to Windsor confessing that he was unable to pay for the wages for the second half of the first year (i.e. October 1374–April 1375) because of the outpouring of money (*effusio expensarum*) made necessary by the expedition of Brittany and Cambridge to Brittany. The parliament's response was to grant him loans to the derisory total of £28.[2] On 30 March 1375 another privy seal letter informed Windsor that the king hoped to be able to give him more news of his plans for Ireland by June. Meanwhile he begged him to keep his retinue in Ireland in the expectation of continued payment at the rate stipulated in the indenture for the first year and sent 2,000 marks towards the wages still due for that year.[3] This was written when the outcome of the Bruges negotiations was still uncertain. In June, when more money had still not arrived, Windsor held a parliament at Kilkenny at which he raised a subsidy of 400 marks and it was agreed to take some offensive action against the Irish.[4] In October he held another parliament at Kilkenny, fortified by a messenger from Edward III, Nicholas Dagworth, bearing an appeal for the Anglo-Irish to help. According to Windsor, the response in parliament was that upkeep of the retinue was the king's business and no grant was made. Accordingly he took two steps: he decided to take the necessary military action against the Irish in the hope that money would come from somewhere and he issued writs requiring the Irish dioceses, counties, and boroughs to send representatives to appear before the king in England by 16 February 1375.[5]

tallagiis sibi concessis ad parliamentum coram se apud Kilkenny et Balidoille tentum et sic idem Willelmus solutus fuit de tallagiis predictis antequam se mouebatur a castro predicto . . .' (E 368/157, Recorda, Hilary, m. 23.)

[1] *Rotulorum Patentium et Clausarum Cancellariae Hiberniae Calendarium* (Dublin, 1828), 87.

[2] *Parliaments and Councils of Medieval Ireland*, 82–3.

[3] Ibid. 55–6.   [4] Ibid. 66–9.

[5] *Parliaments and Councils*, 84–6; Otway-Ruthven, *A History of Medieval Ireland*, 306.

This action precipitated the crisis. The writs required that the representatives sent to England should have power to grant taxation. In spite of efforts by Windsor and Dagworth in the period November 1375 to February 1376 to browbeat the electors by ordering new elections when the returns were unsatisfactory, many communities either refused to elect representatives at all or refused to send them with any powers of consent to taxation. A comprehensive report on the elections sent by Windsor's council to the king on 20 March 1375 made it clear that the plan could not be enforced.[1] By this time the English council had decided (16 February) to summon Windsor to appear at the forthcoming parliament on 30 April, leaving Ireland in the hands of the Earl of Kildare.[2] Windsor appears in fact not to have left Ireland until the end of June but the Anglo-Irish had sent their own representatives to express their grievances before the end of May.[3] Windsor's administration finally went down in the general upheaval caused by the Good Parliament.

It has been suggested that the favourable treatment of Windsor by the king in relation to Irish affairs was due indirectly to the fact that he was already married to Alice Perrers.[4] It is in fact doubtful, to say the least, whether they were married at that time. The *Chronicon Angliae* says that they were married at the time of the Good Parliament,[5] and in 1378 Windsor claimed that at the time of her condemnation in the autumn of 1377 'et long temps devant' she was his wife.[6] On the other hand a later claim by Alice that she was single when she made a loan of £1,000 to Walter Fitzwalter in November 1375 was confirmed by a London jury.[7] Since Windsor was in Ireland then and remained there until June 1376, the probability is that

[1] Clarke, *Fourteenth Century Studies*, 237–41; J. Ayloffe, *Calendars of the Ancient Charters and of the Welch and Scotish Rolls* (1774), 444–62.
[2] *Reports of the Lords' Committees . . . touching the Dignity of a Peer*, iii. 667–8.
[3] Richardson and Sayles, *Irish Parliament*, 84; Devon, *Issues*, 99; Clarke, 155–6.
[4] Richardson and Sayles, *Administration of Ireland*, 13.
[5] *CA* 97.   [6] *RP* iii. 41.
[7] *CPR*, 1385–9, 204; 1374–7, 191. On 26 February 1386 a jury at the Guildhall 'dicunt . . . quod predicta Alicia dum sola fuit tradidit et accomodavit prefato Waltero domino fitz Wauter predictas Mille libras . . .' (E 368/157, Easter Recorda m. 21). On 10 Dec. 1374 Alice made a grant of land to William of Wykeham 'in mea pura et legia viduitate' (Letter from J. Harvey Bloom, *Times Literary Supplement*, 3 July 1919, 364).

the *Chronicon Angliae* is wrong and that they were married after the Good Parliament. Even if they were not married, however, there is evidence of a connection of some sort; Alice received £569 from the Exchequer for Windsor in June 1374.[1] No doubt Windsor did have influence at court. This does not necessarily mean that it was only his influence which prevented him from being replaced by a more suitable representative. It has been argued that the reappointment of Windsor to Ireland was an affront to the Earl of March as the greatest landowner in Ireland and thus a cause of the opposition to the court expressed in the Good Parliament.[2] This seems unlikely. Windsor may well have been sent back to Ireland on terms which were outrageously favourable to him, but the evidence suggests that this was at least partly because a suitable commander was difficult to find: the Earl of March, and even lesser men, had no wish to go instead of him. France was more attractive in 1373. When March did eventually go to Ireland as lieutenant in 1379, it was on radically different and more independent terms with complete control of Irish finances and no accountability to the English Exchequer.[3] It was also at a time when the prospects of war on the continent were less promising than in 1373. The Windsor story from 1373 to 1376 is interesting not as an important cause of the Good Parliament—which it was not—but rather because of the light which it sheds on the condition of English politics. The reappointment of Windsor was a blunder which might not have been made in a court with a coherent policy. The failure to supply Windsor once he had been sent illustrates the dominant poverty and confusion of the crown in 1375. The collapse of Windsor's mission was symptomatic of the failure of court policy.

Between midsummer 1375 when the truce was concluded at Bruges and the end of April 1376 when the Good Parliament met, the English court was in a dilemma from which it must have been difficult to see any constructive outcome. The financial prospects were poor. The last substantial receipts from the lay subsidies granted in 1373 came into the Exchequer in June 1375.[4] The grant of wool customs was unconditional up to Michaelmas 1375; thereafter it was conditional on war being

---

[1] Devon, *Issues*, 197.   [2] Clarke, 148–9.
[3] Richardson and Sayles, *Irish Parliament*, 151–5.   [4] E 401/519.

in progress. The court seems to have got round this by issuing a simple order that no wool should be exported after Michaelmas and then permitting export provided that the usual customs were paid,[1] but wool customs without other subsidies would not support a campaign and circumstances did not promise a favourable response from the commons. The clergy, recently subjected to papal taxation, would probably not be very pliable. The summoning of a parliament was unavoidable if any military activity, offensive or defensive, were to be taken. But the prospects of such action with the French crown dominant and ascendant were poor. It was a vicious circle; still the summoning of a parliament, which the courtiers can only have anticipated with uneasy distaste, was the only hope.

[1] *Foedera*, 1039; *CCR*, 1374–7, 170.

5

The Good Parliament

I. THE COURSE OF THE PARLIAMENT

THE Good Parliament first assembled in the King's Chamber in the Palace of Westminster on Monday 28 April. There were too many gaps in attendance to start business so nothing was done. Next day they assembled again in the king's presence in the Painted Chamber where the Chancellor, Sir John Knyvet, made the usual 'pronunciation' about the reasons for the summons of a parliament. He gave three: to make ordinance for the peace of the realm, to arrange for defence by land and sea 'against the enemies, of which there were great plenty as they well knew', thirdly to maintain the king's war in prosecution of his quarrel of France. He asked for the usual subsidies: a tenth from the clergy (who had been ordered a few days earlier to meet in Convocation) and a fifteenth from laymen and the prolongation of the customs for a year or two.[1] He also commanded the assembled commons to give advice about any cases of misgovernment which needed redress.

Next day, 30 April, the parliament broke into two houses, the lords meeting in the White Chamber in the palace, the commons in the abbey chapter house. A certain air of conspiracy and urgency seems to have been given to the commons' proceedings from the first by their agreement on the first day that they should all take an oath of loyalty and openness in their dealings with each other. After this an unnamed knight 'of the south country' began the process of debate by voicing the suspicion that the heavy taxation experienced by the commons and the king's poverty were unnecessary because 'as I have heard there are some people who have a great store of gold and silver belonging to our lord the king without his knowledge which they have falsely concealed'. Another knight made the

---

[1] *RP* 321–2; *Anon*, 79–80.

first precise point: that the Staple at Calais used to be very profitable to the king because the English merchants there were able to maintain soldiers at no expense to him, whereas now that it had been abandoned in order that Latimer and Lyons could make money out of their impositions the king had to spend £8,000 a year for the defence of the town. A third knight proposed that the commons should ask the king to associate a committee of prelates and lords with them to help their discussion. After other speeches the feeling of the meeting was summed up in a manner which gave general satisfaction by the man who was to become hero of the parliament, Sir Peter de la Mare, representative for Herefordshire and steward of the Earl of March.[1]

The commons now probably debated in a desultory fashion for most of the following ten days until Friday 9 May when they received a message from the king carried by the constable of the Tower, Sir Alan Buxhill, asking for a reply to his request.[2] They then decided to go and put their case to the lords, choosing Sir Peter de la Mare as their spokesman. When they went to the parliament house they found that only a delegation from them was allowed to enter. When he was loftily requested by Lancaster, acting as the king's lieutenant, to state his business, de la Mare therefore asserted that the commons had all come to parliament in answer to the king's writ and that 'what one of us says all say and assent to' and he refused to make any statement until all the commons had been admitted. Only when this had been arranged, laboriously since many of the members had dispersed, did de la Mare make his speech saying that the commons had considered those things which needed amendment in the realm as commanded by the king and asking that they should be joined by four bishops, four earls, and four barons and baronets. Asked whom they would choose, he named bishops Courtenay of London, Despenser of Norwich, Appleby of Carlisle, and Houghton of St. David's, the earls of March,

[1] *Anon*, 80–2.
[2] J. G. Edwards, *The Commons in Medieval English Parliaments* (1958), 36–8, has argued that these events happened on 2 May. The chronicler's phrase 'treterent de iour en iour tanqe la vendredy proschein' suggests a longer period. So does the king's impatience. A case for putting some events a week later than Edwards suggests was also stated by J. S. Roskell in *English Historical Review*, lxxiv (1959), 524.

Warwick, Stafford, and Suffolk, Henry Percy, Guy Brian, Henry Scrope, and Richard Stafford. After the commons had withdrawn, the king was informed of their request and assented to it.[1]

Next Monday, 12 May, the nominated committee of lords joined the commons to discuss with them the points which the latter wished to raise; after which the commons returned to confront the main body of lords again. Once more Peter de la Mare at Lancaster's inquiry declared himself the spokesman. He began by saying that though the king was asking for lay subsidies, wool subsidies, and poundage he need not in fact be short of money. 'but he has with him certain councillors and servants who are not loyal or profitable to him or the kingdom and they have made gains by subtlety thus deceiving our lord the king.' Lancaster asked him to specify. De la Mare then made a series of charges. His first point was the one made earlier in the commons, that the removal of the Staple from Calais deprived the king of the advantage of a rich merchant community there paying for its own defence through the profits of customs and the mint which were levied by the crown. Latimer and Lyons, now directly accused, had made money by patents for evasion of the Staple. Latimer, who was present in the assembly, interrupted to say that the Staple had been moved from Calais only by the king and council. De la Mare, according to the chronicle, produced a statute establishing the Staple unalterably at Calais. No doubt there is confusion here in the chronicler's account: no such statute exists and the Staple had been moved from Calais only for a year in 1369–70 because of danger from hostile Flemings.[2] De la Mare no doubt referred to royal ordinances and letters establishing the Staple at Calais and to the licences for evasion of it of which Latimer and Lyons were accused in the official Parliament Roll and which constituted a practical abandonment of the Staple.[3]

De la Mare's second point was the raising of unnecessary loans to the king's loss and the lenders' advantage. He referred to a particular loan of 20,000 marks made by Latimer and

---

[1] *Anon*, 83–4; *RP* 322.
[2] On the missing statute V. H. Galbraith in *Anon*, 183; on the movement of the Staple in 1369–70 *RP* 301, *CFR* viii. 92, F. Quicke, *Les Pays Bas à la veille de la période bourguignonne 1354–84* (Brussels, 1947), 152–62.   [3] *RP* 323, 325.

Richard Lyons for which the king had paid 10,000 marks premium, which must have been the loan of 23 August 1374 and, when the Duke of Lancaster commented that necessity might drive the king to pay a premium of that size, claimed that two citizens of London, Adam Francis and William Walworth, had offered Richard Scrope, the treasurer at the time, a loan of 15,000 marks without premium provided that no licences were granted for evasion of the Staple. De la Mare called on Richard Scrope and also on Bishop Brantingham, treasurer before him, to give evidence. Scrope immediately promised to speak if the king put him on oath. The third point was that Latimer and Lyons had bought royal debts for half or less of their face value and made great profit. Lastly de la Mare made a direct accusation that Alice Perrers was relieving the king of £2,000 or £3,000 a year, 'and it would be a great profit to the kingdom to remove that lady from the King's company so that the king's treasure could be applied to the war and wardships in the king's gift not be so lightly granted away'. After the discharge of these thunderbolts the parliament adjourned.[1]

On the Sunday at the end of the third week of parliament, 18 May, Thomas Brinton, the Bishop of Rochester, who was one of the Triers of Petitions in the parliament, preached a sermon (it is not known where but it must have been in London) in which he urged the lords and commons not to stop short at public declaration of the faults of the criminals but to insist on 'penalis execucio', on punishment. Brinton's sermon is the only strictly contemporary opinion about the issues of the parliament which survives. He painted a picture which, though conventional enough in its denunciation of dissoluteness, adultery, and simony, was unusually sharp in its pointed references to the court. The king had some good councillors and officers but he acted entirely by the counsel of one, who was a woman. 'It is not fitting or safe that all the keys should hang from the belt of one woman.' The king neglected the proper counsel of nobles and sons of nobles. He was ruled by people of low birth and lascivious boys. It was the duty of both prelates and lords to speak out and correct this scandal. Brinton's sermon shows that ordinary churchmen, even churchmen like himself with a Roman background—Brinton was a Benedictine monk who

[1] *Anon*, 85–8.

had been in the papal household for a decade and had been a papal penitentiary—had no sympathy for the policy of collusion with the papacy which the court had adopted in 1375. On the contrary, he said, the prelates ought to speak out against the spoliation of the church which was taking place because some wanted 'fatter bishoprics'. Clerical opinion of this kind was united with the lay commons in wishing for a decisive attack on the court.[1]

Next day, 19 May, the commons, meeting separately with their committee, decided not to proceed with their charges until they had evidence about the royal finances from the two men who had held the office of treasurer in recent years, the Bishop of Exeter (treasurer June 1369 to March 1371) and Richard Scrope (March 1371 to September 1375). This was reported by de la Mare in a brief meeting of the full parliament and he received the information that the king had approved of the treasurers' giving their evidence. Scrope then confirmed that the expensive loan of 20,000 marks had been accepted in spite of the smaller but much less expensive offer (15,000 marks without premium) made by Francis and Walworth, but seems to have believed that Latimer and Lyons had made the loan. He expressed surprise that the lords of the council had not been able to add the extra 5,000 marks of cash without resorting to a method which involved a premium of 10,000. Walworth, who was one of the members for London in the parliament, was called on to explain. He revealed, correctly, that the loan had been made by Lyons and John Pyel. Pyel was also in parliament as a member for London and was called on in turn. Questioned by Lancaster under oath he said that none of the money loaned was his; it came, 'come ieo suppose', either from the money of the king himself or from Latimer and Lyons. The assembled commons cried out at the successful incrimination of Latimer and Lyons and called for the arrest of Lyons. De la Mare promised to give evidence on a later occasion to show that all the wealth which Latimer possessed would not suffice to repay the sums of which he had defrauded the king.[2]

[1] *The Sermons of Thomas Brinton, Bishop of Rochester (1373–1389)*, ed. M. A. Devlin, ii (Camden Society, ser. 3, lxxxvi (1954)), 316–21.

[2] *Anon*, 88–9. Presumably it was at this point that a group of bishops and lords pledged themselves to produce Latimer in parliament on 26 May, seven days later (*RP* 326–7, § 30).

Later in the same week, Saturday 24 May, the whole parliament met again after separate consultations. Peter de la Mare proclaimed in another outspoken speech that the commons were not willing to proceed further with the business until the king had removed his evil councillors, replaced the Chancellor and Treasurer, dismissed Alice Perrers, and named a new council of three bishops, three earls, and three barons. The lords present agreed with this proposal and the ultimatum was at least partially accepted by the king on 26 May. The councillors named, we do not know on what day, were the Archbishop of Canterbury, bishops Courtenay of London and Wykeham of Winchester, the earls of Arundel, March, and Stafford, Henry Percy, Guy Brian, and Roger Beauchamp. According to the *Anonimalle* Chronicler the king formally entrusted power to these men and removed from his council Latimer, Neville, and Alice Perrers.[1]

By this time another issue had been raised dramatically at Westminster which probably helped to increase the tension and to intensify the commons' attack. Some time in the course of the parliament Sir John Annesley, a Nottinghamshire knight whose wife had inherited a share of the castle of St. Sauveur from Sir John Chandos, accused the former captain Catterton in parliament of selling the castle to the French. Catterton was committed to the custody of Sir John Foxley, constable of Queenborough Castle and a knight of the shire for Berkshire in this parliament, on 25 May,[2] so the case must have been well known before this date. It may have inspired the change in the substance of the commons' charges which now appears in the *Anonimalle* narrative. The chronicle next tells us that the new council of nine appeared in parliament. This may have been on 26 May;[3] it cannot in any case have been much later in view of the administrative actions against some of the accused of which the earliest were dated two days later. As soon as the new councillors appeared, de la Mare resumed his attack but he now

---

[1] *Anon*, 90–2. The chronicle includes Richard Stafford in the list of those ousted but this must be a mistake in view of his inclusion in the intercommuning committee and the nominated council.

[2] J. G. Bellamy, 'Sir John de Annesley and the Chandos Inheritance', *Nottingham Medieval Studies*, x (1966), 94–8; *idem*, 'Appeal and Impeachment in the Good Parliament', *Bulletin of the Institute of Historical Research*, xli (1966), 36–41.

[3] As suggested by J. S. Roskell, loc. cit.

gave prominence to the charge, previously unmentioned, that Latimer was responsible for the loss of Bécherel and St. Sauveur and had been paid for them by the enemy. He repeated the demand that Latimer and Lyons be imprisoned. When Latimer pleaded for time to prepare his defence, William of Wykeham, one of the new council, intervened sharply to say that he should be made to answer now. Eventually Latimer was put in the charge of the Marshall, the Earl of March, and Lyons was imprisoned.[1]

The chronological framework supplied by the *Anonimalle Chronicle* breaks down at this point. But it seems probable that the final collapse of the court's resistance took only a few days. The full list of accused in the parliament roll is Latimer, Lyons, William Elys (Lyons's deputy as customs farmer at Yarmouth), John Pecche (a London merchant who had acquired a monopoly in the sale of sweet wine in the city), Neville, Alice Perrers, and Adam Bury. The earliest datable action suggesting that the court faction was accepting its fate was an order for the arrest of the goods of Bury and Lyons on 28 May. Neville ceased to be Steward of the Household on 2 June. The Earl of Cambridge was appointed constable of Dover in place of Latimer on 12 June.[2] The Black Prince died on 8 June. He had been well enough to attend the opening of parliament and both the *Chronicon Angliae* and the *Anonimalle Chronicle* attribute to him a remote part in its manœuvres. He is said by both to have refused a present from Lyons seeking his protection and by the *Chronicon Angliae* to have rebuked the Chamber knight Richard Sturry for mischievously misrepresenting the commons to the king. Some time before Whitsun, which fell on 1 June, he was struck by his final illness. The *Anonimalle* reports a pathetic last meeting between the old king and his son. The prince's illness and death must have further disrupted the court at the time of crisis.[3]

The parliament dragged on, however, for another month. The Catterton case was apparently still being discussed in the middle of June, for on the thirteenth of that month Foxley, together with a group of other knights including two members of parliament—Sir Thomas Fogge (Kent) and Sir John Saville (Yorkshire)—was ordered to bring Catterton before the king

[1] *Anon*, 93–4.   [2] *CFR* viii. 348; Tout, vi. 43; *CPR*, 1374–7, 278.
[3] *CA* 79–80, 87–8; *Anon*, 92, 94–5.

and lords in parliament.[1] Presumably the possibility of con-
victing Latimer of responsibility for the loss of Bécherel and
St. Sauveur was still being investigated, probably because these
charges were difficult to substantiate. Also a vast mass of
petitions had to be dealt with. On 25 June Prince Richard, the
Black Prince's son, was brought before the commons at their
request and 'they prayed with one voice' that he should be
granted the principality of Wales in the same manner as his
father, probably inspired by the wish to put up any barriers
that could be devised against the rumoured ambitions of John
of Gaunt. After going out to take leave of the king who had
retired to the country at Eltham, the parliament finally broke up
on 10 July. The commons granted the king customs for three
years from Michaelmas 1376 but, in spite of the spectacular
retribution which they had inflicted on his court, they did not
soften the blow by making any grant of lay subsidies. As the
Anonimalle Chronicle said, 'the parliament ended without grant
of tenth or fifteenth.'[2] From the point of view of the court's
finances the parliament had been a failure. For the group who
had controlled it, it had of course been a personal disaster. The
victors, Sir Peter de la Mare and the knights, held a feast which
was attended by the king's younger sons, the Earl of Cambridge,
Thomas of Woodstock, and by the Earls of March, Warwick,
Suffolk, Salisbury, and Stafford.[3]

The parliament was a large and heterogeneous gathering.
Nineteen archbishops and bishops were summoned, two keepers
of the spiritualities of vacant sees, and twenty-five abbots and
priors. The lay lords summoned were Lancaster, seven earls,
and forty lords.[4] There is evidence for the presence of all but one
of the bishops (Llandaff) but only two of the abbots and eleven
of the lords; there is no reason to doubt, however, that most of
the others came.[5] Devon was the only earl missing: Lancaster,

---

[1] *CCR*, 1374–7, 318.

[2] *RP* 330, 322; *Anon*, 94. For the date of the dispersal, Tout, iii. 304.

[3] *Anon*, 94. Norwich paid for its M.P.s' share of the cost of the banquet (W.
Hudson and J. C. Tingey, *The Records of the City of Norwich* (Norwich, 1906–10),
ii. 44).

[4] *Dignity of the Peerage*, 662–5.

[5] According to *Anon*, 79–80, there were two archbishops, thirteen bishops
(probably an underestimate), 'plusours' abbots and priors, the earls of March,
Arundel, Salisbury, Warwick, Suffolk, Stafford (Angus omitted), 'touts les barones
et baneretes de valeur', and 280 commons (probably about forty too many).

Cambridge, March, Warwick, Stafford, Salisbury, Suffolk and Angus, the new earl of Arundel,[1] and the king's youngest son, Thomas of Woodstock, were all there. Writs of expenses were issued at the end of the parliament for seventy-two knights of the shire who are named.[2] If the summonses to cities and boroughs were similar to those issued for other parliaments of the period there must have been about 160 town representatives but on this occasion no record has survived of the writs of expenses issued for most of these so that only fifty-six names are known.[3]

Altogether over 300 men had a voice in the parliament, a very diverse collection of men ranging in status and influence from royal earls to the burgesses of small market towns. What were their attitudes and motives? We are entirely ignorant about the individual actions of the vast majority of them during the parliament. Any attempt to answer the question is therefore bound to be crude. It will, however, be somewhat less crude than it would be if the same question were asked of most other medieval parliaments. The natural way into the problem is through the records of charges made against the accused. Some of these have already been discussed for the light they shed on the financial policy of the court as seen from the court's point of view. The attempt must now be made to look at the rest and to look at the body of accusations and grievances generally from the other point of view, for the light they shed on the motives underlying the movement of indignation against the court.

II. THE FINANCIAL AND COMMERCIAL ACCUSATIONS

The accusations against the courtiers and their associates in the official record of the impeachments may be summarized as follows:

[1] Specially summoned about 22 April (Devon, *Issues of the Exchequer*, 199).
[2] *CCR*, 1374–7, 428–30.
[3] Those named in the close roll plus the following added from independent sources: William Walworth, John Pyel, William Essex, Adam Karlille (London); John Bozoun, John Hulle (Exeter); Bartholomew Appelyerd, William Bliclyng (Norwich); John Brunham, Geoffrey Tolboothe (Lynn); Stephen Adams, John Colbroud (Romney) (*Letter Book H*, 20; M. McKisack, *The Parliamentary Representation of English Boroughs during the Middle Ages* (1932), 147; *Register of Daniel Rough Common Clerk of Romney 1353–1380*, ed. K. M. E. Murray, Kent Archaeological Society Records Branch, xvi (1945), 192). No doubt more names could be discovered by searches in town records.

1. *Evasion of the Staple* (*RP* 323–4, 325–6; *Anon*, 81–2, 85–6). Latimer and Lyons arranged for the issue of licences for the evasion of the Staple for which a charge of 11*s*. per sack was made. This caused loss of revenue at Calais which had been used for the defence of the town and so increased the cost to the king. The burgesses of Calais also petitioned for the restoration of the Staple and a new town constitution (*RP* 358–9).

2. *Tax on letters of exchange.* Lyons imposed a tax of 4*d*. in the pound on letters of exchange (*RP* 323–4).

3. *Loans* (*RP* 323–6; *Anon*, 86–7, 89–90; *CA* 78). Latimer and Lyons arranged for a loan of 20,000 marks in the name of Lyons and Pyel for which the king paid 10,000 marks although Walworth and other Staplers offered a loan without premium in return for restoration of the Staple to Calais.

4. *Brokerage of royal debts* was practised by Latimer, Lyons, and Neville (*RP* 323–4, 328–9; *Anon*, 87).

5. *Extortion in Brittany.* Latimer and his lieutenants were guilty of extortion when he was captain of Bécherel in Brittany (*RP* 324–6; *CA* 76–7).

6. *The loss of Bécherel and St. Sauveur* through Latimer's negligence (*RP* 325; *Anon*, 93; *CA* 77).

7. *Release of spies* and others from prison by Latimer (*RP* 325).

8. *Extortions at Yarmouth*, practised by William Elys as farmer of petty custom and as Lyons's deputy as farmer of the poundage (*RP* 327–8). The roll of the Hilary 1377 parliament also records, without specific charges, a malicious impeachment of Hugh Fastolf of Yarmouth (*RP* 375), not mentioned in the Good Parliament records. There were other related petitions about Yarmouth (*RP* 334, 352, 353, 359).

9. *A monopoly in the sale of sweet wines at London*, granted to John Pecche who exploited it (*RP* 323, 328).

10. *Neville's retinue* on his expedition to Brittany in 1372 pillaged the inhabitants of Hampshire and Neville was overpaid (*RP* 329, 352).

11. *Henry de Medbourne, a clerk of Latimer*, obtained the benefice of Ecclesfield against the king's interests (*RP* 329–30).[1]

12. *Adam Bury* practised deceits as Mayor of Calais and Captain of Balinghem (*RP* 330).

---

[1] Medbourne was later one of Latimer's executors (*Testamenta Eboracensia*, I, Surtees Society, 1836, 115).

13. *John de Leycestre and Walter Sporier*. The roll of the Hilary 1377 parliament records the quashing of impeachments of these two men (*RP* 374). They are not mentioned in the Good Parliament records.

Of the main accusations against Latimer the only ones which are said to have been successfully maintained are the evasion of the Staple by licences for which payment was extracted and the levying of unnecessary loans.[1] The rather garbled version of Peter de la Mare's arguments in the *Anonimalle Chronicle* implies that the Calais Staple was established by statute and that it had in some way been formally abolished or removed. There is no evidence for this version of royal policy. In the form in which the accusation is recorded in the parliament roll, however, it accords perfectly with the record evidence. Since 1371 licences for evasion of the Staple had been issued on a large scale.[2] Something like half the total wool export had been diverted in this way. The financial implications of this are fairly clear. The merchants using such licences paid 11s. a sack into the Chamber (on the admission of Latimer) and 1s. 7d. to the collectors at the ports, instead of the *Calais deniers* which they would otherwise have had to pay at Calais,[3] totalling 12s. 7d. a sack, all of which was gain to the king. The officials at Calais were poorer by 1s. 7d. per sack (4d. on entry, 10d. on exit if bound for Italy, 5d. for seignorage at the mint). The fact that merchants were willing to pay so much to evade the Staple shows how irksome the Staple was to aliens and some English non-Staplers and the degree of artificiality of the monopoly which it conferred upon English Staple merchants when it was enforced. The alleged willingness of Walworth and the other Staplers to lend large sums of money without premium in return for enforcement of the Staple shows the same thing. The argument that in undermining the Staple the king was adding to his own expenses by destroying income at Calais which would have helped to pay for its defence was evidently untenable, for the profit which the king gained by issuing licences was much greater. There was a direct conflict between the interests of the king and those of the

---

[1] *RP* 326, § 28.
[2] See above, p. 80.
[3] *CFR* viii. 145, 31 Dec. 1371, a certificate by the Treasurer of Calais of the amount normally paid there. Regular collection of 1s. 7d. a sack at English ports thereafter is recorded in the enrolled customs accounts, E 356/8.

Stapler wool exporters which must have given force to the commons' attack.

Other parts of the parliament's proceeding were evidently related to the interlocked issues of wool exports and Calais. The petitions included a lengthy one in the name of the burgesses of Calais pleading for the restoration of the Staple on the ground, similar to that advanced in the charge against Latimer, that it paid for some of the costs of defence: 'When the whole Staple was at Calais and the captain made an expedition the mayor set a guard on the town with 100 swords and 200 bows of the merchants and their servants who took no wages from the king. And now they have gone, to the great peril of the town.'[1] The burgesses went on to detailed requests about the constitution and law of the town. This resulted in the issue of a new constitution for the town by letters under the great seal on 23 July which substantially granted the requests made in parliament, especially the wish that the town should be ruled by an elected mayor and twelve aldermen.[2] This municipal constitution was a return to the one which had been set up in June 1365 when Edward III separated the administrations of the Staple and the town into two distinct organizations, one controlled by the merchants of the Staple, the other by the burgesses of Calais.[3] The Staplers had retained their independence in the intervening period, but the town of Calais had been brought under royal control and since 1370 treated like a department of the royal administration. What the burgesses wanted, and got, was a return to their previous independence.

One man had been particularly associated with the royal administration of Calais since 1370, the London alderman Adam Bury. Bury was appointed mayor of Calais on 6 September 1370, with a stipend of £200—the petition of 1376 asked for the reduction of the stipend. He was reappointed in 1371, 1372, and 1373.[4] What happened thereafter is not known but he seems to have been mayor by royal appointment, as opposed to election, for four years. Bury was impeached in parliament for 'deceits and other evils done to the king and his people when

[1] *RP* 358, § 209.   [2] *Foedera*, 1057–8.
[3] *Foedera*, 768–9; cf. discussion in G. Daumet, *Calais sous la domination anglaise* (Arras, 1902), 74–122.
[4] *Foedera*, 900, 957; *Daumet*, 75; C 76/56.

he was mayor of Calais and captain of Balinghem and other-wise'.[1] The pardon issued to him in the following year is slightly more explicit, saying that as mayor of Calais and captain of Balinghem he embezzled money intended for the defence of Calais, and adds that he destroyed the royal mint in London and made bullion in his own home.[2] The addition may refer to the allegation of dishonesty in handling the ransom of King John of France which is the charge reported by the *Chronicon Angliae*.[3] Bury had indeed been involved in the payment of the huge ransom of King John in the 1360s and there is evidence both that the conversion of the French coin into English gave opportunities for illicit profit and that the government was sufficiently worried about the losses to institute an inquiry.[4] That was fairly ancient history in 1376 and is unlikely to have been a compelling reason for denouncing him. It is significant, however, that one of the minor victims of impeachment whose alleged misdeeds are not recorded was John de Leycestre.[5] He appears in 1367 and 1368 as a servant of Bury and was appointed changer and assayer of money at the Tower mint in May 1374. A few weeks before the beginning of the Good Parliament he was nominated with Lyons to a commission to inquire into deceptions at the mint.[6] No evidence has been found to explain what lies behind these accusations about the mint but it looks as though that branch of the royal administration had produced resentment. Bury had been captain of Calais for some years. He had also been 'lord of the castle of Balinghem' with a fee of £200, at least in the year 1375–6.[7] Balinghem was one of the outer forts guarding the marches of Calais, several of which were nominally in the hands of courtiers who drew fees but must have been absentees with deputies—Richard Sturry was captain of Hammes and Robert Ashton of Sangatte. Bury was unusual as a merchant enjoying this kind of knightly sinecure. Whether

---

[1] *RP* 330,§ 47.   [2] *CPR*, 1374–7, 453.   [3] *CA* 94.

[4] D. M. Broome, *The Ransom of John II, King of France, 1360–1370*, Camden Miscellany, xiv (1926), xi, xvi; *CPR*, 1358–61, 582; *CCR*, 1364–8, 115.

[5] *RP* 374. The other accused whose crimes are not specified, Walter Sporier, is more elusive. He may have been a Londoner of that name mentioned in 1380 (*Calendar of Plea and Memoranda Rolls of the City of London, 1364–81*, 272) but nothing has been found to explain his impeachment.

[6] *Calendar of Plea and Memoranda Rolls, 1364–81*, 82; *CPR*, 1367–70, 74; *CPR*, 1370–4, 442; *CPR*, 1374–7, 319 (3 April 1376).

[7] E 101/180/4.

he had been particularly corrupt is impossible to say. What can be said fairly safely is that it was natural to pick him out as the symbol of the hated royal policy about Calais because he was the main instrument of it on the spot.

The main accusation about loans, the case of 10,000 marks paid in order to borrow 20,000, refers clearly enough to the loan made on 23 August 1374 by Lyons and Pyel. The difference between the account given in parliament and the evidence of exchequer records is that the 10,000 marks was allowed for repayment of old royal debts so that the profit to the nominal lenders, Lyons and Pyel, was probably very much less than that.[1] The clinching of the case against Latimer and Lyons depended partly on the evidence of Pyel. Although Pyel was in 1376 a fellow member of parliament with Walworth for London, he had been deeply involved with the court in the preceding years. He had himself been the nominal lender in a similar deal in June 1372. He was chosen as a royal envoy to Flanders in the spring of 1375.[2] He received a favour from John of Gaunt expressed in fulsome terms 'for the love we bear to the person of our very dear and well beloved John Pyel'.[3] Pyel's claim of ignorance about the source of the money for the loan of 20,000 marks, as reported by the *Anonimalle Chronicle,* was disingenuous. His willingness to give evidence against Latimer, however, suggests that by that time he had decided that the plight of the court party was hopeless in the face of the commons' overwhelming hostility.

Two other sets of accusations may be conveniently mentioned here though they do not tell us very much. Lyons admitted a charge of imposing a tax of 4*d.* in the pound on money sent abroad by bills of exchange. The money had been paid into the Chamber instead of the Exchequer. No systematic record of such licences over a long period has survived[4] and there is no means of discovering their importance. They would probably have been bought mostly by Italians but they would, of course, have affected the cost to Englishmen of letters of exchange issued by the licences. Four specific charges of

---

[1] Above, p. 73.
[2] *Foedera,* 1026; L. Mirot and E. Déprez. 'Les Ambassades anglaises pendant la guerre de cent ans', *Bibliothèque de l'école des Chartes,* lix (1898), 192.
[3] *John of Gaunt's Register 1372–1376,* i. 158 (6 February 1375).
[4] A few issued in November–December 1375 are enrolled in *CCR,* 1374–7, 182–3.

brokerage of royal debts were made. Two of them, the debts due to the Prior of St. John and Lady Ravensholm, may, as has been suggested earlier, be related to the loan of 20,000 marks.[1] Lyons was accused of dealing in Lord Despenser's debts. No information about this has been forthcoming. Neville was also accused of procuring the repayment of £400 of debt due to Reginald Love, a grocer of London.[2] The case was reported in parliament by Michael de la Pole, one of the lords who received an individual summons, and Sir William Wingfield, one of the two knights of the shire for Suffolk.

The impeachment of John Pecche was also no doubt a part of the reaction of the London mercantile community against the court. Pecche, like Bury, was a senior London alderman. He had been mayor as long ago as 1361. On 30 November 1373 he had been granted a monopoly in the sale of sweet wines in London in return for a payment of 10s. to the Exchequer on each pipe of wine sold.[3] This had no doubt put up the price of wine. The charge against Pecche was that he had levied a further 3s. 4d. a pipe for himself. His defence was first that he could have charged more if he had wished, secondly that he had acted in consultation with the mayor and aldermen. The grant of the monopoly had in fact been followed by privy seal letters to the mayor asking him to assist Pecche and to fix a reasonable price,[4] but the aldermen of 1376 when summoned to parliament gave evidence that the charge of 3s. 4d. had not been supported by the city authorities. The mayor of London to whom the king had written in 1373 had been Adam Bury. Presumably Pecche had connived with Bury and was now classed with him among the profiteers of the old curial system.

So far our attention has been focused on the reactions of the merchants of London and Calais. There were, however, two scandals ventilated in the Good Parliament which illustrate quite graphically the connections between court politics and the interests of provincial mercantile groups.

One of the impeachments was directed against William Elys, burgess of Great Yarmouth, in his capacities of farmer of the petty custom at Yarmouth and deputy to Richard Lyons as farmer of poundage in the same place. The main accusation

---

[1] Above, p. 77.   [2] *RP* 328–9; *Archives of the Grocers' Company* (1883), 45.
[3] *CFR* viii. 225.   [4] *Letter Book G*, 318–20.

related to the levying of customs from merchants landing goods at a place called Kirkley Road which was supposed to be within the jurisdiction of Yarmouth and therefore within Elys's bailiwick as a collector of customs. His victims were said to have been some Scottish merchants who had been driven by storm to land at Kirkley Road in a Prussian ship, but the accusations were made by John Botild and William Coupere, two men of Lowestoft who came up to London for this purpose—Lowestoft was not a parliamentary borough and had no official representatives, but Elys, it seems likely from the record, was one of the members for Yarmouth. Botild and Coupere further claimed that Elys had procured their imprisonment to prevent them appearing in parliament, while Elys counterclaimed that he had done this because of a report that they were lying in wait to seize him and the customs money which he was bringing up to Westminster.

The attack on Elys as a limb of the curial regime is inextricably bound up with a conflict between the towns of Yarmouth and Lowestoft. In 1372 the king had enlarged the privileges of the borough of Great Yarmouth by allowing it to annex the haven of Kirkley Road and restricting the herring trade within seven leagues of Yarmouth to that port itself or its new haven.[1] The annexation of Kirkley Road was justified by the silting of Yarmouth's harbour. The exact position of the area newly included in Yarmouth is not clear but it certainly involved an extension of the town's jurisdiction down the coast towards Lowestoft[2] and was quickly resented by the men of that town. In a case in King's Bench it was said that in October 1372, John Botild of Lowestoft, the man later involved in the Good Parliament, secretly bought £50 worth of herrings at Kirkley Road and moved them in the night.[3] The proceedings of the Good Parliament included, independently of the case of Elys, petitions by the men of Lowestoft and also by the commons of a wide range of neighbouring counties stating that the Yarmouth charter should be withdrawn, the latter petition pleading on the grounds of the general increase in the price of herring which it caused.[4]

[1] *Calendar of Charter Rolls*, v. 224–5.
[2] *Select Cases before the King's Council 1243–1482*, ed. I. S. Leadam and J. F. Baldwin (Selden Society, 1918), lxxxix.
[3] H. Swinden, *The History and Antiquities of the Ancient Burgh of Great Yarmouth* (Norwich, 1772), 614–18.   [4] *RP* 330, 334.

Elys had met opposition to his activities both as a customs farmer himself and as Lyons's deputy. He had been appointed farmer of petty customs at Yarmouth together with George Felbrigge, a courtier esquire, for five years from 9 August 1371.[1] In February 1376 they procured a judicial commission to investigate smuggling of cloth.[2] Sometime between 1374 and 1376 Richard Lyons, as farmer of poundage, petitioned the king for remedy against the evasions practised at Kirkley Road, among others by John Botild who 'carried away rhenish wine and various other merchandise from the said Road without payment of the custom and subsidy'. He complained that through the 'maintenance' of Botild and others he had been deprived of the whole custom and subsidy of Kirkley Road for two and a half years past.[3] The replies given in an inquisition in this case alleged malicious action by Elys as Lyons's deputy. Botild said the custom and subsidy for the wine had already been paid to Elys. Of another accused, Laurence Rochendale, whose offence was importing herrings from Flanders, 'they all say that Laurence has often proffered to William Elys the money charged to him, and William Elys for malice would not accept it and so in the hall of Westminster he offered it to Richard Lyons who ordered him to go home and pay it to William Elys who would not receive it out of malice.'[4]

Elys was evidently a leading member of the town oligarchy of Yarmouth. He had been one of the bailiffs in 1372, 1374, and 1375.[5] The Good Parliament heard petitions not only from Yarmouth against Lowestoft but also from the commons of Yarmouth against their local masters. One petition from 'the poor commoners of Yarmouth who have come to parliament

[1] *CFR* viii. 133.
[2] *CPR*, 1374-7, 311.
[3] SC 8/10378: 'Item yl se pleint de Johan Botild que come yl encaria vyn renoys et altres diverses marchandises hors de la dite Rode saunz payement dez coustume et subside auauntditz.' The other offenders were William Donmowe of Lowestoft who unloaded 14 weys of salt from Bayonne, Richard Pierles who took away 2 pipes of red wine, William Lacy who impeded Lyons in preventing the illegal export of corn in a ship of Stephen Lacy, Laurence Rochendale who unloaded 4 lasts of herring from Flanders and 10 weys of salt.
[4] SC 8/10379: 'Ils dient touz que le dit Laurence ad souent profre al dit William Elys ceo que luy est surmys et le dit William Elys pur malice ne le voleit resceyuer et sur ceo en la sale de Weymoustier loffri a Richard Lyouns et il luy chargea de repairer a meson et le paier al dit William Elys lequel William ne le voleit resceiuer pur malice.' [5] Swinden, 926.

against the various hardships, wrongs, and oppressions done to them against their franchise by the great men of the town of Yarmouth' begged for the king's protection while their case was examined. Another stated their grievance which was that the 'masters of the town' bought up all the herring, thus enriching themselves and impoverishing their fellows and denying them their right of free trade.[1] A later inquisition established that in the previous year, 1375, a group of men had made 'confederaciones' to maintain each other against Hugh Fastolf and the bailiffs and in particular to fix the price of corn and other victuals in the market at Yarmouth.[2] The record of the Hilary parliament of 1377 reveals a little more of what happened in the Good Parliament. According to this account Hugh Fastolf, who was also one of the leading men of Yarmouth (bailiff in 1373–5, representative in parliament in 1373 and 1377, and possibly in the Good Parliament too and probably under-admiral of the northern fleet under Neville in 1372)[3] 'was impeached by malice and hate of some of his neighbours, his ill-wishers, both by various bills put forward and by clamour at the end of the last parliament, for various extortions, misprisions, champerties, maintenance and oppression done by him . . .' In the intervening period, of course, inquisitions had re-established his good name.[4] Evidently the assault upon the rulers of Yarmouth in the Good Parliament had been severe. The king yielded to this storm of resentment. Yarmouth's charter with the extension to Kirkley Road was solemnly revoked in response to the complaints in parliament. The bailiffs and commonalty were ordered to appear before the king and council on 4 July with the charter itself to give it up for cancellation.[5]

This must have been a severe shock to the regime at Yarmouth. Rumours of unlawful assemblies in the town led the king to order the bailiffs on 11 September to take measures to prevent them.[6] The regime did not fall. Elys was pardoned on 20 April 1377 after inquisitions which cleared him of the charges

---

[1] RP 352, 353.
[2] The Inquisition was taken on 11 January 1377; the confederacy was said to have been made on 18 March 1375 (E 163/5/15). E 163/21/7/5 is a bond in the names of a group of Yarmouth men promising not to make unlawful confederacies dated 28 August 1375.   [3] Tout, iv. 166–7.
[4] RP 375.   [5] CCR, 1374–7, 432, 434.   [6] Ibid. 415.

had led to the summons of Botild and Coupere to the Hilary Parliament and a full reversal of the previous decision.[1] The quarrel between Yarmouth and Lowestoft about Kirkley Road was very far from being settled: it was revived later in 1377[2] and in the long run the Good Parliament was only a brief episode in it. In relation to the political situation of 1376, however, the attack on Elys and Yarmouth shows the court party, through the tentacles of its remarkably comprehensive control of royal finance, compromised by its association with a grasping and rather insecure commercial group in Yarmouth which invited attack by the commons in parliament. It is also likely that the assault on the Yarmouth oligarchy was welcome to country interests in East Anglia which would have resented its influence on food supplies and which were represented in the parliament. Just after the end of the parliament, on 13 July, a group of Norfolk men including Sir Ralph de Poleye, knight of the shire for Norfolk, secured the release of Geoffrey Pulle of Yarmouth from Newgate prison and a summons to appear before the council to Walter Sibille, a London merchant, and Hugh Fastolf and William Pepir, both leading Yarmouth men, who had presumably brought about his imprisonment. Pulle was one of a group whom Sibille, who had had licences to export corn to Bordeaux and to bring it from Yarmouth to London, was at the same time trying to convict of stealing his corn and assaulting him at Yarmouth.[3] Thus it may be that the Yarmouth case gave rise to a fairly complex interaction of commercial and rural interests in London and East Anglia which involved a number of members of parliament.

There is no record of any concerted attack on Italian merchants in the Good Parliament but the petitions did include four which were directed specifically against them and which, taken together, shed some light on English merchants' attitudes and their significance for the court. One petition called for the expulsion of Italians who followed only the trade of 'Brokour'.

[1] *CCR*, 1374–7, 455; *RP* 374–5. SC 8/660 is Elys's petition leading to his re-habilitation; SC 8/661 is another copy with the endorsement 'Soient fait briefs as ditz Johan et William Coupere destre devant le conseil a la XV⁵ de saint hiller proschein chescun sur paine de cc li a respondre a ceste bille. Henry Ly . . . . et William Am . . . . pleg . . . . .'

[2] Swinden, 62 f.; *Select Cases before the King's Council 1243–1482*, xc f.

[3] *CCR*, 1374–7, 431; *CPR*, 1374–7, 81, 157.

That these people were not a figment of the hostile imagination of the commons is shown by a list of those admitted as brokers in the city of London in November 1371. They include nine Florentines, none of whom is otherwise prominent, but all of whom received the backing as sureties of the well-known representatives of the Alberti and Strozzi companies.[1] The second petition concerned an individual Florentine, Giacopo Giacomini, who was cited as an alien who owed large sums to native Englishmen which he escaped paying because of royal protections.[2] Giacomini had been a prominent figure in English commerce at the beginning of the decade as a wool exporter and as a financier. A loan to the crown from him together with Credi and Niccolò di Rossello is recorded in 1371.[3] In 1372 something went wrong and his credit was destroyed. We know about this from a case in the Exchequer. On 23 November the officers of the city of London were ordered to distrain his property which it was said he intended to take abroad though he owed the king great sums of money. The next day a writ of protection was issued for him by Chancery. Giacomini and the mayor and sheriffs of London appeared in Chancery early in Hilary term 1373. The Londoners reported that his goods had all been seized by other creditors. On the king's behalf one particular debt was mentioned: £50 which he had been given to transmit to a member of the diplomatic mission then visiting Genoa, which incidentally included Geoffrey Chaucer. Presumably he had been required to provide a letter of exchange and had failed to do so. He was imprisoned in the Fleet. His financial difficulties seem also to be indicated by a mention of a loan of £168 which Bishop Brantingham of Exeter, who must have known Giacomini from dealings with him as Treasurer, made to him about this time. A further letter of protection was issued on 25 November 1373 but in January of the next year the Keeper of the Fleet reported in the Exchequer that the sheriffs of London had taken Giacomini out of his custody at the prosecution of creditors. He was ordered to be put back and a pardon for outlawry was issued to him on 20 April 1374. That is the last mention of him except for a report in February 1378 when

[1] *RP* 332; *Letter Book G*, 313–14.   [2] *RP* 332.
[3] E 401/505, 15 April (1371), loan of 2,000 marks, repaid in October and November (E 403/444).

he was summoned to the Exchequer again and the Keeper of the Fleet said he had escaped. It seems likely that he had escaped in 1374. The crown and his other creditors had been in competition and there was evidently substance in the complaint that he had been protected. Probably friends at court had helped him to escape his liabilities by fleeing the country.[1]

The third petition referred to captured enemy ships containing goods which ought, according to the petitioners, to have become the property of the king, saving a reward for the capturer. But

the Lombards by collusion and covin, made between them and the governors of our gracious lord the king, sued to these governors by bills suggesting that those goods and merchandise be confirmed as their own property and that of the company of Lombards. Wherefore delivery of them has been made to the said Lombards speciously. But in fact the aforesaid governors, having the goods in their hands and retaining them to their own use and private profit, have come to an agreement with the said Lombards, rewarding them for doing their will and for their work, to the damage of our lord the king of £20,000 sterling and the great destruction of his lieges and simple people who worked for the seizure of those goods and also for the defence of the realm.[2]

The most recent prominent act of piracy to which this petition could refer was the capture of the three *tarits* of Catalonia, Genoa, and Naples in the Channel in the summer of 1374 which had caused great indignation in the Italian cities.[3] There are indeed some features of this episode which do link it in a curious way with the court group. The fleet which made the capture apparently included ships of the Kentish harbours of Hythe, Romney, Lydd, Broomhill, Folkestone, Sandwich, and Rye and also the barge of William Latimer who was active in those parts as constable of Dover. When the royal demands for the restitution of the ships and their cargoes were unsuccessful, a commission of oyer and terminer was issued on 6 August 1374 to Latimer and Thomas Reynes his lieutenant as constable of Dover (also an old soldier and a family friend)[4] with six other

[1] E 368/146, Hilary Recorda m. 3; *Letter Book G*, 302; *CPR*, 1370–4, 221, 370, 408; *The Register of Thomas de Brantingham*, ed. F. C. Hingeston-Randolph (1901–6), ii. 300.

[2] *RP* 335. This petition is echoed in *CA* 78.   [3] See above, p. 84.

[4] M. Bassett, 'Knights of the Shire for Bedfordshire', *Bedfordshire Historical Record Society*, xxix (1949), 82.

commissioners to investigate the robbery, and in the following April Latimer and Reynes together with seven others were commissioned to deliver goods of certain merchants of Genoa and Florence in the ships to their rightful owners. Latimer seems thus to have succeeded in being on both sides, with the pirates and with the officers of the law.[1] A chance survival of a document connected with another similar piratical attack, probably an attack on two Genoese ships in 1371, shows the clerks of Latimer and Robert Ashton restoring large quantities of wool found in them to the Strozzi representatives, Giovanni Credi and Bernardo d'Antonio Ursi, acting on behalf of a large number of Florentine traders.[2] There obviously must have been, as the petitioners claimed, opportunities for influential courtiers to profit by using their good offices to secure the return of goods lost to Italians by acts of English piracy to which their fleets were so vulnerable.

The last anti-Italian petition referred to a *cause célèbre* of the time which sheds some interesting light on the background of feeling in commercial circles. It stated that Italian merchants had fraudulently obtained wool by posing as representatives of the great Alberti and Strozzi companies which then denied all knowledge of them. In particular Tommaso Biancardi and Niccolò di Giovanni Peruzzi had obtained wool in Lincolnshire to the value of £30,000 and £20,000, exported it, and fled without paying.[3]

The fine rolls record licences to a Florentine merchant called Biancardi, sometimes in association with Peruzzi, to export wool

---

[1] *CPR*, 1370–4, 445, 460, 485, 492, 494; 1374–7, 50.

[2] E 404/501/415 an indenture dated at London on 1 December (no year) between Credi and Bernardo d'Antonio of one part and Adam Portelewe and John Baderham, clerks of Latimer and Ashton, of the other part. Portelewe and Baderham had delivered to Credi and Bernardo 'en lour noun et dez autres marchantz de Florence' a number of quantities of wool and other merchandise identified by the marks of their owners. The only other merchants mentioned by name are Giacopo Giacomini and Angelo Cavalcanti. The goods listed are 1,432 pokes of wool (plus three consignments which are illegible), 34 bales of woolfells, 12 bales of 'sondre', and a consignment of 'vesselle de peutre'. One other entry is illegible. The merchants and goods bear some resemblance to those mentioned in an order dated 28 March 1371 to the customers of London to restore to Bernardo d'Antonio, Credi, Niccolò di Rossello, Giacomini, Lodovico d'Andrea, Cavalcanti, and Piero Marchi 1,593 pokes of wool, 33 bales of fells, 12 bales of glasswork, and 51 pieces of woollen cloth found in two Genoese ships (*CCR*, 1369–74, 216), so the indenture may date from the same year. I am indebted to Professor E. B. Fryde for drawing my attention to this document.

[3] *RP* 350–1.

from Hull and Boston in February, September, and October 1372, January 1373, and August 1374.[1] Sometime between then and the autumn of 1375 the Biancardi fled the country. In September the Strozzi and Alberti procured a royal letter stopping the arrest of their wool at Boston.[2] The English reaction, by taking reprisals against the greatest Florentine companies, ensured that the matter was taken seriously at Florence. In October it was stated in the court of the Mercanzia there that $108\frac{1}{2}$ sacks of wool had been shipped from Sluys to Venice by Andrea, Tommaso, and Dino Biancardi and Co. who had fled from England without paying their debts, and that reprisals had been taken by English merchants against the company of Carlo Strozzi so that Strozzi claimed that the wool exported to Italy should be arrested to compensate him.[3] The Strozzi and Alberti procured an official letter from the comune of Florence to Edward III acknowledging that Peruzzi and the Biancardi had fled without paying their debts and assuring the king that they had no connection with the Strozzi and Alberti.[4] In November the king stopped the seizure of their goods at Lincoln and took the representatives of both companies under his protection for a year.[5] One of the aggrieved Englishmen, John Bate, had pursued his case in Bruges and procured the arrest of 9 sarplars of wool belonging to a Strozzi factor there on account of the fact that the Strozzi man had bought wool from the Biancardi earlier in the year.[6] He also got the king to make representations about his case to the comune of Florence.[7]

There the matter rested for the time being but it was stirred into life once more by the representations of the Lincolnshire men in the Good Parliament. Seizure of Strozzi and Alberti goods in London was ordered on 15 July, only to be cancelled

[1] *CFR* viii. 164, 182, 194, 197, 277.   [2] *CCR*, 1374–7, 252 (22 Sept. 1375).
[3] Florence, Archivio di Stato, Mercanzia 1171, fol. 12ᵛ (13 Oct. 1375). The wool had been shipped from Sluys to another merchant at Venice but was in reality the property of the Biancardi 'i quali coll auere di piu mercatanti inghilesi sono fugiti dinghilterra . . . È anchora siamô informati plenamente che Carlo doli strozzi e alla sua compagnia per la detta partenza e stato dannificato e ripresi da detti in piu loro mercantie per colpa e difetto di detti Andrea tomaso e deno.'
[4] Florence, Archivio di Stato, Missive, 16, fol. 35ᵛ (24 October 1375). Bernardo di Antonio Orsi and Bernardo di Georgio Bardi were similarly certified later (fol. 56).   [5] *CCR*, 1374–7, 172; *CPR*, 1374–7, 196.
[6] Missive, 16, fol. 44 (Comune of Florence to Count of Flanders, 15 November 1375).
[7] Missive 17, fol. 47ᵛ (letter to Edward III in reply, 19 July 1376).

again a week later on the grounds that the Italians were to appear before the Great Council in October. Sometime towards the end of 1376 the representatives of the Strozzi and Alberti and of the Lincolnshire men were heard by the council and a formal agreement was made between them. Proceedings were to be stayed until 1 August 1377. In the meantime the Alberti and Strozzi promised full co-operation to the Englishmen in prosecuting their case in Florence and other Italian towns.[1]

One of the thirty-eight Lincolnshire merchants involved in this agreement was John de Hudliston, one of the members for the city of Lincoln in the Good Parliament. He is also recorded as the purchaser of a licence for the evasion of the Staple by export from Boston in February 1372 and had thus clearly been in the same business as the Biancardi.[2] Hudliston and two others, John Bate and Nicholas Cameringham, felt strongly enough to pursue the matter to the extent of going to Florence itself and spending a considerable time there. The case against the Biancardi dragged on interminably and fruitlessly in Florentine courts, probably not because of Italian ill-will but because it was difficult to get satisfaction from escaped and bankrupt merchants. The last we hear of it is a letter dated 22 August 1379 to Richard II, couched in the ingenious and flattering Latin for which the Florentine Chancery was famous. After condemning in the strongest terms the frauds practised by the Biancardi and acknowledging that 'if ever a matter could be called involved, difficult, and perplexed it is this case of the Lincolnshire men', the Chancellor went on to describe how Bate, Cameringham, and Hudliston came to Florence themselves to try to recover their debts. Through the action of the Calimala gild one of the accused was enticed to Florence and imprisoned. Part of the debt, 4,000 marks, was recovered from Biancardi money in Venice and more from property in Florence. In the middle of the proceedings, however, came the revolt of the Ciompi in June 1378 of which the Englishmen were witnesses. Prisons had been broken open, magistrates deposed, and normal justice interrupted. Bate and his friends were discouraged—unreasonably as the Florentines alleged—and went home without seeing their business through to the end. According

[1] *CFR* viii. 357; *CCR*, 1374-7, 440, 472-3.
[2] *CFR* viii. 164. Nicholas Cameringham bought a licence at the same time.

123

to the Florentine account they returned to England determined to put their case again to parliament—presumably the Gloucester parliament in the autumn of 1378—and to obtain reprisals against Florentine merchants. Further representations were then made in their favour by Richard II's envoys, Michael de la Pole, Sir John Burley, and John Sheppey, who visited Florence in the course of their embassy to Milan and Rome in the early summer of 1379, and this stimulated the comune to renewed efforts to compensate the Lincolnshire merchants in order to protect its own citizens in England.[1] This story carries us far beyond the time of the Good Parliament. Its interest is that the member of parliament whose grievance against the Florentines induced him to make the thousand-mile journey to Florence and stay there through a revolution must have felt strongly about the Italian merchants in England and about their courtier allies.

The commercial enemies of the court—that is to say the native merchants as against the Italian and the Staplers as against the non-Staplers—were in a strong position in the summer of 1376 not only because of the political weakness of the court but also because of the general decline of trade and of the alien participation in trade. In 1375–6 the wool export figures derived from the customs accounts reached the lowest point since 1369–70; in 1376–7 they reached the lowest point for nearly thirty years, as far back as the continuous series of statistics stretches. The fragmentary figures for cloth exports suggest that they were distinctly lower in 1375–7 than in 1369–71 but that the decline had begun earlier, at the beginning of the decade.[2] To this general decline was added in 1376 the particular blow to the activity of the Florentines caused by their war with Pope Gregory XI: the War of the Eight Saints. The pope has appeared in earlier chapters in the role which he filled up to the summer of 1375, fighting a great war against Milan with the Florentine commercial network supporting his war effort. In the autumn of 1375 Gregory became embroiled in a totally

---

[1] Florence, Archivio di Stato, Missive 18, fol. 55ᵛ–57ᵛ. There is no record of a protest by the merchants in the Gloucester parliament or of any action against Florentines in England at this time. De la Pole's embassy left England at the end of March 1379 (Perroy, *Schisme*, 138–41).

[2] Carus-Wilson and Coleman, *England's Export Trade*, 50–1, 78–9; cf. above, p. 81, and E. M. Carus-Wilson, *Medieval Merchant Venturers* (1954), 252–5.

different conflict with Florence and with some of the comunes of his own state. The origins of this remarkable conflict are to be found in the local politics of central Italy and do not concern us here. As it progressed, however, the war destroyed the relationship between the papal financial system and the Florentine merchants and considerably affected the position of the Florentines in European trade. The effects of the conflict on Florentine trade and the timing of those effects have some relevance to English politics.[1]

The war between the papacy and Florence became really serious as a straightforward military and political conflict in Italy in the later part of 1375. In December the pope attacked the Florentine merchants at Avignon, an obvious move because Avignon was an important nodal point in the international trading network over which he had complete control and the colony there was a crucial component in the Florentine system of international trade and exchange. At the end of December the papal chamberlain called together all the Florentines 'in curia commorantes' and imposed on them a levy of 30,000 francs (equivalent to about 33,000 cameral florins) to be paid within three days. When the merchants complained to the pope in person he replied with a flaming tirade against everything Florentine. Substantial sums were paid within the next few months.[2] The papal action against Florence on a wider front culminated three months later on 31 March after considerable diplomatic and quasi-judicial activity in the issue of a letter proclaiming an interdict on the city and a prohibition on trading with or giving succour to its citizens.[3] Although, as we shall see later,[4] the papal orders of 31 March were not enforced in England, this papal offensive produced widespread disruption

[1] The effect of the papal interdict has been treated by R. C. Trexler in *The Spiritual Power. Florence under Interdict* (Leiden, 1974). The Florentine-papal conflict in general has been described by A. Gherardi, 'La guerra dei fiorentini con papa Gregorio XI detta la guerra degli Otto Santi', *Archivio Storico Italiano*, ser. 3, v–viii (1867–8), and by G. A. Brucker, *Florentine Politics and Society 1343–1378* (Princeton, N.J., 1962).

[2] A. Segre, 'I dispacci di Cristoforo da Piacenza procuratore Mantovano alla corte pontificia (1371–83)', *Archivio Storico Italiano*, ser. 5, xliii (1909), 84–5. Trexler, 38–9.

[3] This important document has not been printed in full. Large extracts from it are printed in Raynaldus, *Annales Ecclesiastici*, vii. 278–80, and *Lettres secrètes et curiales du pape Grégoire XI (1370–78) intéréssant les pays autres que la France*, ed. G. Mollat, fasc. 3 (Paris, 1965), 10, 32–4.   [4] Below, p. 180.

of Florentine commerce in Western Europe. It also had the particular effect of breaking the close connection between the papal financial administration and the Alberti and Strozzi companies. In April the Alberti were replaced as the main bankers serving the Apostolic Chamber by Lucchese bankers, first by the Interminelli and then by the Guinigi.[1] From May 1376 Garnier, the papal collector in England, made his transfers to the Chamber through Lucchese merchants.[2] Piero Marchi, the chief Alberti factor, appears to have been still in England at the end of November,[3] and it may have been after that date that he and others made the agreement with Lincolnshire merchants about the Biancardi case;[4] but he was gone by 27 April 1377[5] and in the same year petitioned the pope, complaining that he had been driven out of England as a result of papal action though he had been in the country for fourteen years.[6] According to the *Chronicon Angliae* the official papal letters ordering the enforcement of the interdict on the Florentines did not arrive until the end of the Good Parliament.[7] We may surmise, however, that when the Parliament met at the end of April papal hostility to the Florentines was well known, and that the effects of the judgement of 31 March became apparent to the commercial community in London soon after the beginning of the parliament and must have reinforced the feeling that the Italians were in a weak position. It was a period of strength for the native merchants when they would feel confident in attacking Italian rivals, and correspondingly a period of weakness for the court when it could not profitably play off Italians against Englishmen. The various commercial groups which had been injured by the courtiers' favouring of Italians and of non-Stapler Londoners could expect to enjoy their revenge.

III. THE ACCUSATIONS ABOUT BRITTANY AND
ST. SAUVEUR

The time has come to turn our attention from commercial grievances to the other main accusations against Latimer,

---

[1] Y. Renouard, *Les Relations des papes d'Avignon et les compagnies commerciales et bancaires*, 285; G. Holmes, 'How the Medici became the Pope's Bankers', *Florentine Studies* (ed. N. Rubinstein, 1968), 357-9.
[2] *Accounts Rendered by Papal Collectors*, 534-6.   [3] Ibid. 534.
[4] Above, p. 123.   [5] *Accounts Rendered*, 534.
[6] Trexler, 65, citing Vatican Archives, Reg. Avin. 201, fol. 254.   [7] *CA* 102.

extortion in Brittany, and the loss of Bécherel and St. Sauveur. The castle of Bécherel was one of the pledges held by Edward III after 1362 as security for money which had been advanced to John de Montfort, Duke of Brittany.[1] On 18 June 1368 it was committed again to the keeping of Latimer who was by this time in England,[2] and Bécherel was controlled in his absence by his deputies who were, for some of the time at any rate, as the accusers in 1376 correctly stated, Sir John Pert, constable, and Huchoun de Middleton, receiver.[3] The impeachment alleged that they extorted ransoms in the neighbourhood when they should not have done so, that Latimer profited from their activity, and that it led to a protest by some Breton lords. There seems to be no direct evidence to support this. But there are hints that the English command at Bécherel was oppressive to the surrounding population at the time referred to by the article of impeachment. Charles V's siege of Bécherel in 1371 attracted support from some of Montfort's usual followers among the Breton nobility.[4] The instructions for an embassy from Montfort to Charles V in 1372, entrusted with the task of making Montfort's dependence on English help appear consistent with affection for the king of France, contained the following reference to the English at Bécherel: 'Item to explain the causes why those of Bécherel and Derval hold the said places, and that it greatly displeases my lord [the Duke of Brittany] because they do great harm to his country and he has given leave to his subjects to defend themselves and has ordered the payment of wages for this; and my lord greatly desires that they should be out of the said fortresses.'[5] It is highly probable that Latimer's deputies at Bécherel were an affliction to the country, as his accusers said, and rather unlikely that he was innocent of profit from their activities.

If Pert and Middleton were plundering the population around Bécherel this was a continuation of a long-standing form of

[1] *Foedera,* 663–4. On this situation see also C. C. Bayley, 'The Campaign of 1375 and the Good Parliament', *English Historical Review,* lv (1944), and M. Jones, *Ducal Brittany,* 22–69, 167–8.

[2] *CPR,* 1367–70, 123; Jones, 53.

[3] They issued a document in those capacities on 23 April 1370 (Jones, 211).

[4] Jones, 54.

[5] P. H. Morice, *Mémoires pour servir de preuves à l'histoire ecclésiastique et civile de Bretagne* (Paris, 1742–6), ii. 34.

exploitation which had been practised there by Latimer and his representatives in earlier days. In 1359–62, when Bécherel was first entrusted to him, the collection of ransoms from surrounding parishes had been the accepted method of sustaining the occupation. There are accounts of the Treasurer of Brittany for 1359 to 1360 which show that the ransoms expected to be collected at Bécherel in that year amounted to £4,478 11s. 10½d. sterling.[1] Latimer was responsible directly to the king for this source of income.[2] As captain of Bécherel therefore he was used to being in a very independent position which might easily be turned to good account by exploiting the opportunities for local plunder. The sort of activity which had gone on at Bécherel is indicated by a record of a payment of 341½ écus in 1360, described as being for 'a fixed agreement and voluntary concession of the same parishes for the sake of a certain respite so that they should not be pillaged or burned for their rebellion because of the non-payment of their fixed ransoms'.[3] It seems very likely that it had often been arbitrary and oppressive.

In its account of the impeachment of Latimer the *Chronicon Angliae* alleged that the king had fined him for embezzling money from ransoms levied in Brittany but later relented. It is possible that this is an echo of investigations which certainly had taken place into the accounts of the Treasurer of Brittany for the years 1360–2 and which were focused partly on the apparent disappearance of ransom money for which Latimer was responsible. This case was still alive in the years immediately preceding the Good Parliament. In February 1371 it was judged

[1] E 101/174/4, 5. On the ransom system in general see Jones, 164–71.

[2] 'Quarum quidem redempcionum particulas nec non particulas de quibusdam dictarum redempcionum ville de Becherelle debitarum de dictis terminis Pasche et sancti Michelis hoc anno XXXIII [i.e. 1360] et nondum solutarum ex causa impotencie parochiarum que redempciones illas soluisse debuerunt . . . idem Egidius [Guy de Wyngreworth, Treasurer of Brittany] ex precepto predicti Custodis [Robert Herle, Keeper of Brittany] liberauit per manus Simonis de Bloklee Roberto de Lyndeby clerico et deputato Willelmi de Latymer Militis Capitanei predicte ville de Becherelle leuandas et colligendas tam citius quam poterit ad opus Regis per indenturum. De quibus quidem summis idem Willelmus est Regi responsurus.' (E 101/174/4.)

[3] 'Sed respondet de xlv. li. xs. viiid. in precio cccxli. scuttorum et dimidii receptis de quibusdam dictarum parochiarum predicte ville de Becherelle ex certa convencione et voluntari concessione earundem parochiarum pro quadam paciencia habenda. Ita quod non depredarentur seu comburarentur pro sua rebellione causa non solucionis certarum redempcionum suarum predictarum . . .' (E 101/174/5.)

by a committee of royal judges (John Knyvet, Robert Thorp, Thomas Ingelby, John Moubray, and William Fynchedon) appointed to inquire into this matter that Latimer should be summoned to explain the mysteries in the parts of the account of the Treasurer of Brittany which related to the Bécherel ransoms.[1] He was summoned, failed to appear, and was then summoned regularly to appear each term until Easter 1377. The former treasurer in Brittany, Guy de Wyngreworth, whose accounts were the subject of these investigations, obtained letters of pardon exonerating him on 15 April 1376, perhaps in anticipation of an attack in the Good Parliament a fortnight later.[2]

The evidence about the Bécherel ransoms of 1359–62 is not directly relevant to the charge as reported in the parliament roll. It does, however, give some support to the related charge in the *Chronicon Angliae*; the most likely explanation of what happened at the Exchequer is that suspicion of Latimer was strong enough in 1371 for a serious investigation to be threatened but that he managed to fend off the attack by using his influence with the king. The evidence also shows that there had been an official plundering system based on Bécherel which probably persisted unofficially into the 1370s. The investigation of this

---

[1] The doubtful question was the fate of £1,941 19s. 8d. which should have come from the Bécherel ransoms for the year Michaelmas 1359 to Michaelmas 1360. On the Quindene of the Purification 1371 'recitato toto processu predicto coram baronibus huius scaccarii et eciam coram Johanne Knyvet capitali Justiciario ad placita coram domino Rege tenenda Roberto de Thorp capitali Justiciario de commune Banco Thomas de Ingelby secundario Justiciario ad placita coram dicto domino Rege tenenda Johanne de Moubray et Willelmo de Fynchedon Justiciariis de dicto commune Banco de precepto dicti domini Regis ad hoc assignatis, quia datum est dicto domino Regi intelligi et testatum est per fidedignos quod prefatus Willelmus Latymer per se et deputatos suos levauit et recepit diversas summas de redempcionibus predictis concordatum est et consideratum unanimi assensu Baronum et Justiciariorum predictorum quod predictus Willelmus veniat ad reddendum Regi compotum de redempcionibus predictis non habito respectu ad compotum prefati Egidii [Guy de Wyngreworth, Treasurer of Brittany] nec ad aliquod iudicium de onerando predictum Willelmum de aliquibus certis summis de redempcionibus predictis reddita siue ad exoneracionem superius inde factam eo quod accio domini Regio saluata fuit versus prefatum Willelmum ad petendum ab eo summas predictas vel parcellam earundem videlicet tantum quantum legitime inveniri contingeret ipsum Willelmum percepisse vel percepisse potuisse per se vel aliquem deputatum suum sicut in iudicio exoneracionis predicte superius continetur.' Latimer was to appear in Easter term. The case ends with a letter of 6 April 1377, quoting the pardon given to Latimer on 8 October 1376 (below, p. 160) and ordering that he should not be troubled further (E 368/142, Hilary Recorda, rot. 7).   [2] *CPR*, 1374–7, 259.

part of the Good Parliament evidence strengthens the impression that Latimer was an exceptionally successful war profiteer who had managed to continue his gainful career after he had returned from France to the court.

The opportunities for profiteering by courtiers from royal wages—another facet of the finances of the Breton war—were illustrated in one of the impeachment charges relating to Neville's expedition to Brittany in 1372. It was stated in parliament that Neville had taken fewer troops than he had bargained with the king to take and that they had been soldiers of poor quality. It was also said, on the basis of a complaint from the commons of Hampshire, who claimed that the local men had had to arm themselves for protection against Neville's force, that his troops had done much damage and committed many robberies in that county while they were waiting to cross over from Southampton, partly on the pretext that they had not been paid their wages. Neville's defence was that he had mustered his force in accordance with his agreement with the king. He had been paid a quarter of a year's wages in advance but he had also held out in Brittany against a great French army for three-quarters of a year without further payment. Neville in fact probably had used his influence at court to cheat the Exchequer. He said in parliament that he had agreed to take a hundred men-at-arms but in fact it was three hundred. Other records show that when he came back to England in 1374 he persuaded the king to excuse him from rendering any account for the wages he had received.[1] On the other hand it could be said that it was a tough assignment to defend Brest against du Guesclin's army; Neville himself complained in a later parliament that he had been sent to Brittany by the king and had to hold out at Brest for a long time without any help.[2] This makes his force in Brittany seem rather like William of Windsor's in Ireland; a small badly planned expedition led by an unscrupulous swashbuckler.

In 1365 the treaty of Guérande had established an uneasy peace between the Duke of Brittany and the French king. It was

[1] 'De qeconqe aconte arendre dyceux facez descharger le dit Johan et ent estre quitez enuers vous a notre Escheqer suisdit' (privy seal letter to Exchequer, 7 July 1374, E 159/150, Brevia, Trinity, rot. 9ᵛ). The case, *RP* 329, 352, is analysed by Sherborne, 'Indentured Retinues and English Expeditions to France', 725-7.

[2] Jones, 147.

to the period of this peace that the charge about the Bécherel ransoms presumably referred. After 1369 warfare between the Duke of Brittany and the supporters of Charles V gradually increased until Bécherel, still in English hands, was seriously threatened. Latimer was primarily accused of ill counsel leading to the loss of Bécherel and the fortress of St. Sauveur in Normandy. Bécherel, isolated, but controlled still by Latimer's representatives John Pert and John Cornwall, became untenable in 1374. The commanders made an agreement with the besiegers that they would surrender in November if not relieved. They might have been saved if the planned expedition of Brittany and Cambridge had sailed in the autumn of 1374 instead of the spring of 1375, and very likely it was planned partly with Bécherel in mind. As it turned out they were not relieved, they did surrender, and the French allowed them to go unharmed to join the garrison at St. Sauveur.[1] The loss of Bécherel was certainly an important incident in the loss of control of Brittany and the general decline of English power in France between 1372 and 1375. The *Chronicon Angliae* version of this charge[2] states that Latimer impeded the dispatch of help to Bécherel after the ships had been paid to go. It is true, as we have seen, that the Brittany expedition of 1375 left months after the first wages had been paid to soldiers and sailors in September and October 1374. But such evidence as there is suggests strongly that the commanders, not the court, held it up. It is difficult to see how the commons could have hoped to pin responsibility for the loss of the fortress on Latimer or how those with real knowledge of the events could have believed the charge.

The same applies to the loss of St. Sauveur in 1375 which has already been examined.[3] Latimer had at one time been captain of St. Sauveur also but that link no longer existed. Since 1371 it had been farmed for 1,000 marks a year from the king by another courtier, Sir Alan Buxhill.[4] According to the St. Alban's Chronicler, Catterton, the captain of St. Sauveur who acted as deputy for Buxhill, was a squire of Latimer retained 'in pace et in bello, in justis et in injustis, in veris et falsis', as he says in parody of the retainer's oath of loyalty.[5] It is difficult to say

---

[1] *Froissart*, viii. §§ 752, 758; Bayley, 371.   [2] *CA* 77.
[3] Above, p. 44.   [4] *Foedera*, 903, 917.
[5] Walsingham, *Historia Anglicana*, ii. 431.

whether this link, supposing Walsingham to be accurate, had been politically important. No doubt, however, some further drama was added to the proceedings of the Good Parliament by the fact that Catterton was accused of treachery in parliament while the impeachment was proceeding. St. Sauveur had been built by Sir John Chandos. On his death in 1369 his property rights descended to three heiresses: an unmarried sister Elizabeth, who made over her claim to St. Sauveur for £120 to the crown in November 1374, and two married sisters Eleanor and Margaret. Margaret's son Richard Damory had a life interest in St. Sauveur which was held by his assignees for a year after his death. On the date of the expiry of that interest, 29 March 1376, a month before the Good Parliament, one third of St. Sauveur became the right of Margaret's daughter Isabel who was married to a Nottinghamshire knight, Sir John Annesley. The inheritance was of course valueless since St. Sauveur had been sold to the French. At some time, probably between 23 and 25 May, Annesley therefore accused Catterton in parliament of treason, a plausible charge since Catterton had in fact received a large sum of money for the surrender of the castle. Catterton was committed on 25 May to Queenborough Castle whose constable was Sir John Foxley, member for Berkshire in the parliament. He was released for examination on 13 June and released again on 19 July when a group of fellow soldiers mainprized for his appearance before the council in October. Presumably the charge was then dropped. Annesley pursued his vendetta, fought a duel with him according to military law in the more favourable political atmosphere of 1379, and killed him.[1]

The Catterton case may well have contributed to the psychological destruction of the court party: as a link between Latimer and the loss of a vital English stronghold in Normandy it was a godsend to his enemies. There is no evidence, however, that Latimer was regarded as convicted either of the general charge of responsibility for the loss of St. Sauveur or of any more direct involvement in Catterton's bargain with the French or

[1] The story has been worked out by J. G. Bellamy in 'Sir John Annesley and the Chandos Inheritance' and 'Appeal and Impeachment in the Good Parliament' (*Nottingham Medieval Studies*, x (1966), and *Bulletin of the Institute of Historical Research*, xxxix (1966)).

that the two cases were formally connected. The modern historian is in the same position as the parliamentary accusers and judges. Whereas the fiscal and commercial charges are supported by abundant record evidence the accusations about Bécherel and St. Sauveur remain obscure and unproved now as they apparently were in 1376. It seems impossible therefore to maintain the view that it was Latimer's complicity in the loss of St. Sauveur that gave the opportunity for the break-through which enabled the commons to bring about his con-demnation.[1] Whatever one judges to be the *reason* for the attack on Latimer—Bécherel and St. Sauveur no doubt have their place there—it is clear that the effective grounds for his con-viction were provided by his and the other courtiers' manage-ment of the royal finances.

The *Chronicon Angliae* reports a further list of charges against Latimer which, though not mentioned in the official records or elsewhere, may contain some more or less true recollection of statements made in the parliament.

1. Latimer defrauded the king of 8,000 marks out of the 10,000 marks which Robert Knolles had to pay as a fine for the failure of his expedition in France (*CA* 78).

2. The citizens of Bristol paid the king 10,000 marks for safe-guard of their liberties of which Latimer took 8,000 marks (*CA* 78).

3. Latimer and Lyons engrossed goods (*CA* 79).

4. Latimer imprisoned a messenger who arrived from La Rochelle during the parliament to prevent him from being heard by the king (*CA* 81).

5. The king of Navarre discovered from an English knight called William Helingham or Helmham that Latimer had be-trayed his secret negotiations with Edward III to the king of France. When he returned to England the knight was strangled (*CA* 82–3).

They may be broadly divided into charges about embezzlement of the king's money (1–3) and charges about traitorous conduct in relation to the war (4–5). Precise sums apart, the financial accusations are in principle quite plausible. Sir Robert Knolles's expedition in northern France in 1370 did end in a fiasco which

---

[1] As maintained by J. G. Bellamy.

was said to have stirred the king's anger against him and might have involved some financial penalty. The town of Bristol was granted a new charter on 8 August 1373 for which it paid 600 marks into the Chamber.[1] The other accusations might conceivably be true but no evidence relevant to them has been found. Charles of Navarre's talks with Edward III at Clarendon in August 1370, leading to the abortive agreement of 2 December, were certainly a mysterious episode which he would have wished to hide as far as possible from the king of France.[2] Sir William Elmham—if he is the knight to whom Walsingham refers—is quite likely to have given the king of Navarre news of the English court, for he was the defender of Bayonne in 1374 and otherwise played an active part in Spanish affairs; but he was alive long after 1376.[3] The negotiations at Clarendon were revealed to Charles V in the confessions of Pierre du Tertre, secretary of the king of Navarre, after his capture by the French in 1378.[4] Perhaps these are elements in a confused recollection out of which Walsingham constructed this passage, but no other report has been found of the strangled knight.

IV. THE KNIGHTS

In the accounts of the parliament in both the *Anonimalle Chronicle* and the *Chronicon Angliae* it was assumed that it was not the lords or the burgesses but the knights who took the lead in the attack. A knight, Sir Peter de la Mare, presented the commons' case. In the separate commons debates the speeches reported were by 'une chivaler del south pais' and 'une autre chivaler'. In the *Chronicon Angliae* the 'milites de comitatibus' are repeatedly mentioned as if they were the whole commons; the citizens and burgesses are ignored. That chronicle also describes John of Gaunt's reactions to the presumption of the commons. The episode is placed in the course of the unfolding of the commons' attack, presumably some time in the first half of May. When John of Gaunt, discussing a day's business in parliament with his familiars, casts doubt on the power of the knights, one of his squires says that he should not underestimate

---

[1] S. Seyer, *The Charters and Letters Patent . . . of Bristol* (1812), 40: 'pro sexcentis marcis, quas ipsi nobismet ipsis in cameram nostram, de quibus neminem ergo nos onerari volumus, solverunt.'　　　　　　　　　　　　　[2] Delachenal, iv. 363–9.

[3] Russell, *English Intervention in Spain and Portugal*, 209, 218, 443.

[4] Delachenal, v. 180–98.

the support which 'those knights, not plebs as you assert but men powerful in arms and active', command. They have the support of the lords, notably the Black Prince, and of the Londoners. Lancaster, according to the chronicler, was persuaded to adopt a more benign attitude to the knights.[1] It would of course be absurd to regard them as 'plebs'. Thirty-nine of the knights of the shire—more than half—were real knights. Lords and knights belonged to one gentle society and the interconnections between them were multifarious. In the case of the de la Pole family two brothers were in the parliament, one of them, Michael, a lord receiving a personal summons, the other, Edmund, a knight of the shire for Buckinghamshire. Socially the distinction between knights and burgesses was much more significant than that between knights and lords. The knights included men to whom the court was a familiar place such as Sir John Foxley, an old soldier who had received numerous favours from Edward III. At least seven of them were retainers of Lancaster himself: Sir Edmund de Appleby (Derbyshire), Sir John Botiller and Roger de Brokhols (Lancaster), William Fifhyde (Sussex), Sir Thomas Fogge (Kent), Sir Thomas Harcourt (Oxfordshire), and Sir John Saville (Yorkshire).[2] Many of them had experience of fighting and could therefore be expected to share the interests of the lords and the court in that respect. Seven of them had been with the Black Prince in the great expedition to Gascony in 1355–7: Appleby, Sir Thomas Blount (Dorset), Sir Thomas Gissing (Norfolk), John Kentwode (Berkshire), Sir John Ludlow (Shropshire), and Sir John Wood (Worcestershire).[3] At least three had been in the French expedition of 1369: Sir John de Eynesford (Herefordshire), Foxley, who took a retinue of three esquires and nine archers, and Wood.[4] A thorough survey of their military experience stretching back to Crécy where old Sir Thomas Hoo had been present would doubtless reveal that a large proportion had military experience at one time or another.

[1] *CA* 74–5.
[2] *John of Gaunt's Register 1372–1376*, i. 76, 149, 182, 309; ii. 10–11; *1379–1383*, i. 8, 10.
[3] J. R. Hewitt, *The Black Prince's Expedition of 1355–57* (Manchester, 1958), 196–215.
[4] Sherborne, 'Indentured Retinues and English Expeditions to France, 1369–1380', 721–2.

If, as the narrative accounts tell us, the attack on the court was initiated and led by the knights, what was their motive? Peter de la Mare's summary of their view, according to the *Chronicon Angliae*, was that the commons, already oppressed by taxation, were ready to grant more only if they knew that the spending of it was in good hands. The view expressed by the first knight to speak in the *Anonimalle* account is almost identical.[1] The *Chronicon Angliae* also contains the story of a dream of Sir Thomas Hoo, member for Bedfordshire. He fell asleep one evening in the early days of the parliament while thinking 'how or by what means the king could be restored to a more correct life and to employ sounder counsel, and how the abuses hitherto current in the kingdom might be utterly rooted out'. In a dream he saw himself with the other knights discussing these things in their usual meeting-place, the chapter house of Westminster Abbey. Looking down on the pavement he saw seven gold coins which were explained to him by one of the monks as the seven gifts of the Holy Spirit given to the knights 'for the utility and reformation of the state of the kingdom'.[2] Hoo was a characteristic knight of the shire, a well-connected minor landowner and old soldier.[3] There is no good reason to doubt that he and his colleagues regarded the existing court as a discredited and corrupt place which did not deserve to be entrusted with the spending of taxes until it was cleaned up and reformed. They evidently came to Westminster in a militant mood and were glad to make use of the commercial grievances as weapons of attack, even though they did not have very much personal interest in the issues involved in the impeachments.

Apart from the role of Peter de la Mare (Herefordshire) as speaker, the dream of Sir Thomas Hoo (Bedfordshire), and the custody of Catterton by Sir John Foxley (Berkshire), there are very few individual actions or attitudes attributed to knights of the shire in the parliament. The few that we have are intriguing. There is a curious story in the *Chronicon Angliae*. Alice Perrers had been assisted in keeping her sway over the king by a Dominican friar who practised magic. When this was alleged in parliament, Lancaster ordered that the friar should be brought.

[1] *CA* 73; *Anon*, 81. [2] *CA* 70-2.
[3] A. Goodman, 'Sir Thomas Hoo and the Parliament of 1376', *Bulletin of the Institute of Historical Research*, xli (1968).

Two knights of the shire then went in disguise to Alice's manor of 'Palangewyk', caught the Dominican, and brought him before the duke and the magnates. Archbishop Sudbury as protector of the order arranged that he should be handed over to them for imprisonment so that he escaped burning, but the result of the incident was that Alice was forced by Lancaster to swear an oath in the presence of the bishops to keep away from the king. This may seem an improbable story but some of the details can be shown from other sources to be accurate. Alice did have a manor called Pallenswick at Fulham, described in a later inquisition on her property as a big house with a chapel, halls, and chambers.[1] Walsingham named the two knights and it is confirmed by entries on the close roll that they were members of the Good Parliament: Sir John de la Mare (Wiltshire) and Sir John Kentwode (Berkshire). Nothing is known about these men which helps very much to explain their action. Kentwode was a fairly modest Berkshire landowner who had been a squire in the Black Prince's retinue in the 1350s and 1360s and became a knight by 1369.[2] The other man may have been Sir John de la Mare of Langley Burrell in Wiltshire—in any case he belonged to a de la Mare family with lands in Wiltshire and Somerset quite separate from the Herefordshire family to which Peter de la Mare belonged.[3]

The *Anonimalle Chronicle* agreed with the *Chronicon Angliae* in saying that Alice was banished from the king's council though not from his presence.[4] According to the official record, she was condemned only for prosecuting 'en les Courtz du Roi diverses Busoignes et Quereles par voie de maintenance' and forbidden to do it further.[5] The *Chronicon Angliae* story nevertheless may well be true. It shows that some ordinary knights were

[1] *Calendar of Inquisitions Miscellaneous,* iv. 12.

[2] *Victoria County History of Berkshire,* iii. 298, 331; iv. 239 (his property); Hewitt, *The Black Prince's Expedition of 1355–1357,* 206; *Register of Edward the Black Prince* (1930–3), iii. 198–9 (prince owes him 2,000 marks in 1362 for the ransom of Philip son of the king of France), 383; iv. 285, 364; *CCR,* 1369–74, 68.

[3] J. Collinson, *History and Antiquities of the County of Somerset,* ii (1791), distinguishes John de la Mare Lord of Nunney in Somerset who was knight of the shire of Somerset in 1373 from a son John who was sheriff of Wiltshire in 1374 and after. There are frequent mentions of both John de la Mare Kt. and John de la Mare of Nunney Kt. in the chancery rolls of this period but it is not clear whether they were the same person or, if not, how they were related. John de la Mare of Langley Burrell occurs in *Calendar of Inquisitions Post Mortem,* xi. 40.

[4] *Anon,* 91–2.

[5] *RP* 329, § 45.

prepared to act to get rid of Alice Perrers. It does not tell us much about why they were prepared to do this.

The same applies to another story, one of the cases of alleged brokerage of royal debts, Neville's brokerage of £400 due to Reginal Love. This case was reported in parliament by Michael de la Pole, one of the lords who had received an individual summons, and William Wingfield, one of the two knights of the shire for Suffolk. Neville denied the charge and Love, when questioned in parliament, also did so at first. Under pressure he admitted telling the story to Pole and Wingfield.[1] Wingfield was a cousin of Pole's wife, Catherine Wingfield.[2] It is interesting to see the family connection bridging the gap between lords and commons. Apart from that, we can only see the story as another example of the zeal of individual knights, perhaps based on some injury or connection of which we are ignorant, perhaps inspired by a more general hatred of the corrupt court. It is probably significant that twenty-two of the knights of the Good Parliament, only three of whom sat in the parliament of Hilary 1377, were re-elected to the parliament of October 1377 which reasserted support for Peter de la Mare. Of only four of these do we know that they were probably active critics of the court in 1376—de la Mare himself, Thomas Hoo the dreamer, John Foxley who took Catterton into custody, and John Kentwode the accuser of Alice Perrers. Some of the others may actually have been equally significant. Paradoxically the knights, who were probably the most exposed actors in the public attack on the court, are also the most obscure. A great deal of information about the individual knights who sat in the parliament can of course be discovered by reconstructing their biographies out of records.[3] Such a biographical approach to politics is, however, of limited value in this period. Without the

[1] *RP* 329, § 34.

[2] Pedigree in J. M. Wingfield, *Some Records of the Wingfield Family* (1925).

[3] Apart from Hoo (above, p. 136) and de la Mare (below, p. 149), the Good Parliament knights covered by modern biographies are Sir Robert Boynton and Sir John Saville, by A. Gooder, 'The Parliamentary Representation of the County of York 1258–1832', *Yorkshire Archaeological Society, Record Series*, xci (1935), 123–6; Sir John Ragoun by M. Bassett, 'Knights of the Shire for Bedfordshire during the Middle Ages', *Bedfordshire Historical Record Society*, xxxix (1949), 80–91; and Sir Richard Waldegrave by J. S. Roskell, 'Sir Richard de Waldegrave of Bures St. Mary, Speaker in the Parliament of 1381–2'. *Proceedings of the Suffolk Institute of Archaeology*, xxvii (1958).

knowledge of political actions, which we lack except in a hand-
ful of cases, knowledge of background and connections is
difficult to interpret. It may well be significant that Alice
Perrers was attacked in parliament by a retainer of the Black
Prince. It would not help us very much to discover that other
retainers of the prince and of other lords sat in parliament
unless we knew how they acted.

The knights are the most obscure section of the parliament
for two reasons. Unlike merchants they did not have, apart
from resistance to taxation, clear group interests reflected in the
business of parliament. Unlike bishops and earls they did not
have individual political power. Did they frame and promote
the policy which their spokesman presented? All the evidence
we have suggests that they did. But it also suggests that, in their
attack on the court in which they had lost confidence, the
grievances which they presented were mainly not their own
but the merchants' and that the political framework favourable to their attack was created chiefly by the bishops and
the lords.

V. THE BISHOPS AND THE ECCLESIASTICAL BACKGROUND

Among the knights and burgesses it is difficult to discover illu-
minating personal interests and connections so that we are
driven to attribute group interests which may not always be
appropriate to individuals. With the bishops and lay lords the
case is different: it is much easier to ask which among them
probably opposed the ruling group at court and either took the
lead at the time of the parliament or gave indispensable support
to the commons. One crucial piece of evidence relevant to this
problem is the list of names of the prelates and lords nominated
early in the parliament to 'intercommune' with the commons.
Their function was, according to the parliament roll, 'to go to
the same commons to help them to treat and commune with
them of the things declared'—that is, of the Chancellor's pronunciation. According to the *Anonimalle Chronicle*, they went to
the commons 'to hear their counsel and the commons received
them benignly and showed them certain points that they wanted
to pronounce by their assent, and when they were assented they
all went to the parliament'. On a later day the commons were

said to have 'sent for the three bishops, three earls, and the barons and bannerets who were associated with them (*associez a eux*); and when they had come and were seated with the commons, they began to speak of their subject of discussion (*mater*) and to tell the lords that they did not wish to make any further proposals in parliament before the Bishop of Exeter and Sir Richard Lescrope had been sworn and assigned to us.'[1] These passages, which are the only information we have about the activities of the intercommuning committee, seem to justify the conclusion that the policy adopted by the commons was the product of agreement between them and the committee. Unfortunately we have no information at all about the method by which the members of the committee were chosen.[2] We do however know, from the parliament roll, their names. They were four bishops (William Courtenay of London, Thomas Despenser of Norwich, Thomas Appleby of Carlisle, and Adam Houghton of St. David's), four earls (of March, Warwick, Stafford, and Suffolk), and four barons (Henry Percy, Guy Brian, Henry le Scrope, and Richard Stafford).

The four bishops may not have a great deal positively in common but it is immediately clear that the obvious episcopal beneficiaries, associates, and supporters of the court are conspicuously absent from the group. They do not include, for example, Archbishop Sudbury or Archbishop Neville of York, Gilbert of Hereford, the chief ecclesiastical diplomatist, Erghum of Salisbury or Wakefield of Worcester, the beneficiaries of the Bruges agreement. Appleby of Carlisle, an Augustinian canon, had risen to the episcopate through being penitentiary to Pope Urban V[3] and had no known political affiliations in England. Houghton of St. David's was an Oxford civil lawyer who had once been a royal clerk but does not seem to have had any political or administrative importance since his promotion fifteen years earlier in 1361,[4] though he had been associated with Lancaster in the foundation of a college at

---

[1] *RP* 322; *Anon*, 85, 88.

[2] On the intercommuning committee see J. G. Edwards, *The Commons in Medieval English Parliaments*, 14–15.

[3] J. R. L. Highfield, 'The English Hierarchy in the Reign of Edward III', *Trans. Roy. Hist. Soc.*, ser. 5, vi (1956), 122. A. B. Emden, *A Biographical Register of the University of Oxford to A.D. 1500* (Oxford, 1957–9) iv. 2144.

[4] Emden, *Biographical Register*, ii. 972–3.

St. Davids and was to re-enter the royal service as Chancellor in 1377. Despenser owed his appointment to Norwich in 1370 to his military service to the papacy. His whole life, including his later role in the suppression of the Peasants' Revolt and the crusade of 1383, was that of an aggressive champion of his own rights and those of institutions which he represented, but he had so far played no noticeable part in English affairs.[1] Courtenay we know already as a rising star in the episcopate who would certainly have been regarded as hostile by the court and a dangerous defender of ecclesiastical liberties since he had spoken out against the grant of money to the king in 1373 and had apparently been regarded as a rival to Sudbury for the primacy.

The meeting of parliament in 1376 was accompanied as usual by a meeting of the convocation of the province of Canterbury at St. Paul's which, like parliament, was expected by the crown to make a grant of money. The royal command for the summoning of convocation was given four days before the parliament opened; it met on 9 June, soon after the crisis of the parliament was over, and lasted at least until 23 June.[2] The bishops were of course involved in both assemblies; while the critical events in parliament were taking place they were preparing for the other confrontation in convocation. Though this convocation has left comparatively little trace in the records because it made no grant of money, there are some indications that it did see dramatic events. There were disputes in convocation between Sudbury, the archbishop whom the court had chosen as its manager of the church, and the two most prominent bishops on the intercommuning committee, Despenser and Courtenay. They were both disputes of a common type about the exercise of jurisdiction by 'peculiars' subject to the archbishop directly but situated geographically outside his diocese and therefore easy causes of conflict with other bishops.

During the twelve months before the Good Parliament, Sudbury had been abroad taking part in the Bruges negotiations most of the time, from March to June 1375 and from October 1375 to April 1376. It is very likely therefore that the issues which came into the limelight at the time of the Good Parliament blew up during the archbishop's absence when his affairs

---

[1] *Dictionary of National Biography*, v. 860–2.
[2] *Reports touching the Dignity of a Peer*, 668; *Wykeham's Register*, ii. 252.

were in the hands of vicars general.[1] Nevertheless the disputes seem to have had or acquired a colouring of personal rancour. One concerned the jurisdiction of Hugh Bray, Dean of Bocking (in the county of Essex and the diocese of London). A will had been proved before the dean. The commissary of the official in the nearby diocese of Norwich, Despenser's diocese, arrested goods covered by the will which were within that diocese. On 18 June Sudbury issued an order to him to appear before the dean. A few days later on 23 June this apparently trivial conflict of jurisdictions was ended by a personal agreement between the bishop and the archbishop in convocation. This is known from a marginal note in Sudbury's register which says that Sudbury 'at the supplication of the lord bishop of Norwich revoked and relaxed that mandate saving the right of his church of Canterbury in similar cases and that was done out of magnanimity as he said'.[2]

The other dispute seems to have been rather more bitter. Some time before 7 December 1375—perhaps a considerable time earlier because the case was then far advanced—Richard Sutton, master of St. Bartholomew's Hospital, London, was found guilty of incontinence with Joan Pertenhale, a sister of the same hospital. He was convicted by three commissaries of the Bishop of London, within whose jurisdiction the hospital lay: John Appleby, the Dean, Roger Holme the Chancellor, and Adam Mottrom. Sutton then took his case to Master Nicholas Chaddesden, the Dean of the Arches and as such commissary of the official of the archbishop. Chaddesden allowed the appeal; according to Appleby, Holme, and Mottrom, he summoned them to appear before him at unreasonably short notice and quashed their judgement. They then decided to appeal against this interference to the court of Rome and had a notarial document drawn up in February 1376 in which they proclaimed that Chaddesden's intervention was an unheard-of and intolerable interference in the normal jurisdiction of the

[1] I. J. Churchill, *Cantrbury Administration* (1933), i. 29–30; ii. 3–5.

[2] 'Memorandum quod IX Kal Julii anno domini millesimo CCCmo lxxvi in domo capitulari ecclesie sancti Pauli Londonie dominus in convocacione prelatorum et cleri provincie Cantuariensis ibidem per eum tenta ad supplicacionem domini Norwicensis episcopi reuocauit istud mandatum et relaxit saluo iure ecclesie sue Cantuariensis in consimilibus et hoc fuit in curialitate sua ut dixit.' (Lambeth Palace Library, Register of Sudbury, fol. 26.)

Bishop of London. At some stage Sutton also decided to appeal to Rome.[1] The commissaries of the bishop and the archbishop fired summonses and penalties at each other.[2] Sudbury had bestowed rather extended powers on Chaddesden as Dean of Arches on 12 October 1375, which may have sharpened or even caused the dispute.[3] In reaction to the action of the London clergy he went so far as to excommunicate the Dean of St. Paul's for contumacy on 17 May.[4] Quite apart from the bishops, the principal actors in the dispute were themselves weighty personalities. Appleby and Chaddesden were both prominent canon lawyers. Appleby had been dean of St. Paul's since 1365, he had been an advocate at the papal court and a royal diplomatic envoy, and was a considerable pluralist; Chaddesden was also a lawyer of long experience with many benefices.[5]

The manner in which the conflict of jurisdictions was finally settled, as it is recorded in Sudbury's register, suggests that whatever its origin it had become by the summer a bitter personal matter both between Appleby and Chaddesdon and between Courtenay and Sudbury. Sudbury, according to this entry, agreed to make peace only after repeated requests by Lancaster, March, Percy, Wykeham, and the Bishop of St. Davids and after the Bishop of London and his commissaries had humbled themselves before him and begged his grace. He then cancelled his proceedings against them and reasserted the authority of the Dean of the Arches. When Appleby and Mottrom had appeared before him on bended knees he withdrew his penalty of excommunication from them.[6] The letter

---

[1] Sutton was apparently making arrangements to put his case at Rome before 7 December 1375 when a royal letter withdrew an earlier order that Sutton should be taken into custody because he was going overseas to prosecute things prejudicial to king and people (*CCR, 1374-7*, 279, 183; *CPR, 1374-7*, 218). The notarial document was dated 8 February 1376 (St. Paul's Cathedral, Dean and Chapter Archives, A, Box 54, no. 36). [2] Register of Sudbury, fol. 27^v–28.

[3] Churchill, *Canterbury Administration*, i. 144; ii. 189.

[4] Register of Sudbury, fol. 19. [5] Emden, *Biographical Register*, i. 40–1, 380–1.

[6] 'Tandem ad preces et frequentem instanciam incliti principis domini Johannis dei gracia Castelli et Legionum Regis illustris ducisque Lancastrie ac nobilium virorum domini Comitis Marchie et domini de Percy necnon venerabilium fratrum nostrorum Willelmi Wyntoniensis et Ade Meneuensis episcoporum postquam venerabilis frater noster dominus Londoniensis episcopus magisterque Johannes Appelby decanus Londonie et magister Adam Mottrone nobis se reuerenter humiliassent et quatenus ad eos attinebat veniam et graciam in premissis de et a nobis humiliter et singulariter postulassent idemque magister Johannes Appelby

announcing this dramatic end to the case by intervention at the summit was dated 15 July, that is a week after the parliament had dispersed.

Sudbury's attitude in these disputes, asserting that he stayed his hand against the Bishop of Norwich's subordinate out of magnanimity, *in curialitate sua*, pardoning the Bishop of London's subordinates only after dramatic intervention by the greatest magnates and humble submission by the bishop, may certainly be taken as evidence of his firmness.[1] It also shows that Sudbury, although on the losing side in the Good Parliament, was not shaken by it. But the fact that the disputes reached this point at all seems to be evidence of distinctly strained relations between Sudbury and Courtenay, and probably Despenser too, of a rift among the bishops which we may assume to have been a factor in the parliament and to shed some light on its proceedings. The church was divided. The convocation in June met in the chapter house of St. Paul's while its dean was under sentence of excommunication by the archbishop. The division had been produced essentially by the crown's policy of alliance with the pope which had been criticized by Bishop Brinton and had had the effect of intensifying the hostility between Sudbury and Courtenay.

The attitude to ecclesiastical questions expressed by the laity in parliament was, as far as we know it from the records, their traditional and predictable anti-papalism heightened by resentment of the recent surprising success of the papacy in England. The parliament roll contains copies of two quite substantial documents dealing with ecclesiastical matters and emanating from the commons—one described as 'Bille encontre le Pape et les Cardynaux', the other 'Billes et Articles encontre le Pape et le Clergie'.[2] The former, presented as a single subdivided petition on behalf of the knights and burgesses, is a document composed with some elegance of style. It begins with a preamble recalling that the church in England was endowed by the kings and their nobles and looking back to a golden age free of simony when bishoprics and benefices were given to the worthiest holders.

decanus veniam de commissis postulasset et in ordinacione nostra se posuisset in hac parte . . .' (Register of Sudbury, fol. 28.)

[1] As by W. L. Warren, 'A Reappraisal of Simon Sudbury', *Journal of Ecclesiastical History*, x (1959), 148.   [2] *RP* 337–40.

And as long as those good customs were used the kingdom was full of all kinds of prosperity, of good people and good loyalty of clerks and clergy, of knights and chivalry, which are two things that always reign together, of peace and quiet, treasure, corn, cattle and other riches. And since the good customs were perverted into sin of covetousness and simony the kingdom has been filled with divers adversities like wars and pestilences, famine, murrain of beasts and other grievances, by which it is so impoverished and destroyed that there is not a third part of the people or of the other things there used to be.

The twenty-six clauses of the two documents taken together contain a general criticism of the system of papal finance as applied to England. Most attention is directed to the various implications of the papal control of appointments: heavy payments by newly appointed bishops and by others seeking benefices, encouragement of pluralism especially by cardinals and other aliens. The papal collector came in for denunciation. The English clergy were presented as the helpless victims of papal demands for subsidies and procurations. The standpoint of these petitions—normal in lay criticism of the church—was at this time, however, seemingly that of Bishop Brinton when he spoke of 'Christ in his members daily crucified, the innocent condemned, poor clergy despoiled of their benefices, and the liberty of the church so profaned that the holy Church of God is in these days in greater servitude than it was under Pharaoh'.[1]

This anti-papal manifesto is a mixture of fact, fable, and moralizing from which it is difficult to disentangle the grievances and the embellishments. Nevertheless it does clearly enough reflect the situation in the contemporary church—both in the long run and in the immediate past—which can be seen in other records of the time. The holding of English benefices by cardinals and other residents at the papal court was a particular cause of scandal. It was claimed that cardinals' rents from English benefices amounted to 20,000 marks per annum. The slightly hysterical picture of rapacity—'he has newly created about twelve cardinals so that there are now thirty where there used to be twelve and all the benefices in England will not be enough for them'[2]—was not entirely without foundation. The

[1] *Sermons of Thomas Brinton*, ii. 317; and above, p. 103.
[2] *RP* 339; Gregory in fact created twelve cardinals in 1371 and nine in December 1375.

145

cardinals' benefices figure very largely in those parts of Arnaud Garnier's accounts which record his attempts to collect first fruits both because there were a lot of them and because the cardinals made special bargains with the Apostolic Chamber which the Collector had to accept. For instance the Archdeaconry of Taunton was held by the Cardinal Guillaume d'Aigrefeuille who farmed it for £113 6s. 4d.:[1] this is typical of many entries. Among the records of investigations conducted a few years later into the circumstances of the schism of 1378 are some fragments of a conversation shortly after the election of Urban VI between Cardinal Aigrefeuille, soon to be a supporter of the Avignon Pope Clement VII, and the English canonist Adam of Easton, who was later made a cardinal by Urban. Easton reported that he had assured Aigrefeuille that the election of the Italian Urban would be highly acceptable in England because 'all the temporal lords of England thought the former popes were French and that the cardinals were greater enemies of England than the king of France and that but for their urging there would be secure peace between the kings, and therefore it was ordained in England that all the French cardinals should lose their benefices.' Aigrefeuille, when denying Easton's account of the events of 1378, claimed that the cardinals had in fact experienced no difficulty under the old regime about their benefices in England 'for he then received in England peacefully and quietly from benefices which he had there about 3,000 florins annually, and the Cardinal of Poitiers [Guy de Malesec] about 2,000, the Cardinal of Albano [Angelic Grimoard] about 5,000, Cardinal Orsini about 2,000, the Cardinal of St. Eustachius [Pierre Flandrin] a great quantity of money, and various other French cardinals.'[2] Easton's disquiet about the reputation of the largely French Avignonese *Curia* and Cardinal Aigrefeuille's confidence in the financial effectiveness of the old system probably both represented real aspects of the relationship of England and the papacy before 1378.

Like the holding of benefices by cardinals, other ecclesiastical abuses mentioned in the Good Parliament—the farming of benefices by aliens, exaction of *servitia* from bishops and annates

[1] *Accounts Rendered by Papal Collectors*, 494.
[2] L. Macfarlane, 'An English Account of the Election of Urban VI, 1378', *Bulletin of the Institute of Historical Research*, xxvi (1953).

from lesser churchmen, absenteeism, sale of benefices, unfree elections—were age-old grievances which may or may not have been actually more burdensome at this time than earlier. The activities of the papal collector, however, were certainly more impressive than they had been for a long time. The parliamentary petition portrayed him as a most sinister and splendid figure; he

is receiver of the moneys of the pope and holds a great house in London and has clerks and officers as if it were truly the receipt of a prince or a duke and there he receives and sends overseas to the court of Rome each year to the pope's use, from procuracies which the pope takes from abbeys and priories and from first fruits of bishoprics and other benefices and from subsidies granted to the pope from time to time by the clergy, 20,000 marks annually . . .[1]

Garnier did in fact keep a house in London though he claimed it was rather insecure considering the thousands of florins he had to store there (*periculum custodie subcidii* 1 *milium florenorum*).[2] He had substantially raised receipts from annates in the early years of his collectorship and managed to keep them at quite a high level.[3] The great feature of the last year, however, had been the collection of the subsidy agreed to by the crown in June 1375. It was to amount in all to about £9,000 and was supposed to be paid in two instalments at the end of 1375 and midsummer 1376. It began to reach the collector's hands in December 1375. By the time parliament met just under £1,800 had reached him through the Archbishop of Canterbury. He got another £978 from Canterbury in payments made on 12 May and 25 June and £660 from York on 14 May. There was also much resistance to payments. Archbishop Sudbury ordered the Bishop of Lincoln on 6 May to excommunicate the clerics who had not yet paid the long-overdue first instalment.[4] Clerics must have been very conscious of the tax and Londoners of its collection and export through Italian exchangers. The last occasion when the collection of such a tax from the clergy had been permitted was 1362, in the euphoria following Brétigny, and before that 1336. Though the sums were not enormous, the tax itself must have

---

[1] *RP* 339. [2] *Accounts Rendered by Papal Collectors*, 537.
[3] February 1372–July 1374 £1,080 p.a.; July 1374–March 1378 £816 p.a. (Lunt, *Financial Relations*, 379).
[4] Full details of the collection in Lunt, 108–14; *Accounts Rendered*, 531–2.

seemed very remarkable at a time when the crown was so extremely short of money. There was also another kind of exaction mentioned in parliament[1] to which the clergy had been subjected to an unusual degree in the recent past, the payment of the costs of papal envoys and legates. The pope had granted the various papal envoys in the Bruges negotiations the right to collect 'procurations' from the English clergy, that is to say daily subsistence allowances levied according to the normal assessment of the values of benefices. The lively diplomatic activity of recent years and the determination of the pope to make it a charge on the clergy and not on the Apostolic Chamber had led to the issuing of demands for procurations amounting to some 13,640 florins, about £2,000, between January 1373 and March 1376.[2] There had been considerable resistance to their collection. Again the sums were not enormous but they were higher than they had been for many years.

The Good Parliament and the Canterbury convocation both met under the strong impression of an aggressive papal financial policy abetted by the crown and by some of the other great men of the kingdom. As the petition in the parliament put it:

As soon as the pope wants to have money to maintain his wars in Lombardy or elsewhere, to spend, or for the ransom of his friends, French prisoners taken by the English, he wants a subsidy from the clergy of England. And straightway this is granted by the prelates because the bishops dare not refuse him and levy from the clergy without their consent. And the lay lords do not take care or take action to prevent the church being destroyed and the money of the realm wickedly taken away.[3]

This is an accurate statement of the causes of papal taxation and, though there had of course been no formal 'consent' to the subsidy, certain bishops and lay lords had in effect permitted it. The expressions of anti-papal opinion which we have noted in the commons are not in the least surprising in themselves. For once, however, the weight of opinion in the commons and the convocation was united in resentment of the state of affairs which these documents from the commons described. Usually the crown posed as the defender of England against the pope and

---

[1] *RP* 339, § 112.
[2] Lunt, *Financial Relations*, 669–78.
[3] *RP* 339, § 107.

joined with the commons in demanding money from the clergy. The crown now appeared to be the ally of the pope; it had weakened its usual case for clerical taxation by allowing the pope to tax first, and there was a breach between Sudbury, the servant of the crown, and his episcopal enemies. Despenser and Courtenay on the intercommuning committee probably acted as links between the rebels in parliament and in convocation who were united in their refusal to make grants of money and in their hostility to the court's acquiescence in papal taxation of the church. Lancaster had succeeded in the very unusual feat of uniting commons and clergy against himself.

VI. THE LAY LORDS

The four earls on the intercommuning committee had one fairly obvious characteristic in common. All of them were active military leaders. March had been in Lancaster's army in 1369, in the king's naval expedition in 1372, and on the Brittany expedition of 1375; Warwick had been in the army of 1369, the naval force of 1372, and the Lancastrian army of 1373; Suffolk in the forces of 1372 and 1373, and Stafford also in that of 1373. The only other earls who had taken a comparable part in recent expeditions were the king's sons, Lancaster and Langley, and the Earl of Salisbury. Apart from these three and Arundel who had just succeeded his father, the four earls were the only active members of the comital class. It has generally and no doubt correctly been supposed that the close link between March and Sir Peter de la Mare who was his steward[1] was symptomatic of close connections between the lords and the commons; de la Mare could hardly have attacked the court as he did without the approval of his master.

Some fragments of information about the Earl of March's finances in 1374 and 1375 have survived which shed a little light on his attitude and perhaps on that of his fellow earls. March was one of the very greatest magnates in terms of landed property and was closely linked with the royal family. His father's death in 1360 had left him a minor. In 1368 the king married him to Philippa, daughter and sole heiress of his son Lionel Duke of Clarence. In 1369 Philippa's Clare inheritance

---

[1] J. S. Roskell, 'Sir Peter de la Mare, Speaker for the Commons in Parliament in 1376 and 1377', *Nottingham Mediaeval Studies,* ii (1958).

was delivered to him and in January 1373 after reaching his majority he got the whole of the March inheritance.[1] Since then he had been a landowner on a vast scale in both England and Ireland. Nevertheless he seems to have been short of money. He petitioned the king, probably in 1374, for relief from certain debts. The biggest item was a sum of £1,297 8s. 8½d., the rent due to the Exchequer for a portion of his father's estate which had been leased to him for 400 marks a year during the later years of his minority, February 1368–January 1373.[2] Most of the other clauses were about debts which were attached to the lands which he had inherited from Clarence, but there was one about wages of war. March said that he had received an advance of £1,327 2s. ½d. for the wages of his contingent on the royal naval expedition in the autumn of 1372. The expedition was of course a failure and was broken off after a few weeks. March had originally made an indenture with the king to serve for a year.[3] Because of the abandonment of the expedition the period of service had been only 54 days and the wages due for this period were less than the advance so that March was strictly obliged to repay £190 4s. He prayed to be allowed this sum on the grounds that he had lost money by buying victuals for his retinue for half a year in advance.[4] These petitions were granted by the king on 1 October 1374.[5]

This concession was made to March in the autumn of 1374 when the crown appears to have been trying with little success to get the Brittany expedition, in which March was one of the commanders, moving.[6] It reinforces the impression conveyed by other sources that the reluctant commanders had to be bribed and cajoled. Even so they held back right through the winter of 1374–5, either because they did not want a winter

[1] G. A. Holmes, *The Estates of the Higher Nobility in Fourteenth Century England* (Cambridge, 1957), 17–18, 45–6.

[2] *CFR* viii. 356.

[3] *Sir Christopher Hatton's Book of Seals,* ed. L. C. Lloyd and D. M. Stenton (Oxford, 1950), 164 (indenture 24 February 1372 to serve for a year overseas with 19 knights, 60 esquires, and 120 archers).

[4] 'De quel somme le dit Conte prie estre descharge en recompensacion de la perde qil avoit en la deliverance des vitailles qil avoit fait purvoier de comandement de notre dit seigneur le Roi pur toute sa dite retenue pur demye an.' (British Museum, Egerton Roll 8750.)

[5] Privy seal letter to Exchequer, E 159/151, Brevia directa Baronibus, Michaelmas, m. 14[v].

[6] See above, p. 39.

campaign—which English diplomacy and strategy needed to improve the bargaining position against France—or because they were suspicious of the feasibility of the expedition, or because they suspected the diplomatic plans of the court. The fate of the Brittany expedition of 1375 turned out to be in fact in some respects a repetition of the experience of 1372: the expedition was called off after it had lasted only two months.

In this case the commanders do not seem to have done badly in their financial dealings with the crown because substantial payments had been made to them by the Exchequer before they left the shores of England which nearly covered what was due to them for both wages and the passage and repassage of their retinues. The sums still owing to them were not finally paid until some time after the Good Parliament—the Exchequer was ordered to account with March by an order from the king dated 27 November 1376—but they can hardly have had serious grievances on this score.[1] On the other hand the expedition had been a complete failure. The commanders had had no chance to cover themselves with glory, any expenditure which they had made was wasted so far as a return in military achievement or prestige was concerned, and the expedition could only be regarded as a highly unsatisfactory episode. We happen to know that, in spite of his advances from the crown, March had been borrowing money at that time probably to pay for his retinue in the Brittany campaign. The account of his receiver-general for the year Michaelmas 1374 to Michaelmas 1375 records several repayments of debts including 500 marks to William of Wykeham, Bishop of Winchester, £200 to Adam Francis the London merchant, and £120 to an Alberti representative, all apparently borrowed that year.[2] At the end of the

---

[1] March had been paid in all £9,105 12s. 5½d. before the expedition set out. The negotiations about his account between 27 November 1376 and 14 May 1377 determined that his expenses amounted to £9,597 12s. 10½d. and the surplus of nearly £600 was paid to him. Despenser was dead before the Exchequer was ordered on 19 June 1376 to settle the account with his executors. He had been paid £9,223 11s. 11d. in advance and was owed a little over £400. The account of the Earl of Cambridge, who had been paid £9,230 18s. 4d. in advance and was owed just under £400, was settled after an order dated 27 April 1377 (E 364/10, m. 4, 4d, 7d; E 101/34/6).

[2] The loan repayments recorded in the account are: 'Johanni Moryan Lumbardo' a debt of £20 incurred in 45 Edward III; the Bishop of Winchester £233 6s. 8d., incurred this year; Adam Franceys £200 this year; John Organ mercer of London by the hands of John Philpot £73 0s. 9½d. incurred in 45

financial year he still owed 500 marks to Archbishop Sudbury, 50 marks to a shipmaster who had helped to carry his retinue back from Brittany, £200 to Latimer, and £60 to Robert Ashton.[1] It was perhaps particularly galling to have had to turn for money to Sudbury and Latimer. An expedition to France, even if it was well supported by royal wages, was a costly venture which could only be satisfactorily concluded by a materially profitable victory or the acquisition of that military glory to which magnates like March aspired as one of the chief ends of life. In the Brittany expedition, like the expedition of 1372, March had been cheated of both these aims and still had debts to bishops and merchants.

The financial pattern revealed by the records relating to March in 1374–5 is in some respects similar to that revealed by another survival from private magnate archives, the account of Lancaster's receiver-general from Michaelmas 1376 to Michaelmas 1377.[2] Lancaster's landed estates were even broader than March's but here also there are traces of borrowing and of the vital importance of war wages. On 1 December 1376 1,000 marks were repaid to the son of the late Earl of Arundel and on 12 December £100 to Arundel's commercial adviser John Philpot. On the receipt side of the account nearly half of the total (£6,254 14s. 8d. out of £12,803 0s. 4¼d.) came from arrears of wages of war granted by the royal exchequer, most of it (£4,979 4s. 2d.) from one big assignment secured by Lancaster in October 1376, immediately after his recovery of control of the court, in payment of wages due since 1371.[3] Lancaster had also had to borrow fairly heavily for his preparations for the French expedition of 1373: his loans in the summer of that year included at least 4,000 marks from Arundel.[4] For the active

Edward III; Roger Beauchamp £100 this year; 'Lawrencio Frose Lumbardo de societate Albertinorum' £120 13s. 4d. this year. (Egerton Roll 8727.)

[1] A list of 'Creditores domini Comitis Marchie ad festum Sancti Michelis anno regni regis Edwardi tercij post conquestum xlix^mo finiente' includes £333 6s. 8d. 'Simoni Episcopo Londoniensi per compotum Johannis Blake [the Earl's Treasurer] anno xlix°'; £33 6s. 8d. 'Johanni de Weston domino nauis le Margarete de Plumouthe pro repassagio domini de partibus Britannie'; £200 to Latimer ('Domino de Latemer') and £60 to Robert Ashton, both unexplained. (Egerton Roll 8751.)   [2] DL 28/3/1.   [3] See below, p. 161.

[4] On 17 April 1373 Lancaster ordered his receiver general to pay to his treasurer of war 1,000 marks received by loan from Arundel and on 7 May £3,977 15s. 10½d. and £2,000 received from the royal treasurer for the next expedition and 2,000

soldier–politician–magnate like March or Lancaster, the payment of wages of war and the success of expeditions were matters of financial and emotional concern large enough to determine their political behaviour.

March would no doubt have liked the Brittany expedition to be remembered in the terms used by his family's chronicler some years later: 'This most kindly Edmund, with the Duke of Brittany who was allied to the King and the kingdom, was sent with a great army on an expedition to subdue the rebellion of the Bretons.'[1] This description concealed the fact that the expedition had been a failure. Within four years, March had been involved in the fiasco of 1372, the court had pressed him to go to Ireland instead of France in 1373, and he had been a leader of the ill-fated expedition of 1375. It is not surprising that he resented the way the managers of royal policy were spoiling his career and encouraged his steward to attack them in parliament. Though they may not have had quite such strong reasons for discontent, his magnate colleagues on the intercommuning committee probably sympathized with him. None of them can have felt that their military interests had been well served by the court since 1372.

The four barons who constituted the third rank of the committee are harder to characterize as a group and difficult to see as severe critics of the court. Henry Percy, thirty-five years old, was an outstanding rising member of the baronage, soon in fact to become an earl. He had been a Knight of the Garter since 1366 and had a long record of military activity on the Scottish border, where he had been warden of both marches, and in France, where he had taken part in Lancaster's expeditions of 1369 and 1373.[2] In 1376 he was already a great man in the north and growing in importance by the expansion of his estate.[3] The *Alnwick Chronicle* describes a grand occasion in August 1376 when he dined at the abbey with a huge company including thirteen knights.[4] The men whom he most resembled

marks received by loan from Arundel; on 11 July he acknowledged a loan of 4,000 marks to be repaid at the house of John Philpot, Arundel's financial agent on 1 November (*John of Gaunt's Register, 1372–1376*, ii. 154, 189; i. 79).

[1] W. Dugdale, *Monasticon Anglicanum*, ed. J. Caley, H. Ellis, B. Bandinel (1817–30), vi. i. 353. [2] Biography in *Complete Peerage*, ix. 708–12.
[3] J. M. W. Bean, *The Estates of the Percy Family 1416–1537* (Oxford, 1958), 7–8.
[4] 'Cronica Monasterii de Alnewyke', *Archaeologia Aeliana*, ser. 1, iii (1844), 43–4.

in background and interests were the similar northern barons Scrope of Bolton and Neville of Raby. His most obvious connections were with Lancaster, in whose household he had been brought up,[1] and with Neville, whose sister was his first wife. He was Lancaster's most active collaborator in the reconstruction of court policy which followed the Good Parliament.

Guy Brian was one of the most famous of the courtier knights. Now an oldish man, he had received a grant for long service as a king's yeoman as long ago as 1339. He had borne the king's standard at Calais, been made a Knight of the Garter in 1369, and was, in short, the pattern of the king's brother-in-arms, though not like Percy a man of great family but one who had risen up by service in the king's household.[2] He had been closely associated with the court in the period before the Good Parliament and had been entrusted with presenting the king's request for a grant of money for war expenses to the parliament of 1372.[3] Henry Scrope of Masham was also an old soldier whose roll of honour included many of the most famous battles of Edward III's reign. In recent years he seemed to have been a good deal about the court or on missions from it. In 1369-70 he had been Captain of Calais, in 1370 Warden of the Marches in Northumberland, in 1371 Steward of the Household for a few months. In 1374 and 1375 he had been negotiating with the Scots and in December 1374 he got continuation of an annuity of 200 marks granted to his father.[4] Richard Stafford, the last of them, was again an oldish soldier, uncle of the present Earl of Stafford. He had been a life-long follower of the Black Prince for whom he had been steward as long ago as 1347.[5] In the autumn of 1374 Stafford together with Guy Brian had been ordered to judge two disputes about the ownership of prisoners because the office of constable was vacant through the death of the Earl of Hereford.[6] This adds to the impression that they were exceptionally respected exponents of the chivalric life. None of these three could be regarded as outsiders and if they had personal grievances against the court they are unknown to us. They seem to have been chosen as a group of impeccably

[1] Ibid. 42.
[2] For his biography see *Scrope and Grosvenor Controversy*, ii. 245–50; Tout, iv. 255.
[3] *RP* 310.
[4] *Complete Peerage*, xi. 561–3; *Scrope and Grosvenor Controversy*, ii. 112–19.
[5] Tout, iii. 328.   [6] *Foedera*, 1014–15; *CPR*, 1374–7, 54, 57, 58.

orthodox representatives of the way of life which the knights of the shire admired.

The study of the proceedings of the Good Parliament leaves us with certain fairly clear impressions about the reasons for, and methods of, the attack on the court. The success of the attack depended in one sense on the ability to convict the courtiers of charges relating to their financial policy and the most obvious victims of these financial misdemeanours, now bent on revenge, were commercial groups. The study of the impeachments themselves emphasizes strongly the commercial implications of the court's policy. But it would be a mistake to draw the deduction that the financial and fiscal policies were the most important matters in the political situation. Financial policy had created clear and easily definable grievances and was therefore a good ground for attack; the Staple merchants had a straightforward reason as a group for objecting to the courtiers and could prove their case. The attack on the court, however, was certainly not solely the work of the merchants and they may not even have been very important in it except as witnesses. The attitudes of other groups involve us in a less manageable world of conjecture but are probably more important. There was a feeling of resentment among some sections of the nobility about the humiliating and—to them—damaging failure in France which was vented in the attack on Latimer over Bécherel and St. Sauveur even though that was unsuccessful. There was a general dislike, shared by bishops, nobility, and commons, of the corrupt court ruled by a concubine. The recent Lancastrian policy towards the church pleased no one except its few direct beneficiaries; clergy, nobility, and commons all resented the plunder of the church by the pope with the connivance of the king. It was the combination of a variety of grievances affecting all important political groups which made the situation so explosive in 1376, but probably the factors which did most to determine the political atmosphere were the French and ecclesiastical policies adopted by Lancaster in 1375. By these policies Lancaster united the lords and commons with the bishops against the crown and made it impossible to pursue the usual plan of browbeating convocation with the support of parliament. Thus for a short time the court was severely shaken by an irresistible outburst of criticism and indignation which, though it may have been chiefly motivated by other considerations, found its most satisfactory outcome in the condemnation of a number of courtiers and agents of the court for financial abuses. The court bowed to the storm by making a limited and, as it turned out, temporary redistribution of office and influence.

One of the points made by Bishop Brinton in his sermon on 18 May was that the king's sons ought to be more prominent at court: 'The king is bound to reward his followers (*obsequiales*), who ought to be nobles and the sons of nobles, but according to their rank so that he sets his own sons before his servants (*famuli*) for it is not right or just that servants should be lords and lords should be beggars.'[1] The relative deprivation of the king's two younger sons, Edmund of Langley and Thomas of Woodstock, was a feature of the court before the Good Parliament. Neither of them figured much among the recipients of favours. Edmund was by this time 35 years old. For money he presumably depended chiefly on the Yorkshire lands of the old Earl Warenne which had been granted to him in 1347 when the Warenne family became extinct—the rest of the inheritance going to the Earl of Arundel.[2] Since then he had not received very much more land and his marriage in July 1372 to Isabel, the co-heiress of Peter the Cruel of Castile, though it may have seemed to carry great promise in the event of a successful overthrow of Henry of Trastamara, must have been materially valueless. The other son, Thomas of Woodstock, was much younger, only 21, and had not even begun a serious military career. The inheritance of the Bohun earls of Hereford, who died out in the male line in 1373, was earmarked for him and he must sometime between 1374 and 1376 have married Eleanor, one of the two heiresses. It was a rather unsatisfactory provision, partly because there were two co-heiresses—the other was Mary, later to be wife of Henry Bolingbroke—between whom it would have to be divided and partly because some of it was tied up in a trust in favour of a young widow Joan who survived her husband by 46 years.[3] Thomas had been granted

[1] *Sermons of Thomas Brinton*, 320.
[2] *Calendar of Charter Rolls*, v. 63 (grant 1347); *Calendar of Inquisitions Post Mortem*, ix, no. 54.
[3] Holmes, *Estates of Higher Nobility*, 24–5, 56.

nine of the Bohun manors to maintain his estate in April 1374.[1]
Both he and Edmund must have been aware that in spite of
their naturally superior rank they had not been treated with
the open-handedness which marked the king's dealings with
Latimer, Neville, and Alice Perrers. This was partially put
right when the victims of impeachment fell. Edmund succeeded
Latimer as constable of Dover with a fee of £300 on 12 June
and was granted another 1,000 marks a year in October.[2]
Thomas was given the hereditary Bohun office of constable with
1,000 marks a year and got the Bohun castle of Pleshey.[3] Both
of them were given property seized from the hated Richard
Lyons, including a ship called the *Grace Dieu* which went to
Edmund.[4]

Apart from the improvement in the position of the King's
two younger sons there was no great upheaval in the court and
certainly no successful rush by rivals to reap the material
benefits of a palace revolution. In fact there was no palace
revolution: the damage which the parliament inflicted on the
court group was superficial. The lay Chancellor and Treasurer,
John Knyvet and Robert Ashton, survived the crisis as office
holders. Guy Brian, who was a prominent courtier soldier
before the Good Parliament, was also in the continual council
after it. Though it was limited and temporary, however, there
was some withdrawal of royal favour. Latimer as Chamberlain was replaced by Roger Beauchamp, a distinguished
courtier soldier who had been a king's yeoman in 1337 and
since then had been, among other things, steward of Queen
Philippa and captain of Calais.[5] Neville as Steward of the
Household was replaced by Sir John de Ypre, another courtier
knight who was also a long-standing retainer of John of Gaunt.[6]
After the end of the parliament the council was compelled to
deal with the pressing problem of Ireland. The complete aboli-
tion of Windsor's administration which took place in July and
August,[7] though it would probably have been dictated in any
case by the events in Ireland in the winter and was certainly
not a result of the Good Parliament, was probably helped on by

---

[1] *CPR*, 1370–4, 472.   [2] *CPR*, 1374–7, 276, 347.
[3] Ibid. 279, 337, 407–8.
[4] Ibid. 297; Myers, 'The Wealth of Richard Lyons', 323.
[5] Tout, iii. 307.   [6] Tout, iv. 157.
[7] Described by M. V. Clarke, *Fourteenth Century Studies*, 157–61.

the damage done to Windsor's friends at court. Windsor himself was actually imprisoned briefly at the end of August, not for his deeds in Ireland, but on the king's order 'for a certain quarrel that arose between him and other our lieges in our presence' at the Carmelite house in Fleet Street.[1] This is the only piece of evidence pointing to quarrels within the court. One would like to know where Alice Perrers stood.

The parliament attempted to prolong its influence over the government by the imposition of a nominated council. It was agreed that 'the council of our lord the king be afforced by lords of the land, prelates, and others to remain continually to the number of ten or twelve according to the king's will, in such a way that no great matter shall pass there or be delivered without the assent and advice of all and other lesser matters by the advice and assent of six or four as the case requires'.[2] Little is known about this council beyond a list of nine names of members given by the *Anonimalle Chronicle*: Archbishop Sudbury, bishops Wykeham and Courtenay, the earls of March, Stafford, and Arundel, Henry Percy, Guy Brian, and Roger Beauchamp.[3] If ever effective, it was so only for a short time.

[1] Order for his arrest 16 August (H. T. Riley, *Memorials of London and London Life* (1868), 402; *Letter Book H*, 44), superseded 18 August because he had surrendered at the Tower (ibid.); order for release 20 August on mainprize of Ralph Basset of Drayton, Guichard d'Angle, Ralph Ferrers, Lewis Clifford, Mathew Redmayne, Henry Ferrers, and Thomas Rokeby (*CCR*, 1374–7, 443).

[2] *RP* 322, § 10.

[3] *Anon*, 91.

6

The second reversal of court policy
in 1376 to 1377

I. THE COURT AND THE PROBLEM OF DEFENCE

WE have seen how the proceedings of the Good Parliament
reflected the political situation created by Lancaster and the
courtiers in the previous two years. In the aftermath of the
parliament the rulers of the court did their best to escape from
this situation and largely succeeded. Their policies in the next
eight months were aimed at dispelling the highly unfavourable
impression which their previous actions had created. What they
did after the parliament therefore sheds light on the situation
during the parliament which they were trying to change.

According to one of the chronicles the government of the
continual council set up in the Good Parliament lasted scarcely
three months.[1] The evidence of the records is that the restitution
of manifest power to the former courtiers, in so far as it had been
interrupted, took place by the beginning of October and
probably followed quickly upon the onset of the serious illness
which attacked the king in late September, and continued until
the beginning of February 1377.[2] Writing to London on 29 July
the king told them 'we have decided to be in person at our
palace of Westminster on the feast of St. Michael [29 September]
next and to have before us there at the same time the prelates
and lords of our great council for certain great business touching

---

[1] *Polychronicon*, viii. 385.

[2] According to *Anon*, 95, Edward was ill at Havering from Michaelmas, 29
September, until 3 February. A large number of letters entered on the patent and
close rolls were dated at Havering from early September to the beginning of
February. The date of the onset of the illness is confirmed by a payment for cloth
for the king 'pro infirmitate' on 2 October (E 101/397/20) and a letter from
Archbishop Neville from London to his official at York on the same day calling for
prayers for the king's health (*Historical Papers and Letters from Northern Registers*, ed.
J. Raine, Rolls Series, 1873, 410).

the estate of us and our kingdom.'[1] Illness probably prevented this great stocktaking and facilitated continued control by the old group of courtiers. According to the chronicle tradition of the continuators of Higden the continual council had also lost credit with the king because of attacks by the tenants of the Earl of Warwick (one of the councillors) on the property of Evesham Abbey.[2]

However it was done, the key figures in the condemned group were openly in favour again in October. On 8 October at Havering the sick king 'with his own hand' and in the presence of Lancaster, the bishops of Lincoln and Worcester, Roger Beauchamp the Chamberlain, Ashton the Treasurer, and Nicholas Carew the Keeper of the Privy Seal handed a petition for pardon from Latimer to the Chancellor with orders that it should be granted.[3] On the previous day the same group of men who had been present at the pardon of Latimer, with the addition of Latimer himself and John Gilbert, Bishop of Hereford, had been named as executors in Edward's will.[4] Alice Perrers received a pardon on 22 October which carefully covered indebtedness for any money, gold, silver, jewels, or clothes which she might have received from the Chamber or the Exchequer;[5] on the same day an entry in the wardrobe accounts recorded payments for gowns for her together with the Countess of

[1] 'Nous avons ordenez destre en notre persone a notre Paleys de Westminster en la feste de Seint Michel prochein venant et dauoir delez nous a mesme le temps illoeqes le Prelatz et Seignours de notre grant conseil pur certeines grosses busoignes touchantes lestat de nous et de notre roialme avant dit.' (Corporation of London Records Office, Letter Book H, fol. 44.)

[2] *Polychronicon*, viii. 386–7; Walsingham, i. 322.

[3] The pardon is in *CPR*, 1374–7, 353–4. Latimer's petition (SC 8/180/8960) is endorsed thus: 'Memorandum quod dominus Rex manu sua propria tradidit istam billam domino Johanni Knyvet militi tunc cancellario suo apud Haveryng atte Boure in presencio dominorum tunc assistencium videlicet Johannis Regis Castelle et Legionis Ducis Lancastrie ac Episcoporum Lincolniensis Wygornensis Rogeri de Bello Campo Camerarii Roberti de Assheton Thesaurarii Nicholi de Carreu Custodis privati sigilli ipsius domini Regis Ricardi de Rauensere, Archidiaconi Lincolniensis Magistri Walteri de Skirlawe Archidiaconi Estrithing clericorum Cancellarii Regis ac aliorum precipiens eidem Cancellario quod faceret eidem Willelmo de Latymer cartam ipsius Regis de pardona de contentis omnibus in ista billa quam dictus dominus sic tradidit eidem Cancellario octauo die Octobris anno presenti.' Latimer had been granted a special pardon of Bécherel debts on 7 October (*CPR*, 1374–7, 361).

[4] *Foedera*, 1080; a number of the king's manors were given in trust to the executors, including Latimer, on 5 October (*CPR*, 1374–7, 347).

[5] *CPR*, 1374–7, 364–5.

Bedford and the Countess of Oxford.[1] On 11 October Lancaster received a very large payment of arrears of wages, £4,979 4s. 2d., from the Exchequer.[2]

The political problem facing the court in the autumn was the same as it had been before the Good Parliament: the threat of increasing French power and the need to find a substantial source of money to counter it. The parliament had done nothing to provide money except to authorize the levy of customs for a further three years from Michaelmas 1376. The background to the next phase of English politics, the autumn of 1376 to the spring of 1377, was a diplomatic stalemate and a growing menace.

From mid-July to early September an English delegation consisting of the Bishop of Hereford, John Cobham, Henry Scrope, and John Sheppey was in Bruges for continued negotiations with the French under the auspices of the papal mediators.[3] At the end of this phase of talks the papal mediators sent King Edward a proposal for a threefold division of the enlarged Aquitaine of the Treaty of Brétigny, one part to be held by the king of England in complete sovereignty for his life (but presumably held by the king of France thereafter), one to be held by Prince Richard of the king of France, one to be held by the king of France himself. With the proposal they sent the king a letter in which they confessed failure to persuade either party of negotiators at Bruges to give any ground over the question of sovereign jurisdiction and their inability to induce them to accept any compromise. The English team, with John Montague substituted for Scrope, was back at Bruges on 11 November and remained until 14 January. On 25 November the mediators wrote to Charles V again confessing complete deadlock but asking for his reaction to two possible modifications of their previous plans: first that the king of France should buy Prince Richard's third share, abandoning sovereignty over the king of England's third, secondly that the prince's third should be enlarged at the expense of the king of England's but the latter remain quite independent. Charles replied by sending an extra

[1] E 101/397/20.
[2] E 403/461, assignment by tallies for wages due to Lancaster for his army in Aquitaine June 1370-1. Also entered in the receipts of his receiver general, DL 28/3/1.
[3] Mirot and Déprez, 'Les Ambassades anglaises', 195.

negotiator, an expert lawyer, Jean le Fèvre, abbot of St. Vaast at Arras, bearing a document which reiterated the French king's absolute refusal to give up any sovereignty over Gascony. The abbot's commission ended with an outspoken denunciation of John of Gaunt who was accused of maintaining a rigorous line so that he could emerge out of the dissension in England as king after the death of his father or else lead a great army to France with which he could then conquer England as Julius Caesar had returned from Gaul to conquer Rome.[1]

In the middle of January the English and French envoys dispersed to report to their kings and then return to Bruges. On 7 February the papal mediators wrote a rather frank letter from Paris to Edward. Their task, they said, was made difficult by the fact that there were people around the French king advising him against any prolongation of the truce because he was well prepared for war. Also there were Castilian envoys at Paris working against peace.[2] The nuncio's letter reflected the real political situation. The main factor was that Charles V was preparing ambitiously for war, his preparations were far advanced, and he would extend the truce beyond 1 April only so far as he needed time to complete his alarming arrangements. Since the successful completion of his last major project, the assault on St. Sauveur, Charles had been preparing another, this time a naval, attack on England. His preparations were very formidable. In June 1374 the king had ordered the building of a large number of ships at the royal dockyard at Rouen, *le Clos des Galées*.[3] Accounts of the building works in the spring of 1376 indicate that some of the ships were large vessels designed on the model of the Castilian galleys—a new venture for the Channel powers.[4] In January 1377 Charles V apparently sent an envoy to Henry of Castile asking for naval help.[5] In May he paid a visit to Rouen accompanied by his treasurer of war to see the preparation of his fleet and army.[6] Throughout the

[1] *Anglo-French Negotiations*, 48–65.

[2] Ibid. 66–8.

[3] C. de la Roncière, *Histoire de la marine francaise*, ii (Paris, 1900), 50.

[4] Terrier de Loray, *Jean de Vienne, amiral de France 1341–1396* (Paris, 1877), 77–8, pièces justificatives no. 30.

[5] Delachenal, v. 24. See also for this whole episode, Russell, *English Intervention*, 237–41.

[6] H. Moranvillé, *Etude sur la vie de Jean de Mercier* (Mémoires présentées par divers savants à l'Académie des Inscriptions et Belles-lettres, ser. 2, vi (1888)), 309.

winter no doubt Charles's eyes had been fixed on the naval assault on England which was to be made in the summer of 1377 and the negotiations for peace must have been of subsidiary importance. Everything suggested that a devastating assault would be made on England after the expiry of the truce on 1 April. So poor was the outlook that England's precariously placed ally, the Duke of Brittany, had decided that the prospects of succour from England in the conditions following the Good Parliament were small and travelled to Flanders to investigate the possibility of changing sides in August 1376, making his own separate approach to the court of France[1] while Anglo–French talks were going on at Bruges.

The detailed evidence of diplomatic history provided by the *Liber Abbreviatus* of the papal mediators comes to an end early in February 1377. It is clear, however, that the English envoys reappointed on 20 February did meet the French again— during Lent (11 Feb.–27 March) we are told by Froissart— and did secure a prolongation of the truce until 1 May.[2] On 26 April new envoys were appointed: Adam Houghton, Bishop of St. Davids, the new Chancellor, the Bishop of Hereford again, the Earl of Salisbury, Robert Ashton, Guichard d'Angle, Aubrey de Vere, Hugh Segrave, Walter Skirlaw, and John Sheppey.[3] Little is known about these negotiations, but the instructions issued by Charles to the French envoys have survived and make it clear amongst other things that they were not to accept any truces which would hinder his naval plans.[4] Some time during this period the truce was extended to 24 June, but probably both the extensions beyond 1 April were admitted by Charles only because it was convenient to have more time for preparations at Harfleur. Within a few days of midsummer, which was three days after the death of Edward III, the Franco-Castilian fleet was launched against the south coast of England. When it came in the late summer the French attack turned out to be no more than a series of destructive raids and was perhaps less formidable than had been expected. That, however, is not important for the present argument. Throughout the winter of 1376–7 and especially from January onwards the English

---

[1] Jones, *Ducal Brittany*, 81.
[2] *Anglo-French Negotiations*, 68; Froissart, viii, § 774.   [3] *Foedera*, 1076.
[4] Printed *Anglo-French Negotiations*, 80–5, analysed by Delachenal, v. 8–14.

government had good reason to believe that a sword of Damocles was hanging over its head. The Chancellor told the parliament in his opening speech at the end of January that

the Adversary, during the truce and under its protection, is preparing formidably for war both by land and by sea with a great number of galleys, barges, and other large ships, and also strengthening himself in every way he can with the help of the Spaniards, Scots, and our other enemies to whom he is allied, who make us almost surrounded on all sides, so that he can destroy our lord the king and his realm of England and drive out the English language.

The danger may have been exaggerated to arouse sympathy but the statement of the essential nature of the French threat was correct. The English negotiators showed no signs of making concessions to the French at Bruges such as would open up serious chances of peace and thus force the French king to abandon his plans for attack. The court had evidently decided even now not to give any ground to French demands for sovereignty over Gascony. The truce therefore would inevitably soon be replaced by bloody and expensive warfare. A parliament had to be faced again and persuaded to pay for it.

Some preparations were made for resistance to naval attack during the spring of 1377. On 13 February the admirals to the north and west, Michael de la Pole and the Prior of the Order of St. John of Jerusalem, were empowered to arrest ships for a fleet to assemble in the Thames by 16 March. In March landowners were ordered to defend the Isle of Wight and other coastal lands.[1] Walsingham tells us that a large fleet was in fact assembled at London about Easter, which fell on 29 March, and reports that a fracas broke out when an esquire protected by Alice Perrers killed one of the sailors.[2] But limited measures of naval defence were not the main aim of the government. An attacking expedition to divert the enemy's military effort was also in the minds of the courtiers. The names of the leaders of this intended expedition are incidentally significant: John of Gaunt, Thomas of Woodstock, Prince Richard, and the Duke of Brittany who returned to the English alliance when the prospect of helpful action made it more attractive.[3] The French

---

[1] *Foedera*, 1071, 1076, 1073, 1075.
[2] *CA* 138.   [3] Jones, *Ducal Brittany*, 82–3.

attack in June came too soon for English plans to mature, so that it is not clear whether the army was intended simply to go to sea or to land in Brittany. By this time the Exchequer had got as far as issuing advances on wages.

II. WYCLIFFE'S ANTI-PAPAL DOCTRINE

The month of October 1376 thus saw the restoration of the old personnel of the court to some extent as it had been before the Good Parliament, but more firmly under the leadership of Lancaster who was indisputably the senior prince of the blood after the death of the Black Prince and did not now indulge in long absences from the court as he had done in the previous year. The court faced the same political difficulty of raising money from unwilling taxpayers in a situation of depressing and ominous military failure. The same group faced the same political situation for the next nine months until the old king finally succumbed to death in June 1377. It is in one sense surprising therefore that the relations of the court with the next parliament which met in January to April 1377 were quite different in character from the intensely strained and hostile encounter with the Good Parliament. This has often been explained by the argument that, while the personnel of the court remained substantially the same, the personnel of the Parliament was dramatically changed; John of Gaunt took care to 'pack' the Hilary 1377 parliament with knights of the shire who were well disposed to him, led by a speaker who was his own steward, while the speaker of 1376, who had been March's steward, languished in prison. No doubt there is some truth in this interpretation. The concentration on personalities, however, misses the importance of issues. However much Lancaster exercised his powers of patronage and influence in the knightly class, it is unlikely that he could have controlled the Hilary parliament if there had not been a fairly radical change in the political situation. This was partly brought about by the change in the international scene; the threat from France was more immediately alarming in February 1377 than it had been in April 1376. But there was another change which can only be explained as a quite deliberate reversal by Lancaster: he dropped the eccentric policy of allowing the pope to exploit the English church and returned in an exaggerated and ostentatious fashion to the more normal policy of demanding money from the church for the king.

Even if the ecclesiastical policy of 1375 were judged to have been correct at the time, there was every reason for reversing it now. The crown could expect no further advantages in England from alliance with the papacy. In the international scene the position of Pope Gregory was also very different from what it had been in June 1375. At that time he had been at the height of his power, at the end of the exceedingly arduous but successful war with Milan which was concluded by the treaty with Bernabò Visconti in the following month. He looked forward to a peaceful return to Rome from a pacified northern Europe. But in the autumn of 1375 the papal position in Italy was shaken by the Florentine-inspired risings in many parts of the papal states. Throughout 1376 the pope was fighting the bitter War of the Eight Saints against Florence and attempting to restore his position in his own dominions. Nevertheless he pressed on with his plans to return from Avignon to Rome and actually started the journey on 13 September, a long journey to cover such a short distance, fraught with every kind of misfortune, which came to a weary end when he entered Rome on 17 January 1377 just ten days before the Hilary Parliament met at Westminster. The position in Italy to which he returned could only be insecure and difficult. The king of France, whose brothers the dukes of Burgundy and Anjou had both visited the pope in his last days at Avignon in the hope of persuading him to stay, was bound to be displeased, and the influence of the *Curia* in northern European politics was bound to be diminished.[1] When the English court embarked on its anti-papal demonstrations it could do so confident that it was not losing a valuable ally.

One of the first signs of the new line of thought is an entry in the Exchequer issue roll dated 23 September 1376 which records the sending of a messenger to Oxford to summon John Wycliffe before the council.[2] During the next few months Wycliffe was to play a dramatic part in events at London, first,

---

[1] The return to Rome is described by L. Mirot, *La Politique pontificale et le retour du Saint-Siège à Rome en 1376* (Paris, 1899). For the last-minute attempts to prevent it see especially pp. 98–100.

[2] F. Devon, *Issues of the Exchequer* (1837), 200.

according to the *Chronicon Angliae* and the *Anonimalle Chronicle*, preaching in the churches against the prelates,[1] and then facing Bishop Courtenay in a famous scene at St. Paul's. The courtiers must have thrust Wycliffe forward deliberately as a mark of their new aims, and the enthusiasm with which they supported him for the time being was presumably generated by the urgent need to emphasize that their aims had changed. They were now following a strategy in one respect diametrically opposed to that of the previous twelve months. Wycliffe was already known as an outspoken opponent of papal taxation and intervention in England and a supporter of lay control. He stood for the attitude to the church which Lancaster had rejected and affronted in the last year, the attitude which was expressed by the commons in the Good Parliament. Lancaster showed by his patronage of Wycliffe that he had seen the error of his ways and returned to the commons' point of view.

In November 1376 a Benedictine correspondent at Avignon (probably Adam Easton whose conversations about cardinals' benefices in England we have noticed earlier) wrote to the Abbot of Westminster asking him to obtain a copy of

the sayings of a certain master John Wycliffe which as is said he sows against our order at Oxford. I cannot obtain a copy of them. Since you are the father and principle lord of our order, I beg you to arrange for me to have a copy, and also of those things which he disputed against the church, and a copy of a little book which the same doctor issued concerning royal power in several chapters.[2]

The book referred to must be the first part of Wycliffe's *De Civili Dominio*. How was it that England threw up at this period an anti-papal theorist whose writings not only expressed in an extreme form the anticlerical prejudices of English laymen but also were powerful enough to acquire a European notoriety? The answer to this question is of interest to us because it is closely connected with the peculiar atmosphere of ecclesiastical politics which had been created by John of Gaunt's manœuvres in 1375.

Wycliffe had probably been implicated in politics, in some way which cannot now be discovered but involved preparation

[1] *CA* 116; *Anon,* 103.

[2] W. A. Pantin, *Documents Illustrating the . . . Chapters of the English Black Monks 1215–1540,* iii, Camden Society, ser. 3, liv (1937), 76–7.

of the crown's case against the papacy or the church, since about 1371 if not before.[1] His report of an argument in favour of the right of the secular power to use the property of the church in case of necessity, which he said he had heard in parliament, probably referred to the parliament of February to March 1371.[2] On 12 May 1371 the king granted him a portion of the tithes of Ludgershall in Buckinghamshire of which he was rector. The tithes belonged properly to the Prior of Bermondsey and were in the king's hands because it was an alien priory. The grant, though it was small—tithes assessed at 20s. for a rent of 26s. 8d.—may have been a royal favour for services rendered.[3]

Within the next few years Wycliffe produced his first extended discussion of church-state relations or at least the first that has survived, the 'Determinationes' in which he replied to the arguments put forward against him at Oxford by two Benedictine masters, Ughtred of Boldon and William Binham. The *Determinationes* are undated but seem most likely to have been written in the later part of 1373.[4] Wycliffe describes his

---

[1] The most reliable account of Wycliffe's life is in K. B. McFarlane, *John Wycliffe and the Beginnings of English Non-conformity* (1952) but it is without references to sources. The fullest collection of references is in H. B. Workman, *John Wyclif* (Oxford, 1926), but the conclusions are unreliable. The biography in Emden, *Biographical Register of the University of Oxford*, iii, is also valuable.

[2] *De Civili Dominio*, ii (ed. J. Loserth, London, 1900), 7.

[3] A patent dated 12 May 1371, *teste* Scrope the Treasurer, announced the grant to Wycliffe, rector of the church of Ludgershall, of 'custodiam porcionis quam Prior de Bermondesey alienigenus singulis annis percipere tenetur in eadam ecclesia' taxed at 20s., which is in the king's hands because of seizure of alien priories, from Easter last, rendering 2 marks a year rent at the Exchequer. Wyclliffe finds as mainpernors Robert Wycliffe clerk and John de Santon of Yorkshire (E 159/147, Commissiones . . . , Easter). On 3 February 1372 the Prior of Bermondsey exhibited in the Exchequer an indenture between himself and Master John Wycliffe dated at Bermondsey in the convent chapel 29 June 1371 by which the convent granted at farm to Wycliffe two parts of the tithes of the demesne of Ludgershall from the last feast of the Nativity of St. John Baptist for six years, for a rent of 26s. 8d. (E 159/148, Commissiones . . . Hilary). Cf. *Victoria County History of Buckinghamshire*, iv. 73.

[4] Published in *Opera Minora*, ed. J. Loserth (1913). Loserth's view (lii–lvi) that the *Determinatio* against Binham is later than *De Civili Dominio*, iii, depends on a reference (*Opera Minora*, 415–16) to a reply which Wycliffe said he had made to William Woodford. This does not, however, seem to be the same as the argument which Wycliffe puts in *De Civili Dominio*, iii (ed. J. Loserth, 1903–4, 351). The arguments against the payment of tribute to the pope which Wycliffe says he had heard expressed by lay lords in a council (*Opera Minora*, 425–9) seem to tally with the chronicle account of the council probably held in June 1373 (*Eulogium Histori-*

position thus: 'Since I am one of the king's own clerks (*peculiaris regis clericus*) I gladly accept the role of replying [to a critic of English law], defending the view that the king may justly govern the kingdom of England, by denying tribute to the Roman pontiff, and that the errors imposed upon the kingdom are false and without the support either of reason or of law.'[1] In the case of Ughtred of Boldon Wycliffe had to reply to three opinions: that priestly is better than lay rule; that the priest-hood cannot be judged by the secular power; that no one should teach that priests can be deprived of tithes or oblations. He accepted the correctness of these views as they stood but went on to add to them the view that laymen may judge whether their endowments to the clergy are misused and may deprive them of these if they are. The *Determinatio* against Binham in the first place also argued the same point. It then went on to attack a second main point raised by Binham, that the king ought to pay tribute to the pope. This led Wycliffe to quote a series of arguments against the validity of King John's submission to Innocent III which he said he had heard ex-pressed by secular lords in a council.[2] The *Determinationes* read as though they reflect the arguments between leaders of church and state provoked by the secular taxation of the clergy in 1371 and the papal attempt to impose taxation in 1372. They con-tain defences of current royal positions in the period 1372–4 put forward on a fairly superficial level. There is little discussion of the philosophical foundations of an anti-clerical position and Wycliffe—in claiming that he essentially agreed with Ughtred and that he spoke 'as a humble obedient son of the Roman Church', *tamquam humilis obediencialis filius Romane ecclesie*[3]—was trying to argue his brief without compromising his fundamental orthodoxy. He received his reward when he was presented to the living of Lutterworth on 7 April 1374 and nominated to the embassy to negotiate with the papal representatives at Bruges in July. But he was among the first to return from the embassy on 14 September. Thereafter there is no record of employment

arum, 339; cf. above, p. 14). McFarlane (p. 62) dates the work to 1372–3 and suggests that the Benedictine's assault on Wycliffe had been encouraged by the chapter of the order which met in September 1372. Boldon was out of England as an envoy from 25 July 1373 to 20 February 1374. Wycliffe himself was abroad from 27 July 1374 to 14 September 1374.

[1] *Opera Minora*, 432.　　　[2] See above, p. 14.　　　[3] *Opera Minora*, 425

by the government for two years, until he was summoned from Oxford to the council in September 1376.

It was probably during those two years that he composed the first book of *De Civili Dominio* which set forth a comprehensive and radical theory of the nature of human authority in general and the relationship between secular and ecclesiastical powers[1] and first made him into a dangerously revolutionary thinker. *De Civili Dominio* is the fourth part of Wycliffe's *Summa Theologie*. The earlier sections—*De Dominio Divino, De Mandatis Divinis*, and *De Statu Innocentiae*—which were composed in the years 1373–5 contained nothing of immediate political or ecclesiastical importance. In contrast the first book of *De Civili Dominio*, in spite of its rambling and turgid prolixity, was a shattering attack on the ecclesiastical order and was quickly recognized by contemporaries as a dangerous work. Wycliffe's main purpose in this book was to show that all claims by priests to property rights or to coercive jurisdiction were by their nature invalid, in other words to demonstrate the theoretical impropriety of the whole system of ecclesiastical government. For this purpose he used the conception of lordship (*dominium*) as a condition of rightful control over or enjoyment of created things which was an attribute of men in a state of grace. 'Every just man has the use of the whole sensible world; but he has the use of nothing of which he does not have lordship (in as much as he is just). Therefore every just man has lordship of the whole sensible world.'[2] This conception of lordship as an attribute of the just had been elaborated a generation earlier by another Oxford

---

[1] *De Dominio Divino* (ed. R. L. Poole, 1890, xxiii) contains no indications of date but is certainly prior to *De Civili Dominio*. Book I of *De Civili Dominio* (ed. R. L. Poole, 1885, Bks. ii–iv, ed. J. Loserth, 1900–4) was probably referred to by a writer at Avignon on 18 Nov. 1376 (Pantin, *Chapters of the English Black Monks*, iii. 76–7) and the papal bull issued at Rome on 22 May 1377 (Wilkins, 116–23; cf. J. H. Dahmus, *The Prosecution of John Wyclyf*, New Haven, Conn., 1952, 38–54) was certainly based upon it. Book ii, p. 90, contains a reference to the papal action against Florence on 31 March 1376 which might have been known in England in the summer of 1376 but was more topical in January 1377 when Courtenay published the bull (see below, p. 180). Book iii, p. 334, contains a reference to Wycliffe's loss of the prebend of Caistor and so must be after January 1376 (see below, p. 175). A passage in Book i, pp. 387–8, contains a possible reference to the same thing. It is probable therefore that *De Dominio Civili*, Book i, was completed by the autumn of 1376 and that it had been composed in 1375–6.

[2] 'Item, omnis iustus utitur toto mundo sensibili; sed nullo utitur cuius non habet dominium (cum sit iustus), ergo omnis iustus dominatur toti mundo sensibili' (*De Civili Dominio*, i, 48).

thinker Richard Fitzralph in his treatise *de Pauperie Salvatoris* and had been used, less extensively, by Wycliffe in *De Dominio Divino*. In *De Civili Dominio* it was used more fully to provide the basis of a general investigation of the relations between church and state.

As far as the government of the church and its relation with that of the state were concerned, the essence of the argument was that the two institutions worked within separate frameworks, priests being concerned with evangelical law and lay rulers with civil law. The function of promoting the religion of the gospel which was the priest's proper business gave him no authority whatever in temporal matters.[1] The prevailing conception of canon law as a legal system with coercive force analogous to that of civil law was a misconception. Canon law was a mixture of fragments of divine law and human inventions; only the divine law was the concern of the clergy and that had nothing to do with temporal coercion.[2] Canon law was not, as canonists claimed, an authority in competition with civil law. The only ecclesiastical art was theology and only that study, not law, should be the concern of all clergy including the pope.[3]

The critique of the contemporary church, which was entwined in Wycliffe's exposition with general theoretical propositions of this kind, is easy enough to correlate with other contemporary criticisms. And in broad terms Wycliffe's standpoint is that which he had maintained while he was in the royal service, extended into a more radical and far-reaching exposure of the attitude of the conventional defenders of ecclesiastical liberties at that time. It may be summarized, in terms which he used, by saying that the English church was not in a Becket situation but in a Grosseteste situation.[4] The enemy of the church's true function was not the king but the pope with his provisions, exemptions, and courts of appeal. The attempts of some clerics to present themselves as candidates for martyrdom like Becket in defence of the church against the king were absurd because the defence of property could not make a martyr. Wycliffe scorned the papal system of regulation which

---

[1] *De Civili Dominio*, i. 74.   [2] Ibid. 125.   [3] Ibid. 118, 124.

[4] 'Et patet quod hodie (si phas est dicere) sunt episcopi Anglie quoad Romanam ecclesiam in casu consimili, ut Lincolniensis in sermone suo conqueritur Romano pontifici . . .' (*De Civili Dominio*, i. 290), following a passage rebutting clerical pretensions to be acting in the spirit of Becket.

the clergy accepted. It was wicked and simoniacal for the clergy to promise the payment of annates or to pay for bulls in order to get benefices.[1] It was absurd for the pope to pretend to declare in his bulls ability or inability to hold a benefice for by so doing he claimed the power of conferring or withdrawing grace which was God's.[2] The later part of the book contained a more general demolition of the papal position. Since the true church was the community of the predestined, the pope and the cardinals were unnecessary to it and had no claim to obedience except in so far as their commands conformed with God's law.[3] On the other hand the clergy ought not to resist the claims of the lay power. There were two kinds of authority which the state should exercise over the church. The first was the ordinary exercise of its power over the clergy like other subjects. Thus the clergy had no right to object to the exaction of tenths by the king when they themselves used secular law in defence of their property. The echo of contemporary ecclesiastical debate is clear in Wycliffe's ironical sentence: 'How inconsistently and greedily it seems our ecclesiastics grumble about secular princes requiring tributes or tenths for the defences of the kingdom when they incessantly long for temporal acquisitions and submit to human laws and take counsel according to civil law so that they may be defended.'[4] Secondly it was a proper function of laymen to correct the clergy. Thus it was proper for parishioners to refuse tithes or oblations to incumbents who did not perform their duties, among whom Wycliffe mentioned alien cardinals as possible offenders.[5] The secular authority in general had a duty to confiscate the property of churchmen if it was a hindrance to their furtherance of the law of Christ. Wycliffe expressed a studied agnosticism as to whether the present state of the church required such a disestablishment. 'Whether the church is today in that case is not for me to discuss but for the statesmen who direct the business and the condition of kingdoms . . . I know, however, that it is for temporal lords to examine this matter and if there is a defect they ought to correct it in accordance with charity.'[6]

Wycliffe thus presented theoretical objections to the views of the defenders of ecclesiastical liberties and of papalism; there is

---

[1] *De Civili Dominio*, i. 201–2.   [2] Ibid. 255.   [3] Ibid. 358–92.
[4] Ibid. 200.   [5] Ibid. 310–14.   [6] Ibid. 269.

no doubt that that was his main aim and that it was correctly recognized by contemporaries. But the method by which he did it—and this is what especially links this book with the political situation of 1375-6—was potentially almost as dangerous to lay as to ecclesiastical authority; in the mood in which he composed this treatise Wycliffe was not particularly concerned to guard against such a danger. According to the conception of lordship on which his book depended, lay authorities were set up because of man's sinful post-lapsarian nature as a necessary restraint and a punishment. The power of kings, though established by God, was not of a very superior or estimable kind. Monarchy was better than aristocracy, but kings were good only in so far as they acted in accordance with divine law. The best form of government would be that of judges ruling in accordance with the law of God, the state from which Israel had declined into monarchy.[1] Although put there by God, kings and property owners had no rights to authority except those which were conferred by being in a state of grace. Property rights in this regime had a rather limited validity: 'the consent of the people to someone holding civil lordship who was more free of sin was not just except on the assumption that the person holding lordship be accepted by God for that office . . .'[2] Neither conquest nor hereditary succession were in themselves titles to lordship; the lordship must be merited by the conqueror or the inheritor himself and this applied in particular to the king of England.[3] And behind all the gradations of right and wrong, justice and injustice of various parts of the political and ecclesiastical systems, was the true church, the church militant, the only repository of absolute right. It was in Wycliffe's eyes a crass error to suppose that any earthly authority could enjoy or convey a right to property or jurisdiction which had any absolute validity.[4] Ultimately the community of property could be the only just condition because the just would all have an equal dominion over the whole of creation.[5]

This book of the *De Civili Dominio* contains in essence the most radical parts of the doctrines which Wycliffe was to elaborate in later years concerning the essential nature of the church. The

[1] *De Civili Dominio*, 185-99.　　　　　　　　　　　　　　　　[2] Ibid. 130.
[3] 'Et patet plane solucio de successione regum Anglie, quomodo contingit sanctum post tyrannum succedere, sed non in iure suo, quod non remansisset in posteros sed novo iure acquisito a Domino capitali.' (Ibid. 153.)
[4] Ibid. 32-3.　　　　　　　　　　　　　　　　　　　　　　　　[5] Ibid. 96-103.

true church was for him the invisible community of the righteous, and the visible church therefore had no rights against lay powers. Crises of church–state relations in the fourteenth century naturally called for anti-clerical political theories. Wycliffe's theory in one sense shows the extreme difficulty of producing a watertight anti-clerical theory with scholastic tools. Whereas Marsilius of Padua, returning directly to Aristotle, had been able to disarm the visible church without touching the validity of temporal institutions, Wycliffe's theory subverted all human institutions whatsoever. This is the nature of his doctrine which, as defenders of the established order realized, was potentially anarchistic. It seems to be a mark of the period when this book was written, however, that he accepted these implications with equanimity. When he returned to political philosophy about two years later to write the *De Officio Regis*[1] at a time when he was again an honoured servant of the crown, Wycliffe produced a theory of monarchy which, though consistent with *De Civili Dominio*, was very different in tone. It was a respectful and adulatory account of the duties and rights of kings. In the evolution of Wycliffe's political thought Book I of *De Civili Dominio* stands between the *Determinationes* of *circa* 1373—the judicious and moderate statement of the royal case against the papacy—and the *De Officio Regis* of *circa* 1378—the enthusiastic analysis of kingship. It is a bitter and revolutionary book written by a man careless of the consequences of his theories.

Wycliffe's book was quickly recognized as a dangerous work containing theories which subverted the authority of the pope and the church. Adam Easton's inquiry from Avignon dated 18 November 1376 led in quite a short time, and in spite of the administrative upset of the move to Rome, to the issue of a papal bull on 22 May 1377 denouncing a list of propositions selected from the *De Civili Dominio*, Book I.[2] Adam Easton himself in the next few years composed a treatise—the *Defensorium Curatorum*—attacking the more famous anti-papal theories of Marsilius and Ockham and very likely inspired by the new threat from Wycliffe.[3]

[1] *Johannis Wyclif Tractatus de Officio Regis*, ed. A. W. Pollard and C. Sayle (1887); on the date of composition, pp. xxvii–xxviii.

[2] Analysis of the bull by Dahmus, *Prosecution of John Wyclyf*, 37–55.

[3] W. A. Pantin, 'The Defensorium of Adam Easton', *English Historical Review*, li (1936).

In order to explain the particular characteristics of the theories which Wycliffe evolved in the years 1375–6 it is necessary to place those years in the perspective of his own career as an ecclesiastic. At the beginning of his two-year period of exclusion from royal service, September 1374–September 1376, Wycliffe was in possession of three benefices. First the rectory of Ludgershall which he had acquired in 1368 in exchange for the rectory of Fillingham to which he had been presented by Balliol College in 1361 when he was Master. Secondly a canonry of the collegiate church of Westbury-on-Trym with the prebend of Aust which he had been granted as a result of a petition by the university in 1362. Thirdly the rectory of Lutterworth which, as we have seen, he had received in 1374 from the crown.

He also had some expectations. According to a much later report (by Robert Hallam Bishop of Salisbury, quoted by Thomas Netter in the early fifteenth century),[1] he hoped for the bishopric of Worcester which was vacant from November 1373. It was filled in the autumn of 1375 by the royal clerk Wakefield at the same time as Wycliffe's colleague in the Bruges negotiations, John Gilbert, was promoted from Bangor to Hereford. His design on Worcester may have been a malicious rumour. A more certain piece of information is that Wycliffe had obtained a papal letter granting expectation of a canonry and prebend of Lincoln. The grant was originally made on 28 January 1371 and confirmed on 26 December 1373 with the concession that he could continue to hold the Westbury canonry and prebend as well.[2] The first vacancy to which this expectation could be applied arose when Henry de Ingelby, canon of Lincoln holding the prebend of Caistor, died between 15 June and 20 October 1375.[3] Wycliffe must have received the canonry and prebend: on 14 January 1376 he is recorded as witness to a document drawn up at Oxford with the titles 'sancte theologie

---

[1] *Thomae Waldensis . . . Doctrinale Antiquitatum Fidei Catholicae* (Venice, 1571), 326, 'ut dixit Robertus Sarisburiensis episcopus in magna synodo Cantuariensis cleri, Vigoriensis episcopatum non assecutus fuerat, quem optauit.' Hallam was Bishop of Salisbury from 1407 to 1417.

[2] M. E. H. Lloyd, 'John Wyclif and the Prebend of Lincoln', *English Historical Review,* lx (1946); J. A. Twemlow, 'Wycliffe's Preferments and University Degrees', *English Historical Review,* xv (1900).

[3] *Testamenta Eboracensia,* i (Surtees Society, 1836), 94.

doctor, canonicus Lincolniensis'.[1] But he had a rival who had also been promised benefices by the pope and whose goodwill was much more urgently needed. The rival was Philip Thornbury who was son of John Thornbury, one of the chief mercenary captains in the service of Gregory XI in Italy. At some unknown date, probably after 14 January 1376, Wycliffe was deprived of the prebend and it was given to Thornbury. This is known from an entry in the accounts of the papal collector where Wycliffe's name appears in a list of debts outstanding at 6 March 1378, owing £45 for first fruits of the prebend although he had been replaced as holder of it by Thornbury. Wycliffe seems to have been a victim of the papal policy of charging annates on benefices obtained from expectancies which was applied from 17 April 1371 to March 1374.[2] The double injury of losing a benefice and having to pay for it after it had been lost explains Wycliffe's quite precise reference to his own experience in Book III of De Civili Dominio: 'the lord pope gave me a prebend in the church of Lincoln, and having taken care to collect the £45 of first fruits conferred the same prebend on a youth overseas by way of a concealed reservation without making any inquiry into my unsuitability nor into any effort made by me for a dispensation in this matter.'[3] In more general terms a remark in the later part of Book I may refer to the same experience:

What I ask is to be believed, if today the head of the church grants me something, not privately but publicly, by open letters obtained at no little cost and effort, and tomorrow, without any opportunity for me to defend myself, as a result of a change in his wishes because of a relationship or a question of money or blood or some other

---

[1] H. E. Salter, 'John Wyclif, Canon of Lincoln', *English Historical Review*, xxxv (1920).

[2] Lunt, *Financial Relations*, 353; *Accounts Rendered by Papal Collectors*, 504. The words of the entry (Vatican Archives, Collectorie 12, fol. 182) are: 'de prebenda de castre in ecclesia lincolniense ex causa provisionis facte per expectationem Johanni Wicliff per gregorium anno V pro taxa sexaginta octo marce que valent xlv libras. folio   . fructus sunt sequestrati et monitus est dictus Johannes in secundo et quarta die maij anno etc. lxxvii soluit pro eo Robertus Wiclef tresdecim libras sex solidos et octo denarios et sic remansit in istis restis pro xxxii libris. Sed post fuit prorogatus ad octauas sancti hillarii quia fuit expoliatus per philippum thornbury possessorem. Restant xxxii libre.'

[3] *De Civili Dominio*, iii. 334. On the meaning of this passage see Lloyd, 'John Wyclif and the Prebend of Lincoln', 390.

personal matter, the pope declares the letters and the decision made the day before to be wrong?[1]

About the time when he came into fleeting possession of the Lincoln prebend, Wycliffe also, it seems, had to defend his Westbury prebend against an English rival. On 6 November 1375 he obtained a royal mandate to the Chancery ordering that a letter patent should be issued confirming his tenure of the prebend. This might seem an unnecessary precaution. On 18 November, however, another patent granted the prebend to a clerk called Robert Faryngton on the grounds that it was in royal hands because of the vacancy in the bishopric of Worcester from October 1373 to October 1375.[2] Faryngton was a royal clerk, probably a chancery clerk, who had collected a few benefices.[3] One explanation of his action would be that, on the look-out for a prebend and knowing that Wycliffe had just been successful at Lincoln (where he secured one himself the following year),[4] he thought that this might open the way to a claim at Westbury. Wycliffe in fact had a dispensation to hold both, of which Faryngton may have been ignorant. Nothing is known of the fate of the prebend for the next year. On 22 December 1376, when he was back in favour, Wycliffe secured another royal letter issued on the information of Lancaster saying that the prebend had been granted to Faryngton in the belief that it was vacant and in the king's gift but now, 'for certain reasons presented to us and our council', the grant was revoked.[5] Whether or not Faryngton ever actually held the prebend is not certain. The incident does, however, show that Wycliffe did not have friends at court to protect him at the end of 1375. He was out of favour both at Avignon and at Westminster, a victim of their temporary alliance.

At the time when he was writing Book I of *De Civili Dominio*, we may conclude, Wycliffe had good reasons for a deep hatred of the papal system and all its works and also had little reason to love the royal court of which he had earlier been a valued

[1] *De Civili Dominio*, i. 387–8.
[2] Documents in full in H. J. Wilkins, *Was John Wycliffe a Negligent Pluralist?* (1915), 33–5; *CPR*, 1374–7, 121, 195.
[3] *CPR*, 1374–7, 32, 44 (presentations to churches of Harlow and St. Dunstan in the East, 1374) and various references in this volume to him receiving attorneys.
[4] *Fasti Ecclesie Anglicane*, i, ed. H. P. F. King (1962), 46.
[5] Wilkins, *Was John Wycliffe a Negligent Pluralist?*, 36–7.

servant. His hopes of preferment had been dashed by an alliance of his friends with his enemies. Gilbert and Wakefield, who had been rewarded with sees, belonged to a class of beneficiaries of royal favour which he might have hoped to join, but the turn of political events which had made their fortunes had given him less than nothing. All that we know about the circumstances of his withdrawal from royal service in 1374 is that he came back from Bruges at the beginning of September earlier than had been expected; but the coincidence of this with the change from a policy of firmness to one of pliancy in dealing with the pope suggests that he had been dropped because his talents were no longer useful. It is clear in any case that he suffered personally from the new political course. This background is reflected in the content and tone of the book. If his relationship to politics had been different, it is unlikely that Wycliffe would have written such an extreme work or taken so little care to mask its anarchistic tendencies. The general significance of this for the interpretation of Wycliffe's character and the evolution of his thought is a question which does not concern us here. What does concern us is the instructive paradox that the book which made Wycliffe such a suitable ally of the court party after September 1376 and a symbol of their new extreme anti-clericalism was inspired by resentment of the policy of the same court in the previous two years. This paradox is a measure of the completeness of the reversals of the court's policy before and after the Good Parliament.

III. THE HILARY PARLIAMENT 1377

Before the parliament assembled in January 1377 those in control of the court had made their general political position clear. It contained one major shift in policy, a whole-hearted return to the anti-papalism and anti-clericalism of the early 1370s. This is most spectacularly symbolized for modern observers by the adoption of Wycliffe. But of course in January 1377, though his fame had spread to learned ecclesiastics at the *Curia*, Wycliffe was for most Englishmen still a rather obscure clerk. A more effective demonstration of its stance was the onslaught which the court launched against William of Wykeham. Wykeham was probably arraigned before some sort of conciliar tribunal in the later part of 1376.[1] He was accused of various corrupt practices when he had been chancellor. Thus the court resumed the attitude which had been most clearly expressed by the dismissal of Wykeham and Brantingham from the chancellorship and treasurership in 1371. The *Anonimalle Chronicle* tells us that Wykeham came before the council at Westminster 'well attended with men but with a pensive face and with him the Bishop of London to comfort him'. Courtenay again appears as the new champion of the church. The chronology of the proceedings against Wykeham is obscure. He was summoned for a second examination on 20 January but a royal letter of 7 January (the earliest official information about the proceedings) cancelled the summons and forbade him to come to Westminster. He was also at some time deprived of his temporalities —we do not know when.[2] Whatever the precise timing of these events Wykeham was certainly in disgrace long before the parliament met. As the richest English bishop and a notable beneficiary of the papal system of provisions he was an appropriate victim for the court. Extra piquancy was given to the proceedings by the fact that when he asked for time to consider his reply to the charges his interrogators were able to remind him that he had called for an immediate answer when Latimer was questioned a few months earlier in the Good Parliament.

The court also showed its inclination in ecclesiastical politics by the line which it took about the quarrel between the pope and the Florentines. Florentine envoys bearing a request to the king for protection against the operation of the papal interdict probably arrived in the late summer or autumn of 1376.[3] A special letter to Edward III demanding the execution of the papal sentence againt the Florentines had been sent on 18 May and so must have reached England in the summer.[4] No action

[1] The *Anonimalle* account of the trial, the fullest (*Anon*, 95–100), places it in a great council which met from 13 October to 6 December. An issue roll entry under 29 August records letters sent to bishops, magnates, and barons summoning them to a council at Westminster on 22 September (E 403/460), but there is no confirmation of the particular dates given by the chronicle. The *Anonimalle* chronology agrees with the short *CA* account (106–7). The charges against Wykeham are in the later pardon (*Foedera*, 1079). On these see Tout, iii. 310–12; *Anon*, 184.

[2] *Foedera*, 1069, 1075.

[3] *Foedera*, 1061, safeconduct 12 August for Nofferi de' Rossi and Donato Barbadori. *CA* 101–2, puts their arrival immediately after the end of the Good Parliament. [4] *Foedera*, 1050.

seems to have been taken. On 21 August the court imposed a severely worded prohibition on the publication of papal letters prejudicial to the interests of the king and his subjects and this was sent to prelates.[1] There is no indication of the kind of letters which the king had in mind but the prohibition would have had the effect of preventing the publication of the interdict. Nevertheless sometime after this, probably at the beginning of January 1377, Bishop Courtenay of London with another display of audacity published the papal bull at St. Paul's cross.[2] The king reacted first by ordering the arrest of the Florentines and their goods in London and then declaring on 30 January that they were to be released as the king's serfs to trade under his special protection.[3] Thus the object of the papal interdict was frustrated without strictly infringing its orders that Florentines were to become serfs of their captors and to have their goods confiscated. It seems probable that the Florentine embassy had remained in England through these events and helped to bring about the protection of the Florentine community in general and also the settlement of the Biancardi affair which was made about the same time.[4] In June the comune of Florence sent fulsome letters of thanks to the king and Lancaster for the generous reception of the embassy of Donato Barbadori and for the support given to its citizens in their resistance to those 'apostolic rescripts to which by the consensus of Christians we see supreme authority attributed as if to divine oracles'.[5] The affair of the Florentines, as this letter showed, brought briefly into alliance Italian and English anti-clericalism with two very different sets of origins and forms of expression at a moment of dangerous weakness for the papacy. For Lancaster and the court in England the defence of the Florentines served as an expression of defiance both to the pope and to the London merchants.

The Londoners were also victims of the resurgent court. To explain how this happened it is necessary to go back to the previous summer. With the exception perhaps of Yarmouth, the

---

[1] Wilkins, 107–8; *Wykeham's Register*, ii. 58, 263, 586.
[2] *Eulogium Historiarum*, iii. 335 (erroneously placed several years earlier); *CA* 109–11 (placed between Christmas and the beginning of the Hilary Parliament).
[3] *CCR*, 1374–7, 422, 478; *Foedera*, 1071.
[4] See above, p. 123.
[5] Florence, Archivio di Stato, Missive 17, fols. 111—12 (4 June 1377).

Good Parliament had nowhere had such a disruptive effect as in the city of London which was much more disturbed by the proceedings than the court itself. The attack in the parliament on the fiscal and commercial policies of the court had also been a dispute between groups of London merchants (Lyons, Pecche, and Bury on one side, Walworth, Francis, and their friends on the other), rivals for enjoyment of the financial advantages which resulted from political influence. This dispute produced a rift within the governing oligarchy of the city and discredited it sufficiently for its rule to be severely shaken so that the consequences of political exposure descended upon both the accused and the accusers, a spectacle which must have been enjoyed by the courtiers. London was ruled by an oligarchy of aldermen. The proceedings of the Good Parliament discredited that oligarchy because the three Londoners condemned were all aldermen. An opportunity was therefore given for the enemies of the system within the city to couple an attack on the three culprits with a demand for constitutional reforms. The earliest mention of the trouble was in a royal letter to the city on 29 July which said that news of dissension had reached the king's ears. According to the city records the crisis came on 1 August when an assembly of aldermen and commonalty deprived Lyons, Pecche, and Bury of their aldermanic rank and decreed that in future the mayor and aldermen should make ordinances only with the participation of a common council of men elected by the guilds. The names of those elected were presented at the Guildhall on 9 August. This was a fundamental weakening of aldermanic authority.[1]

More was to come. On 2 November the king, acting, he said, in response to a petition presented to the great council, declared that aldermen should have a term of office of only one year and should not be re-eligible until a year elapsed. This was an interpretation of an old grant of privileges. In practice aldermen had in the recent past retained their offices indefinitely. The new ruling was a powerful blow against them.[2] In October the crown launched what appears to have been a deliberate offensive, though based on a very trivial case, against the indepen-

---

[1] R. Bird, *The Turbulent London of Richard II* (1949), 17–29; 36–9. The crucial documents are in *Letter Book H,* 35–44.
[2] *CPR,* 1374–7, 387; Bird, *Turbulent London,* 30–6.

dence of the London Hustings Court. On 20 October the mayor and sheriffs were ordered to bring the record of proceedings in a case between Adam Houghton, Bishop of St. Davids, and the late Prior of the Hospitallers before the king's justices sitting in a case of error in St. Martin le Grand. The case dated from 1365 and concerned a rent of 30s. 4d in the suburbs of London; it cannot have been very important. The Bishop of St. Davids was soon to become chancellor. In the letter of the same date appointing the judges, the king gave judgement in advance: 'error intervenit manifestus ad gravem dampnum ipsius Episcopi sicut ex querela sua accepimus.'[1] Nothing more appears to have been done about this until 20 January 1377 when the judges ordered the mayor and sheriffs to appear before them with the record on 19 February.

Meanwhile to these offensives there was added probably at the end of 1376 an attempt by the new marshal Henry Percy, appointed some time shortly before 1 December, to extend the jurisdiction of his office over the city. The beginnings of this movement are obscure, but the commons petitions in the Hilary Parliament include three complaints about the marshal's jurisdiction which had presumably been drawn up before 2 February when petitions were presented and are therefore evidence of friction before the parliament. One alleged that the Marshalsea jurisdiction in Southwark was a refuge for felons and asked that the city officers might be allowed to prosecute them. The second complained that

the officers of the Marshalsea take upon themselves cognizance of various pleas more largely than was ever done before these times to the great disinheritance of lords of franchises, claiming waifs, strays, and other profits . . . And in ancient times they used not to have cognizance of pleas of felony and trespass against the peace and within the verge and after their coming and contract and covenant of debt between the king's retinue and those who follow the court.

A third complained of infringement of city and borough franchises by the steward of the household, the marshal, and clerk of the market.[2]

---

[1] Corporation of London Records Office, Letter Book H, fols. 55–6. The entries dealing with this affair in the printed calendar, *Letter Book H*, 56, contain large omissions and have to be supplemented from the manuscript.

[2] *RP* 366, 368, 369; cf. Bird, *Turbulent London*, 15, 25.

The vindictiveness shown by the court to the London oligarchy is nowhere fully explained. Hypothetically we may suppose that it was caused by a mixture of motives. Revenge for the damage done in the Good Parliament was obviously the occasion. Presumably the dependence of the *seigneurs* on the money of merchants like Philpot and Walworth made political revenge sweeter. The length to which the revenge was carried suggests a deep-seated lack of sympathy between merchant and magnate. However it is to be explained, the court appeared by the beginning of the Hilary Parliament to be waging systematic war on the city as it was on the church. The attacks on the church and on the Londoners were so spectacular that they may obscure the positive purpose of the court's policy. That was evidently to restore a united front of the court, the lay magnates, and the gentry—in other words of the whole lay gentility at the expense of relations with clerics and merchants who were the natural victims of their common prejudices. The restoration of lay unity was made much easier by the clear lead which Lancaster was able to give to the court now that the Black Prince was dead and the king so far declined. He did not displace the other leading personalities at court who had survived the Good Parliament: Alice Perrers, Latimer, and Ashton. He added to the circle one new baron who became his closest ally in the next few months, Henry Percy. He also wished to have good relations with his brothers and the other nobility. Even the Earl of March who had taken a hostile stand in the Good Parliament was willing to act at the beginning of February as one of the usual delegation which put the crown's case for a grant of money to convocation. March did this in spite of the fact that his steward, de la Mare, had been imprisoned in November—he was the only enemy on whom the court was able to inflict this punishment[1]—and that he himself about the same time had been deprived of the office of marshal which was conferred on Percy.[2] These must have been humiliating reprisals. March's acceptance of them suggests either that he was personally ineffective or that his position was weak. Once the circumstances

---

[1] *CCR*, 1374–7, 397.

[2] The first record evidence of this is the attribution of the title to Percy in his summons to parliament dated 1 December (*Reports of the Lords' Committee . . . touching the Dignity of a Peer*, iii. 67). Cf. *CA* 108.

which had formed the opinion of the Good Parliament had passed, magnates showed no desire to challenge Lancaster's leadership.

The parliament had been summoned on 1 December. In December and January, if we are to believe the *Chronicon Angliae*, Lancaster exerted his influence to secure the election of members who would be favourable to him, so that only twelve of those who had been in the Good Parliament remained who were obstinately supported by their communities.[1] Apart from this chronicler's remark and the official writs and returns no record survives of the elections so that it is very difficult to know what degree of credence or importance to give to it. The knights of the shire re-elected were in fact only eight or nine in number.[2] This was a small number but not spectacularly small in comparison with the custom of the recent past. Of the Good Parliament knights only thirteen had sat in 1373; of the 1373 knights nine sat in 1372 and in 1372 twelve were re-elected from the 1371 parliament.[3] So one would expect new men to be elected in most shires anyway, and in this respect the chronicler gives a misleading impression. The Hilary Parliament also included at least one man who must have been rather obviously unwelcome to the court: John de Annesley, who had appealed Latimer, was newly elected for Nottinghamshire. Perhaps more significant, however, is a comparison between the Hilary Parliament and the October Parliament of 1377 which met in a new reign and a new atmosphere and showed itself in some respects anxious to reverse the record. Thirteen knights came in both January and October, but the surprisingly large number of twenty-two Good Parliament knights (only three of whom had sat in January) were re-elected in October. It looks as though the Shire electors consciously reasserted their anti-Lancastrian or anti-court sympathies. It is perhaps significant also that a plea in the Good Parliament that 'knights of counties

[1] *CA* 112.

[2] John Hamely and Thomas Blount (Dorset), John de Eynesford (Hereford), John Westwycombe (Herts.), John Botiller and Roger de Pilkyngton (Lancaster and therefore the Duke's nominees), William Flaumville (Leics.), Robert de Stafford (Warwick). John de la Mare (Somerset) may or may not have been the man who sat for Wiltshire in 1376 (above, p. 137).

[3] A more elaborate statistical study was made by H. G. Richardson, 'John of Gaunt and the parliamentary representation of Lancashire', *Bulletin of the John Rylands Library*, xxii (1938), 201–5.

should be elected by common election of the best people of the counties and not certified by the sheriff without due election' was disregarded in the wording of the writs of 1 December.[1] Investigation does not add much to the statement of the *Chronicon Angliae* but on the whole it supports it: it suggests that so far as national political considerations were a factor in the shire elections, the court had a favourable, though not completely favourable, body to deal with in January. Though the chronicler is wrong about the expectation of re-election, he probably reflects the atmosphere at the beginning of the parliament correctly in saying that 'they had nearly all been replaced by the duke so that the few of the more faithful who remained could not prevail over such a multitude.'[2]

The Hilary Parliament, when it came, was in essence a return to the situation of 1371–3; the court manipulating parliament and convocation by imposing a burden on the clergy sufficiently large to reconcile the laity to making a moderate contribution themselves. In 1377, however, the conflict was much sharper and more dramatic because the crisis of the previous year had produced intense feelings between some of the main actors: Lancaster, Courtenay, Wycliffe, and the Londoners in particular. Parliament assembled for the first time on 27 January in the Painted Chamber with the young heir of the Black Prince, Prince Richard, in the king's throne. Next day the real business began with two speakers. Bishop Houghton the new chancellor, appointed less than three weeks before, set out the strategic situation which required money. Robert Ashton who had become chamberlain at the same time also spoke, setting the tone of the parliament by saying that he had words to utter which could not come from the mouth of a prelate because they touched the pope: the usurpations of the see of Rome in England would require 'certaines articles' to be declared later in the parliament. There is no evidence that this threat was carried out in the sense that anti-papal legislation was made in the parliament and in fact the replies to commons petitions about papal provisions and the collector were negative;[3] it was presumably intended to make clear to

[1] *RP* 355, § 186; *Reports of the Lords' Committee . . . touching the Dignity of a Peer*, iii. 671; Richardson, op. cit. 194–5.
[2] *CA* 112.
[3] *RP* 367, 373.

the commons where the king's ministers now stood. The lords and commons then separated with an intercommuning committee appointed as in the Good Parliament to link them. This time the bishops were Buckingham of Lincoln, Reade of Chichester, Gilbert of Hereford, and Erghum of Salisbury; two obscure men and two obvious followers of the court. The earls were Arundel, Warwick, Salisbury, and Stafford, a fair selection of the active members of the class. The barons were Percy, Roos, Fitzwalter, and Basset.[1] Percy was certainly a political partisan of Lancaster at this time. Thomas Roos of Hamelak was a feed retainer.[2] Walter Fitzwalter's allegiance is uncertain. So is that of Ralph Basset of Drayton, an old warrior of fifty who is not known to have had great political importance.[3] Evidently, however, the intercommuning committee, whether imposed upon or suggested by the commons, was distinctly favourable to Lancaster, and the appointment of Thomas Hungerford his steward[4] as speaker was a neat reversal of the previous appointment of de la Mare. According to the *Chronicon Angliae* Lancaster had asked for a generous grant—either two subsidies in one year or a sales tax, a hearth tax, or a tax on knights' fees.[5]

Little can have happened in parliament before 3 February when convocation met at St. Paul's, on the same day as the release of the Florentines from the Tower was ordered. After formalities convocation began with the usual deputation of lay lords to present the king's demands. This time they were the earls of Cambridge and March, showing that unity had been restored in the comital class, Robert Ashton, and John Knyvet. Ashton, who had made the anti-papal speech in parliament a few days before, spoke for them in English asking for generous help to resist the king's enemies. Next day convocation met again, the archbishop absent but represented by Nicholas Chaddesden, the Dean of the Arches (whom he had defended at the time of the Good Parliament), and Roger Sutton his

[1] *RP* 361–4.

[2] *John of Gaunt's Register 1372–6,* i. 47; *John of Gaunt's Register, 1379–1383,* ed. E. C. Lodge and R. Somerville (Camden Society, ser. 3, lvi–lvii, 1937), i. 7.

[3] *Complete Peerage,* ii. 3; he is not in the list of those who received summonses to the parliament (*Dignity of a Peer,* iii. 670) but he was appointed a trier of petitions (*RP* 363).

[4] J. S. Roskell, 'Three Wiltshire Speakers', *The Wiltshire Archaeological and Natural History Magazine,* lvi (1956), 274–300.

[5] *CA* 112; *Anon,* 100–1.

chancellor. The absence of certain proctors was inconsequentially discussed. The day after, 5 February, they met again with Sudbury present and the contention began. Bishop Courtenay read out a series of articles concerning injuries done to the church and to the Bishop of Winchester. These were perhaps the basis of the list of grievances of the clergy of the province of Canterbury which were entered later on the parliament roll: they consist of five fairly innocuous complaints about conflicts of lay and ecclesiastical jurisdiction and an article complaining that the Bishop of Winchester had been deprived of his temporalities without good cause shown and also prevented from staying in the religious houses of his diocese.[1] This was acclaimed by the assembled clergy.[2]

Sudbury met the bishops alone at St. Paul's on 9 and 11 February. The next full meeting was on 13 February when 'having propounded certain difficult matters concerning the state of the English church he charged the clergy in their consciences that they consider among themselves what ought best to be done for the good of the church' and prorogued the convocation until the 16 February.[3] On 16 February the clergy were joined in the chapter house for the first time by the outlawed Wykeham whom, at the instigation of Courtenay, they had insisted on summoning in spite of Sudbury's opposition.[4] The representatives of the lower clergy presented excuses for refusing a grant to the king until the laymen in parliament had made a grant.[5] Two days later on 18 February the archbishop

---

[1] *RP* 373; Wilkins, 104.

[2] 'Propositis quibusdam articulis ex parte domini Londoniensis Episcopi in scriptis redactis super reformacione quorumdam grauaminum sibi et ecclesie sue ac Episcopo Wyntoniensi et ecclesie Wyntoniensi illatorum et ipsis ibidem publice lectis, clerus predictus provincie Cantuarie petivit instanter et universaliter quod dicti articuli proponentur eciam pro ipso per dominum Regem et eius consilium reformandi et habita altercacione aliquali super articulis predictis inter dictos prelatos et clerum et discussione demum dictus dominus Cantuariensis Archiepiscopus continuavit dictam convocacionem cum presentibus expectando absentes ad diem veneris proximam tunc sequentem.' (Lambeth Palace Library, Register of Sudbury, fol. 33ᵛ.)

[3] 'Propositis per dominum ibidem dictis prelatis et clero quibusdam arduis concernentibus statum ecclesie anglicane onerauit dictum clerum in eorum conscienciis ut deliberarent inter se quid esset melius faciendum pro vtilitate dicte ecclesie et continuavit dictum convocacionem . . .' (Register of Sudbury, fol. 34.)

[4] *CA* 114; *Anon*, 101.

[5] ' . . . a dictis quibusdam excusacionibus dicti cleri super non concedendo ali-

presented to the assembled clergy the royal reply to the grievances about the treatment of the church in general and of Wykeham in particular—presumably in the latter case unfavourable.[1]

We are much less well informed about the progress of negotiations in parliament. 'And of these matters', says the *Anonimalle Chronicle*, 'they treated for a long time, for some wanted to grant tenths and fifteenths, some a mark on the wool customs, some a hearth tax, some fourpence a head, but at the end they agreed to give fourpence a head from all those above the age of fourteen years.'[2] The same chronicler also tells us that the grant of money was resisted in parliament by Bishops Courtenay of London, Despenser of Norwich, and Brinton of Rochester and the new bishop of Bangor, John Swaffham.[3] The first three were evidently trying to keep alive the resistance in which they had participated at the time of the Good Parliament. Whether the chronicler is right in putting their resistance in parliament rather than convocation is less certain but it may be that they were trying to repeat the tactics of joint resistance in parliament and convocation. Evidently no grant was made by either commons or clergy before 16 February when the clergy were still waiting for news from Westminster. The commons may have given their grant by 19 February.[4] On that day, however, came an extraordinary explosion caused by Lancaster's determination to make an aggressive demonstration of his power against his enemies among the Londoners and the clergy.

quod subsidium domino nostro regi priusquam communitas laicorum certum quid eidem domino nostro regi concesserit . . .' (Register of Sudbury, fol. 34.)

   [1] 'Dominus in prefata domo capitulari sedens exposuit dictis prelatis et clero voluntatem domini regis quo ad peticiones eorum concernentes statum in parte uniuersalis ecclesie anglicane et in parte domini Episcopi Wyntoniensis et habita deliberacione per dictos prelatos et clerum super huiusmodi responsione dominus continuauit dictam convocacionem.' (Register of Sudbury, fol. 34.)

   [2] *Anon*, 101.

   [3] *Anon*, 100–1. Swaffham, translated to Bangor in 1376, had formerly been Bishop of Cloyne in Ireland and had been one of the delegates sent to England in 1373 to plead for the sending of March to Ireland (Clarke, *Fourteenth Century Studies*, 150).

   [4] The commons' grant must have been made between 16 and 22 February. It seems likely that it was before 19 February because the events of that and the following day probably disrupted the proceedings. The *Chronicon Angliae* says 'Post paucos dies regressus est dux ad parliamentum quod intersumptum fuerat ex causis expressis superius' (*CA* 130).

According to the *Chronicon Angliae* Lancaster proposed in parliament on the morning of 19 February that the mayor of London should be replaced by an appointed captain and that the marshal should have powers of arrest. He was answered by John Philpot. The name sheds doubt on the story for, though he was an appropriate spokesman of the London merchants, he was not elected to this parliament. The general idea of a confrontation about city liberties at this time, however, is plausible.[1] As we know from another source, 19 February was also the day when the mayor Adam Stable and the sheriffs John of Northampton and Robert Launde appeared before the king's judges at St. Martin le Grand to answer the summons about the bishop of St. Davids's case in the hustings. They pleaded that the king's judges had no right to summon them with the record of a case in the hustings and that they could not produce it without damage to the liberties of the city.[2] The custom of the city would allow the 'mayor and aldermen after forty days' deliberation to reply to the justices through the recorder. This stubborn reaction to court provocation may possibly have been the occasion for the threat to the city which the *Chronicon Angliae* recorded. But the question of the marshal's jurisdiction was also very much in the air. At some time not far distant from that day the mayor, sheriffs, and aldermen were summoned to appear before the council at Westminster to answer charges about the marshal's jurisdiction.[3]

On the same day John Wycliffe had been summoned to St. Paul's to answer before the bishop for his seditious preaching. He came attended not only by four mendicant theologians but also by Lancaster and Percy bearing the marshal's staff and prepared to behave provocatively. Courtenay rebuked Percy for entering the church in this manner. Percy ordered Wycliffe to sit in the bishop's presence, which the bishop forbade. Lancaster and Courtenay exchanged threatening words.[4] This

---

[1] *CA* 120.

[2] 'Per quod recordum et processum loquele predicte coram justiciariis hic sine offensione consuetudinis civitatis predicte habere non possunt . . .' Corporation of London Records Office, Letter Book H, fol. 56; cf. *Letter Book H*, 56.

[3] A writ dated 22 February postponed the summons for 23 February 'propter quedam immensa et ardua negocia que instanti die lune proxima futura coram consilio nostro tractari oportebit' to 28 February (Letter Book H, fol. 57; cf. *Letter Book H*, 56–7).

[4] *CA* 117–20; *Anon*, 103–4.

dramatic confrontation, together with the hostility between the court and the city oligarchy, started a riot. The following day the Londoners met to discuss the threat to their constitution. The meeting was interrupted by two baronial intruders, Guy Brian and Fitzwalter, whose intervention seems to be explicable only on the grounds that they wished to create trouble for Lancaster and Percy. Fitzwalter pointed out that Percy had a prisoner in his house whose detention was a further affront to the liberties of the city. The citizens, whoever they were, took arms and went to release the prisoner. A crowd advanced on Lancaster's manor at the Savoy, and Lancaster and Percy in fear fled to Kennington. Courtenay and the Black Prince's widow intervened to quell the rioters. According to the *Chronicon Angliae* they showed decided hostility to Lancaster and his policy by attacking a critic of de la Mare, unhorsing a retainer who was wearing the duke's badge, and demanding that the Bishop of Winchester should have a fair trial.[1]

These dramatic events took place according to the *Chronicon Angliae* on 19 and 20 February. After this it becomes much more difficult to establish the order of events. It seems probable, however, that there was a general reconciliation with London on 22 February. On that day Lancaster and certain of the lords went to see the king at Sheen and the answers to the commons petitions were read in his presence. It was probably on the same day that a London deputation (led according to the *Chronicon Angliae* by Philpot) also went to Sheen and received the king's assurance that no threat was intended to the city's liberties.[2] On the following day, Monday 23 February, the king's answers to the commons petitions were read out in parliament, and on the same day the speaker presented a request for the reversal of the judgements in the Good Parliament against Lyons, Alice Perrers, John de Leycestre, Adam Bury, Pecche, Elys, and Hugh Fastolf.[3] This is described in the parliament roll as 'the last day of this parliament'. The grant of the first poll tax must therefore have been made and accepted before this. It was not until a week later, on 1 March, that the cost of the banquet to celebrate the end of parliament was entered in the royal wardrobe accounts,[4] and the writs of expenses for the commons were

---

[1] *CA* 121–6; *Anon*, 104.   [2] *CA* 127; *RP* 364.
[3] *RP* 364, 374–5.   [4] Tout, iii. 318.

issued the day after that. The explanation is perhaps that the clerical subsidy was as yet undecided.[1] The members of parliament waited for the outcome of that issue and convocation and parliament ended on the same day.

A number of bishops met with the clergy at St. Paul's the day after the interrogation of Wycliffe (the archbishop with Ely, Salisbury, St. Davids, Hereford, Rochester, Llandaff, Winchester, Bangor, and St. Asaph). There was a further meeting on Monday, 23 February, with only Sudbury and the Bishop of Ely (many of the prelates must have been in parliament on that day). After two meetings without the archbishop a full convocation met on 26 February and decided on a grant of fourpence a head from beneficed clergy 'and in case that concession should not please the king, to obtain his happy grace in the matter of the petitions of the prelates and clergy' they were willing to grant a further fourpence from beneficed persons. This grant was to be in addition to the fourpence a head voted in parliament; all beneficed clergy and all regulars male and female would pay twelve pence.[2] The convocation assembled once more on 28 February to hear from the archbishop of the king's acceptance of this grant. The archbishop said he wished to explain the grant in parliament. Convocation met formally therefore for the last time the following day, 1 March.[3]

The only substantial point which the court conceded in the Hilary Parliament was the substitution of the poll-tax for the traditional lay subsidy. This turned out to be an important concession with considerable repercussions ending in the Peasants' Revolt, but it is possible that in 1377 the court was as vague about its quantitative implications as it had been in making its famous error about the number of parishes in England in 1371. Whatever assumptions the government had made about the probable yield of the tax the acceptance of a poll-tax was a concession to the knights of the shire and their constituents. It was an abandonment of the traditional principle, embodied in the tenths and fifteenths, that the laity should be

[1] The parliament roll (*RP* 364) contains the words 'ceste Subside ore grante [by the commons] et del Subside que le Clergie d'Engleterre q'est encores a granter al Roy nostre Seigneur . . .'
[2] Cf. Galbraith's note, *Anon*, 185.
[3] Register of Sudbury, fol. 34: 'dominus dixit quod voluit explanare dictam concessionem in parliamento consilio regio . . .'

taxed according to their wealth and an acceptance of the novel principle of universal taxation by head which was bound to shift the burden partially from the electors of the knights of the shire on to the lower, unrepresented classes. This emphasizes the general impression that Lancaster and the courtiers had staked everything on recovering the common front with the lay magnates and knights, which had been broken in the Good Parliament, at the expense of their enemies among the clergy and the London merchants. By this strategy they had succeeded in their aim of getting linked grants of taxation from the commons and convocation and thus had successfully returned to the relationships of 1371 and 1373. They had done this without making other political or personal concessions and without compromising in their acts of revenge. Lancaster and and the court had deliberately sought a dramatic confrontation with church and city on 19 February which repaid the humiliations of the previous year. Peter de la Mare remained a prisoner in Nottingham Castle, to be released only in the next reign. In spite of the stirrings of convocation Wykeham continued to be treated as a criminal. His temporalities were granted to the new Prince of Wales on 15 March. He was pardoned on 18 June, presumably because the king was then close to death; it may or may not be true that, as the *Chronicon Angliae* said, he had to humble himself to plead with Alice Perrers.[1]

The court's action against London was also pressed home. The *Chronicon Angliae* and the *Anonimalle* contain independent accounts of a further crisis in the relations between the court and London soon after the end of the parliament. The gist of the story is this. Lancaster was thirsting for revenge against the Londoners. According to one account Londoners had put up placards on which his arms were reversed and the legend of his illegitimate birth was proclaimed. Lancaster therefore arranged for them to be summoned before the sick king at Sheen where, in the royal presence, they were arraigned (*Anonimalle Chronicle* says by Lancaster, *Chronicon Angliae* by Robert Ashton the chamberlain). The chronicles agree that as a penance the city leaders carried a candle marked with Lancaster's arms to St. Paul's. The *Anonimalle* says they were also ordered to change the

---

[1] *Foedera,* 1075, 1079; *CA* 136–7.

mayor, sheriffs, and aldermen. Both accounts say that the common people of the city were more hostile to Lancaster than the aldermen and unwilling to bow to him.[1]

This story is to some extent confirmed by the city records. A meeting of the mayor, aldermen, and representatives of the guilds on 6 March agreed in effect to accept the constitutional revision which the crown had imposed upon them on 2 November, that is to make the aldermen due to go out of office six days later ineligible for re-election for twelve months.[2] On 21 March they bowed to a royal demand for the replacement of the mayor. Adam Stable was discharged and Nicholas Brembre elected in his place for the rest of the year.[3] It seems very likely then that a showdown such as that described by the chronicles took place in the early part of March, soon after the dispersal of parliament, and it is certain that the court wreaked its revenge on the London leaders to the extent of ending permanent aldermen and unseating the mayor. But it also seems that the court commanded too little sympathy in the city to be able to control it effectively. At a meeting of mayor, aldermen and guilds on 27 March five members of common council (William Essex, John More, Richard Norbury, John Willoughby, and Robert Francis) were removed for betraying the council's secrets and failing to support the city's policy about the marshal—a reference presumably to the events of 19–20 March.[4] The council went on to make plans for the fortification of the city. Although the London victims of the Good Parliament—Bury, Pecche, and Lyons—were completely rehabilitated by parliament and court, the city never received them back into favour or gave any of them office again.[5] Lancaster's revenge against his adversaries in London was therefore incomplete. Nevertheless by the end of March he and his courtier allies could congratulate themselves on having injured or humbled in some way most of their enemies.

The end of the Hilary Parliament saw the process of rehabilitating the Good Parliament victims almost complete. Royal pardons were issued to Lyons on 17 March, Pecche on 10 April, and Bury and Elys on 20 April.[6] Lyons's confiscated

---

[1] *CA* 131–4; *Anon*, 104–6. [2] *Letter Book H*, 59. [3] Ibid. 60–1.
[4] Ibid. 64; Bird, *Turbulent London*, 26, n. 8. [5] Bird, 24.
[6] *CPR*, 1374–7, 439–40, 444, 448, 453, 455.

property in the hands of the London sheriffs was restored to him.[1] The St. George's Day celebrations on 23 April were turned into a demonstration of the solidarity of the court and its magnate allies. Three princes of the royal blood had knighthoods conferred on them, namely Prince Richard, Thomas of Woodstock, and Lancaster's son Henry of Bolingbroke. Three sons of Henry Percy, Lancaster's chief ally, were honoured in the same way. With them were Robert de Vere, the young heir to the earldom of Oxford, the young John de Mowbray, and Henry Beaumont, the sons of the earls of Stafford and Salisbury, and finally, fantastically exalted into this glittering array, Alice Perrers's bastard son, John de Sotherey.[2]

[1] A. R. Myers, 'The Wealth of Richard Lyons', 329. In the Exchequer it was emphasized that restitution to Lyons was to be complete: 'recordabantur quod non est intencio Regis quod ipse aliquod avantagium haberet seu reportaret de aliquibus exitibus et proficuis terrarum et tenementorum predicti Ricardi Lyons . . .' (E 159/153, m. 136).

[2] G. F. Beltz, *Memorials of the Order of the Garter* (1841), 11.

Epilogue: conclusions

THIS study has treated the Good Parliament as an event, a focus of political interests, passions, and influences, not as a stage in a linear development of institutions. It offers no conclusions on the 'importance' of the Good Parliament in the evolution of institutions. It makes no claim of course to exhaust the implications of the subject or the sources for it, but its aim has been to shed some light on the complex influences which affected the actors in the drama at Westminster in May 1376 simply as a dramatic event and for its own sake. To do this it has been necessary to travel backwards and forwards in time and also to take into account the interests of a wide variety of Englishmen and the impact of distant events in Brittany, Avignon, and Tuscany. They have been invoked with the primary aim of explaining the situation at Westminster in May 1376. The interest of that situation, however, must be chiefly what it revealed under the stress of crisis about the nature of politics at the time, and we shall end with a brief attempt to summarize this.

The most obvious interest of the Good Parliament proceedings from the historian's point of view is that, taken in conjunction with other records, they do shed some light on the behaviour of the court. Naturally the court under an aged and decrepit king was disorganized and corrupt. What the records chiefly show us, however, is the tendency of the court to arrange its finances by playing off mercantile interests—Stapler and non-Stapler, English and Italian—against each other. The court was only partially dependent on mercantile capital for loans; the sums of money borrowed from Arundel and, under cover, from Latimer probably outweighed those advanced by merchants. Its system of control of trade by means of the customs allowed it not only to raise a large income but also to provide artificial commercial advantages—by enforcement or evasion of the Staple—for which merchants were willing to pay. The court was therefore very important to merchants. The attack on the court's financial policy was motivated by rivalries between groups of merchants and facilitated by the unlucky circumstances of trade depression which reduced Italian activity in England and thus strengthened the Staplers.

From the point of view of the government the most important event in the parliament itself was not the successful impeachment of the courtiers but the joint refusal of parliament and convocation to grant subsidies. The damage inflicted on the court group by the impeachments was superficial and quickly repaired. A few offices changed hands but none of the leading personalities at the court except Neville can have left it for more than a short time. After the Good Parliament Lancaster, who in earlier years had been abroad a great deal in France and at Bruges, evidently decided to take the court more firmly under his control than he had done before. During the winter of 1376–7 he was in command of it as he had not been before and perhaps could not have been before his elder brother's death. But he also decided to work in collaboration with the existing courtier group and did not essentially disturb their position except by a new elevation of Henry Percy who became his chief political ally. The Good Parliament showed that even the most violently hostile demonstration—short of physical rebellion or executions—could not do very much to alter the conditions at the court. Parliaments were brief; the court was there all the time.

The refusal to grant subsidies, however, was a serious blow which implied a profound and general criticism of the whole policy carried out in the king's name and not merely of the fiscal manipulations which affected small and relatively unimportant groups. Apart from the unsavoury situation at court the political alignments of the moment had been chiefly created by the two major decisions of 1375 to abandon the Brittany expedition and to make an agreement with the pope. These decisions can probably be explained quite straightforwardly as based on calculations of the best interests of the king's government without recourse to the nefarious designs or purely personal interests of Lancaster. In 1375 the government was so incapable—for lack of money—of pursuing an active military policy and the Brittany expedition was so slow in starting and so far from being an effective deterrent to the French that a truce probably seemed the best way out. Apart from the difficulty of facing a resurgent France, everything suggests that court policy in France, as in Ireland, was weak, probably because the court was headless, the king, the prince, Lancaster, and Latimer all controlling sectors of it, but no one effectively directing it. To many of the nobility and gentry, however, the government seemed to have failed in its primary duty of framing a successful military policy within which the active soldiers could enjoy the exercise of their prowess. March probably felt himself to be particularly the victim of treachery and was therefore willing to take a lead in the action against the court.

The concordat with the pope was also probably the result of a rational calculation that a pliant bench of bishops was worth a few thousand pounds. That may have been an even more damaging political mistake than the abandonment of the army in Brittany. At the beginning of the decade the king's finances had been quite successfully based on a balance between lay and clerical taxation which was fairly onerous to the clergy, offered nothing to the pope, and appealed to the anti-clericalism of the lay tax-payer. The government now seemed to have abandoned unnecessarily all the advantages of its previous stance. It had aligned itself with the pope, allowing him to take money from the English clergy on a scale unprecedented for many years. By doing this it had very much weakened its case for taxing the clergy and forfeited the sympathy and respect of the laity who could see no reason why they should bear the whole cost of the war themselves and despised a court which favoured the papal system and allowed money to be taken out of England to the papal Chamber. Thus the government got no money from either the clergy or the laity. The ecclesiastical side of the situation in 1376 is the one which has been most ignored by historians interested in domestic politics. This has been a serious failure of perspective. An analysis of the political background to the parliament reveals the great importance of the balance between lay and ecclesiastical power which is not made clear by the narrative sources. The policy of friendship with the pope was perhaps the factor which most isolated the court in 1376, and it could be argued that in the long run the most momentous results of the political crisis of 1375–6 were the writing of Wycliffe's *De Civili Dominio* with its ideological consequences and the intensification of anti-clerical prejudices and clerical resistance.

It is natural to see the Good Parliament as a stage in the evolution of a political system and perhaps reasonable to suppose that the impeachments helped to establish a tradition of independent action by the commons. A study of the background to the parliament, however, emphasizes that the crisis took place at a time of disaffection influencing all the politically important classes which resulted mainly from the king's government pursuing for a short time a peculiarly offensive policy. The aftermath of the parliament shows how quickly the government could re-establish its leadership once it had changed its policy. In the nine months after the parliament the ruling group was able to take revenge on its leading critics at the same time as re-establishing tolerable relations with lords and commons and extracting taxes once again from clergy and laity. The packing of the commons with friendly knights of the shire may have helped in this restoration but it must chiefly have been made possible by a reversal of the circumstances which dominated the Good Parliament. While the Good Parliament took place just after a renewal of the truce for a year, in February 1377 the government could argue plausibly that French attack was imminent and dangerous. While the government appeared in 1376 as the ally of papalism, by 1377 it had taken pains to present itself clearly as hostile to the pope and to ecclesiastical property. Those in control of the court were safe until they lost their hold on it when the king died in June.

Index

Adams, Stephen, 108 n

Aigrefeuille, Cardinal Guillaume d', 146.

Aire, Diocese of France, 35.

Alberti family and companies, 82, 84–6, 119–23, 126, 151, 152 n.

Alberti, Andrea di Benedetto, 82 n.

Alberti, Nerozzo, 82 n.

Amedeo VI, Count of Savoy, 9.

Amiens, Bishop of, see Lagrange

Angle, Guichard d', 158 n., 163.

Angus, Gilbert de Umfraville, Earl of, 107 n., 108.

Anjou, Louis, Duke of, 28, 58–61, 166.

Annesley, Sir John de, 105, 132, 184; Isabel, wife of, 132.

Appelyerd, Bartholomew, 108 n.

Appleby, Sir Edmund de, 135.

Appleby, John, Dean of St. Paul's, 142–4.

Appleby, Thomas, Bishop of Carlisle, 101, 140.

Aragon, English relations with, 26, 29, 51, 54.

Arundel, John de, 72 n.

Arundel, Richard Earl of (died 1376), 31, 43 n., 48, 71–7, 152, 156, 195.

Arundel, Richard Earl of (succ. 1376), 105, 107 n., 108, 152, 158, 186.

Arundel, Rape of, 75.

Arundel, Thomas, Bishop of Ely, 48, 75, 191.

Ashton, Sir Robert, 40 n., 88, 112, 121, 152; Keeper of Ireland, 93; Treasurer (1374–7), 64–5, 105, 157, 160, 163; envoy to Bruges (1377), 163; Chamberlain (1377), 185–6, 192.

Auray, (Brittany), 25, 30.

Aust, (Glouc.) prebend of, 175.

Auvergne (France), 26.

Baderham, John, 121 n.

Balinghem (France), 109, 111.

Ballyduagh (Ireland), parliament at (1371), 92, 95.

Bamburgh Castle (Northumberland), warden of, 94.

Bangor, Bishop of, see Gilbert; Swaffham.

Barbadori, Donato, 179 n., 180.

Bardi company and family, 71–3, 77–8, 82, 87–90.

Bardi, Alessandro di Bartolomeo, 73 n.

Bardi, Bartolomeo di Rodolfo, 73 n.

Bardi, Bernardo di Giorgio, 82 n.

Bardi, Gualtiero, 73 n., 82, 87–90.

Bardi, Piero, 73 n., 87, 89.

Bartolommeo di Giovanni, 82 n.

Basset, Ralph Lord, of Drayton, 23, 158 n., 186.

Bate, John, 122–3.

Bayley, C.C., 45 n.

Bayonne (France), 51, 116 n., 134; diocese of, 35.

Bealknap, Robert, 20.

Beauchamp, John, 88 n.

Beauchamp, Roger, 105, 152 n., 157–8, 160.

Beaufort, Roger, 8, 41, 43, 46, 55.

Beaumont, Henry, 66, 69 n., 194.

Bécherel, (Brittany), 25, 32, 37, 106–7, 109, 127–9, 130–1, 133, 155.

Bedford, Isabella, Countess of, 41, 68, 161.

Bees, (or Besse), Thomas, 83 n.

Bellamy, J.G., 132 n., 133 n.

Benedict, Sir Walter, 29.

Bermeo (Castile), 57.

Bermondsey (Surr.), Prior of, 168.

Bernes, John, 74.

Beverley, Richard, 47.

Biancardi family, 82, 84–5, 121–3, 126 180.

Biancardi, Andrea, 122.

Biancardi, Dino, 122.

Biancardi, Tommaso, 121–2.

Binham, William, 168–9.

Black Prince, see Edward.

Blake, John, 152 n.

Bliclyng, William, 108 n.

Bloklee, Simon de, 128 n.
Blount, Sir Thomas, 135, 184 n.
Boerius, 47.
Boldon, Ughtred of, 14, 168–9.
Bologna (Italy), 8–9.
Bordeaux (France), 22–3, 25–6, 28, 30 n., 31, 118; diocese of, 35.
Borstall, William, 47.
Boston (Lincs), 73, 122–3.
Botild, John, 115–16, 118.
Botiller, Sir John, 135, 184 n.
Boulge, Gilbert, 85.
Bourges, Cardinal Pierre de, 9.
Bourgneuf (France), Bay of, 56.
Boynton, Sir Robert, 138 n.
Bozoun, John, 108 n.
Brantingham, Thomas, Bishop of Exeter, Treasurer, 17, 65, 103–4, 119, 140, 179.
Bray, Hugh, Dean of Bocking, 142.
Bredon (Worc.), Prior of, 73 n.
Brembre, Nicholas, 193.
Brest (Brittany), 22–3, 25, 30 n., 37, 94, 130.
Brétigny, Treaty of, 22, 147, 161.
Brian, Guy, 39, 64, 74, 102, 105, 140, 154, 157–8, 190.
Brinton, Thomas, Bishop of Rochester, 103–4, 144–5, 156, 188, 191.
Bristol, 56, 67, 133–4.
Brittany, Duchy of, English interests in, 22–3, 26–32, 43, 127–31; expedition to (1375), 36–41, 43–6, 49, 52–3, 96, 150–2, 196; see John IV.
Brive (France), 28.
Brokhols, Roger de, 135.
Broomhill (Kent), 120.
Bruges (Flanders), 84, 122; negotiations at (1374), 19–20; (March–June 1375), 33–6, 41–56, 96, 148; (Dec. 1375–March 1376) 58–62, 141; (July 1376–March 1377), 161–4.
Brunham, John, 108 n.
Buch, Captal de, 8 n., 43.
Buckingham, John, Bishop of Lincoln, 147, 160, 186.
Bureau de la Rivière, 61.
Bures, John, 74.
Burghard, John, 73 n.
Burgundy, Philip, Duke of, 28, 34, 54, 58, 60, 62, 166.
Burley, Sir John, 124.
Burton, Sir William, 14, 19–20.

Bury, Adam, 106, 109, 111–12, 114, 181, 190, 193.
Buxhill, Sir Alan, 32, 38, 101, 131.

Caistor (Lincs), prebend of, 170 n., 175–7.
Calais, 19, 22–3, 26, 28, 34, 70, 111–13, 157; mayor and burgesses of, 111–13; see Staple, Ermyn.
Calveley, Hugh, 23.
Cambridge, Edmund of Langley, Earl of, 26, 58, 64, 149, 186; and Brittany expedition (1375), 37–46, 96, 131, 151 n.; and Good Parliament, 106–8, 156–7.
Cameringham, Nicholas, 123.
Canterbury, Christ-Church, 75; St. Augustine's, 86; Archbishop of, see Sudbury; Whittlesey.
Carew, Nicholas, Keeper of the Privy Seal, 18, 64, 76, 160.
Carlisle, Bishop of, see Appleby.
Carpentras, Bishop of, see Lestrange.
Castile, English relations with, 25–6, 29, 56–8, 162–4; see Henry of Trastamara.
Catalan shipping, 84, 120.
Catherine, St., of Siena, 8.
Catterton, Thomas, 38, 44, 131–2, 136, 138.
Cavalcanti, Angelo, 121 n.
Cavendish, John, 64.
Chaddesden, Nicholas, Dean of the Arches, 142–3, 186.
Chandos, Sir John, 38, 105; Eleanor, Elizabeth, and Margaret, daughters of, 132.
Charles V, King of France, 21, 36, 38, 41, 45, 50–5, 57, 61–2, 127, 130–1, 133–4, 161–6.
Charles VI, King of France, 50.
Charles II, King of Navarre, 51, 134.
Chaucer, Geoffrey, 119.
Cher, river, (France), 28.
Cherbourg (Normandy), 37, 51.
Chichester, Bishop of, see Reade.
Chichester (Sussex), Rape of, 75.
Clarence, Lionel, Duke of, 65, 92. 149–50.
Clarendon (Wilts), 134.
Clark, M.V., 2.
Clement VI, Pope, 11.
Clement VII, Pope, 146.

Clifford, Lewis, 158 n.
Cloyne, Bishop of, *see* Swaffham.
Cobham, John Lord, 34, 58–9, 161.
Cokyn, John, 73 n.
Cognac (France), 43, 50.
Colbrond, John, 108 n.
Constanza, d. of Peter I of Castile, Duchess of Lancaster, 25–6.
Controne, Pancius de, 73.
Convocation of Province of Canterbury (1370) 16–17; (April, 1371), 17, 71; (December, 1373), 18–19, 72; (June, 1376), 141–9; (February, 1377), 186–8, 190–1.
Cook, John, 44 n.
Cornwall, John, 131.
Coupere, William, 115, 118.
Courtenay, Edward, 66.
Courtenay, Hugh de, 74.
Courtenay, Hugh de, Earl of Devon, 107.
Courtenay, William, Bishop of Hereford (1369–75), of London (1375–81), in convocation (1373), 18–19; translation to London, 47–9, 53; in parliament and convocation (1376), 101, 105, 140–4, 149, 158; defence of Wykeham, 179; publication of anti-Florentine bull, 167, 170 n., 180; during convocation (1377), 185, 187–90.
Cradock, Roger, Bishop of Llandaff, 107, 191.
Crécy, Battle of, 66, 135.
Credi, Giovanni, 82, 83 n., 85–6, 119–21.
Crevalcuore (Italy), battle of, 9.

Dagworth, Nicholas, 96–7.
Damory, Richard, 132.
Dauphiné, 54.
Dax (France), diocese of, 35.
Daywatre, John, 73.
Derval (Brittany), 25, 30 n, 127.
Despenser, Edward Lord, 23, 114; and expedition of 1375, 37, 39, 151 n.
Despenser, Henry, Bishop of Norwich, 101, 140–2, 144, 149, 188.
Devereux, John, 37.
Devonshire, Commons of, 40.
Donmowe, William, 116 n.
Dordogne, River (France), 28, 30.
Dover, 26; Constable of, 66, 94, 106, 120, 157.

Dublin, 91, 95–6.
Durant, Thomas, 44 n.
Dytton, William, Clerk of Privy Seal, 64.

Easton, Adam of, 146, 167, 174.
Ecclesfield (Yorks), 109.
Edward III, King, 51, 90, 107, 133–4; expedition led by (1372), 22, 29; relations with Duke of Brittany, 23–5, 127; with Alice Perrers, 68–9, 160; illness of, 159–60; death, 198.
Edward, Prince of Wales (the Black Prince), 13–14, 17, 22, 25–6, 51, 64, 68, 88 n., 90, 106, 135, 139, 165, 183.
Edwards, J.G., 101 n.
Egremont castle (Cumb.), 69.
Eight Saints, War of, 124–6, 166.
Elmham, Sir William, 29, 56, 133–4.
Eltham (Kent), 90, 107.
Ely, Bishop of, *see* Arundel.
Elys, William, 106, 109, 114–16, 118, 190, 193.
Erghum, Ralph, Bishop of Salisbury, 48–9, 140, 186, 191.
Ermyn, William, Treasurer of Calais, 62.
Essex, William, 108 n., 193.
Evesham abbey (Worcs.), 160.
Exeter, Bishop of, *see* Brantingham.
Eynesford, Sir John de, 135, 184 n.

Faryngton, Robert, 177.
Fastolf, Hugh, 109, 117–18, 190.
Felbrigge, George, 116.
Felton, Sir Thomas, Seneschal of Gascony, 26, 56.
Fernandez de Velasco, Pedro, Chamberlain of Castile, 57.
Ferrers, Henry, 158 n.
Ferrers, Ralph, 39, 158 n.
Fèvre, Jean le, Abbot of St. Vaast, 162.
Fifhyde, William, 135.
Fillingham (Lincs), rectory of, 175.
Finisterre (Brittany), 40.
Fitzralph, Richard, 171.
Fitzwalter, Walter, 69, 97, 186, 190.
Flanders, English relations with, 80.
Flandrin, Cardinal Pierre, 146.
Flaumville, William, 184 n.
Fleet prison, 119–20.
Florence, merchants of, 60–1, 81–7, 118–26, 179–80, 186; relations with

John IV de Montfort, Duke of Brittany, 61, 68; relations with Edward III and England 22–5, 56, 127, 130–1, 163–4: and expedition to France (1373), 26–30, 72; and expedition to Brittany (1375), 31–2, 37–41, 43–6, 50, 53, 96, 131, 153.

John II, King of France, ransom of, 12, 112.

John XXII, Pope, 11.

Karlille, Adam, 108 n.
Kennington (Surrey), 190.
Kentwode, Sir John, 135, 137–8.
Kildare, Maurice, Earl of, 93, 97.
Kilkenny (Ireland), Parliament at (1371), 92, 95; (1373), 93; (1375), 96.
Kilmainham (Ireland), Prior of, 93.
King's Lynn (Norfolk), 73 n.
Kirkley Road, 115–18.
Knaresborough (Yorks), honour of, 24.
Knolles, Sir Robert, 28, 37, 133–4.
Knyvet, Sir John, Chancellor, 18, 64, 76, 100, 105, 129, 157, 160, 186.
Kyngeston, Sir John de, 88.

Lacy, Stephen, 116 n.
Lacy, William, 116 n.
Lagrange, Jean de, Bishop of Amiens and Cardinal, 60–1.
Lancaster, John of Gaunt, Duke of, 17, 22, 24, 48–9, 64–5, 90–1, 113, 140, 149, 153–4, 157, 160, 164, 180, 183, 194, 196–7; finances of, 68, 75, 152–3, 161; claim to Castile, 25–6, 29, 51–2, 56; expedition to France (1373), 23, 25–31, 72, 94; envoy to Bruges (March–June 1375), 34–41, 44, 50, 53–4; (Dec. 1375–March 1376), 58–62; and Good Parliament, 76, 101–4, 107, 134–7, 143, 155; and Hilary Parliament (1377), 165, 184–6; and Wycliffe, 167, 177, 189; and London, 188–90, 192–3.
Langham, Simon, Cardinal, former Archbishop of Canterbury, 48, 86.
Langley, Edmund of, see Cambridge.
Langley Burrell (Wilts), 137.
La Rochelle (France), 56; Battle of, 21–2, 57, 71, 133.
Latimer, William Lord, 18, 31, 94, 152, 195; missions to Bruges (1375–6), 36,

58, 61; position at court, 64–8, 76, 90–1, 197; accusations against in Good Parliament, 90, 101–7, 109–11, 113, 120–1, 126–33, 155; position at court after Good Parliament, 157, 160, 183.
Launde, Robert, 189.
Laurencius de Nigris, and his brother Angelo, 85.
Lesparre, Florimund of, 57.
Lestrange, Guillaume de, Bishop of Carpentras, Archbishop of Rouen, 31, 59.
Leycestre, John de, 110, 112, 190.
Libvre du bon Jehan duc de Bretagne, 30.
Lincoln, Bishop of, see Buckingham; canonry of, 175, 177.
Llandaff, Bishop of, see Cradock.
Lodovico di Andrea, 82, 121 n.
Loire, river, 28.
London, Bishop of, see Courtenay, Sudbury; mayor and alderman, 114, 119, 181, 189–90, 193; customs at, 73; disturbance after Good Parliament, 180–2; Hustings court, 182; Marshalsea jurisdiction in, 182; conflict with court (March 1377), 192–3.
Louis, younger son of King Charles V, later Duke of Orleans, 50.
Love, Richard, 114, 138.
Lowestoft (Suffolk), 115–16, 118.
Lucca (Italy), merchants of, 126.
Ludgershall (Wilts), 168, 175.
Ludlow, Sir John, 135.
Lutterworth (Leic.), rectory of, 169, 175.
Lydd (Kent), 120.
Lyndeby, Robert de, 128 n.
Lyons, Richard, 56, 157, 181, 190; and royal finances, 65–7, 72–4, 78–9, 89; accusations against in Good Parliament, 101–4, 106–7, 109, 112–14, 116, 133; pardon of, 193–4.

McFarlane, K.B., 29 n.
Majorca, Kingdom of, 58.
Malesec, Cardinal Guy de, 146.
Malines (Brabant), 54.
Mantua, envoy of at Avignon, 29, 54–5.
March, Edmund Mortimer, Earl of, 18, 64, 186, 197; and Brittany expedition (1375), 37, 39, 45, 150–3; and Ireland, 93–5, 98; and Good

March (*cont.*)
Parliament, 101, 105–8, 140, 143, 150–3, 158; finances, 149–53; marshal, 183; Philippa, wife of, 149.
Marchi, Piero di Jacopo, 82, 85–6, 121 n., 126.
Mardisley, John, 14.
Mare, Sir John de la, 137, 184 n.
Mare, Sir Peter de la, 101–5, 107, 110, 134, 136–8, 149, 183, 186, 190, 192.
Marignolli family, 83 n.
Mariole, Francis, 83 n.
Marsilius of Padua, 174.
Mary, d. of Edward III, w. of John Duke of Brittany, 24.
Meath, Bishop of, 94–5.
Medbourne, Henry de, 109.
Merstham (Surr.), 75.
Middelburg (Zeeland), 85.
Middleton, Huchoun de, 127.
Milan, war of Papacy with, 8–9, 54, 124, 166; merchants of, 84.
Mint, royal, 87.
Mohun, Joan, 89.
Mohun, John de, 89 n.
Montague, John, 161.
Montechiari (Italy), battle of, 9.
Montluçon (France), 28.
More, John, 193.
Morton, Robert de, 72 n.
Moryan, John, 151 n.
Mottrom, Roger, 142–3.
Moubray, John, 129.
Mowbray, John de, 194.
Multon, Simon de, 20, 34.
Munster (Ireland), 96.

Najera (Castile), battle of, 25.
Naples, kingdom of, 50; attack on ship of, 84, 120.
Navarre, English relations with, 29, 51, 54.
Netter, Thomas, 175.
Neville, Alexander, Archbishop of York, 34, 140, 159 n.
Neville, John Lord, of Raby, 34, 117, 154, 196; expedition to Brittany (1372), 23–5, 130; Steward of Household, 64, 66–8, 106, 157; and royal finances, 77, 138; and Good Parliament, 105–6, 109, 157.
Neville's Cross (Durham), Battle of, 65.
New Forest, keeper of, 94.

Niccolò di Giovanni, 82 n.
Niccolò di Luca, 82.
Norbury, Richard, 193.
Normandy, 37–8, 43.
Northampton, John of, 189.
Norwich, Bishop of, *see* Despenser.
Nottingham Castle, 192.

O'Brien family, 95.
Organ, John, 151 n.
Orgrave, Thomas, 47.
Orsini, Cardinal Giacomo, 86, 146.
Oxford, 86; Balliol College, 175.
Oxford, Maud, Countess of, 161.

Pallenswick manor, Fulham (Middlesex), 137.
Pamplona, Bernard Folcant, Bishop of, 19.
Papacy, *see* Clement VI, Clement VII, Gregory XI, Innocent VI, John XXII, Urban V, Urban VI.
Paris, 26, 28.
Parliament (Feb.–March 1371), 17, 71; (Nov.–Dec. 1373), 16, 52, 72; (April–July 1376), 100–58; (Jan.–April 1377), 165, 178, 184–91.
Payn, John, 88 n.
Pecche, John, 106, 109, 114, 181, 190, 193.
Pembridge, Sir Richard, 94.
Pembroke, John Hastings, Earl of, 21, 71.
Pepir, William, 118.
Peraglie, Piero di Geri, 82 n.
Percy, Henry Lord, 23, 64, 153–4; and Good Parliament, 101, 105, 140, 153–4, 158; activity after appointment as Marshal, 182–3, 189–90, 194, 196.
Perrers, Alice, 79, 157–8, 164, 183, 192; position at court, 68–9, 88–92, 194; and William of Windsor, 97–8; accusations against in Good Parliament, 103, 105–6, 135–9; pardon to, 160, 190.
Pert, Sir John, 127, 131.
Pertenhale, Joan, 142.
Peruzzi, Arnaldo, 82.
Peruzzi, Niccolò di Giovanni, 82, 121–2.
Peter I, King of Castile, 25, 156.
Peter III, King of Aragon, 26.

Phillipa, Queen, 70, 157.
Philpot, John, 72 n., 73, 75–7, 151 n., 152, 153 n., 183, 189–90.
Pierles, Richard, 116 n.
Pilkington, Roger de, 184 n.
Pisa, 84.
Pleshey (Essex), castle of, 157.
Plymouth, 25–6, 39, 40.
Poitou, English position in, 21–2.
Pole, Edmund de la, 135.
Pole, Michael de la, 73, 114, 124, 135, 138, 164; Catherine, wife of, 138.
Poleye, Sir Ralph, 118.
Portelewe, Adam, 121 n.
Portugal, 54.
Prata, Pileo de, Archbishop of Ravenna, papal legate, 31, 33, 59, 61.
Pulle, Geoffrey, 118.
Pyel, John, 66, 71–4, 78–9, 104, 108 n., 109, 113.

Queenborough Castle (Kent), 132.
Quimperlé (Brittany), 45.

Ragoun, Sir John, 138 n.
Raniero di Domenico, 82 n.
Ravenna, Archbishop of, see Prata.
Ravenser, Richard, keeper of the Hanaper, 47, 160 n.
Ravensholm, John de, 73 n., 77.
Ravensholm, Margaret de, 77–8, 114.
Reade, William, Bishop of Chichester, 186.
Redmayne, Mathew, 158 n.
Reims (France), 28.
Reynes, Sir Thomas, 120–1.
Richard, Prince, later King Richard II, 51, 87, 107, 161, 164, 185, 192, 194.
Richmond, earldom of, 24.
Roche, Jean de la, 41, 43.
Rochendale, Lawrence, 116.
Rochester, Bishop of, see Brinton.
Rokeby, Thomas, 158 n.
Romney (Kent), 120.
Roos, Thomas Lord, of Hamelak, 186.
Roskell, J.S., 101 n., 105 n.
Rossi, Nofferi de', 179 n.
Rouen (Normandy), 162.
Rounhey, Nicholas, 88 n.
Rubiera (Italy), battle of, 9.
Rye (Kent), 120.

Saint Albans (Herts), Abbot of, 69.
St. Asaph, Bishop of, 191.
St. Bartholomew's Hospital, 142.
St. Brieuc (Brittany), 40.
St. David's (Pembs.), 140–1; Bishop of, see Houghton.
St. John, Prior of order of, in England, 73 n., 77, 114, 164, 182; in Ireland, 94.
St. Malo (Brittany), 23.
St. Paul's cathedral, London, 167, 189; convocations at, see convocation; dean of, see Appleby.
St. Sauveur-le-Vicomte castle of (Normandy), 32, 37, 43–5, 50, 62, 105–7, 127, 131–3, 155, 162.
Salisbury, Bishop of, see Erghum; Hallam.
Salisbury, William Montague, Earl of, 18, 23, 25, 34, 58, 61, 64, 94, 107–8, 149, 163, 186, 194.
Sánchez de Tovar, Fernán, Admiral of Castile, 56.
Sandrus Boni, 82 n.
Sandwich (Kent), 25–6, 58, 120.
Sangatte (France), 112.
Santon, John de, 168 n.
Sarlat (France), 30.
Savage, Sir Arnold, 34.
Saville, Sir John, 106, 135, 138 n.
Savoy, see Amedeo
Savoy, manor of, 17, 190.
Scrope, Henry Lord, 102, 140, 154, 161.
Scrope, Richard Lord, Treasurer, 18, 64–5, 68, 76, 103–4, 140, 154, 168 n.
Segrave, Hugh, 163.
Sencler, Lardy Mary, 88 n.
Sheen (Surrey), 90, 190, 192.
Sheppey, John, 14, 34–6, 124, 161, 163.
Sibille, Walter, 118.
Sinigaglia, Bishop of, 19.
Skirlaw, Walter, 160 n., 163.
Sleaford, John, 47.
Sluys (Flanders), 122.
Smithfield (London), 68.
Sotherey, John, 68–9, 194.
Southampton, 58, 130.
Sporier, Walter, 110, 112 n.
Stable, Adam, 74, 189, 193.
Stafford, Hugh, Earl of, 23, 102, 105, 107–8, 140, 149, 154, 158, 186, 194.
Stafford, Richard, 102, 105 n., 140, 154.
Stafford, Robert de, 184 n.

205